REFLECTIONS ON PHILOSOPHY

■ *Introductory Essays*

REFLECTIONS ON PHILOSOPHY

■ *Introductory Essays*

Edited by

LEEMON McHENRY
Wittenberg University

and

FREDERICK ADAMS
Central Michigan University

ST. MARTIN'S PRESS   NEW YORK

Senior editor: Don Reisman
Manager, publishing services: Emily Berleth
Project management: Denise Quirk
Cover design: Sheree Goodman
Cover photo: Parmigianino, *Self-Portrait in a Convex Mirror.* Kunsthistorisches
         Museum, Vienna. Reprinted by permission of Art Resources, NY.

For information, write:
St. Martin's Press, Inc.
175 Fifth Avenue
New York, NY 10010

ISBN: 0-312-06777-1

PREFACE

Reflections on Philosophy: Introductory Essays originated when one of us suggested to our colleagues in the philosophy department at Central Michigan University that we write essays *for students*. After the initial shock and outrage, the notion slowly gained acceptance, and a few of us produced essays that were put to a trial run in classes in the academic years 1989–90 and 1990–91. The success of this venture then led us to expand the book to include topics by philosophers outside CMU, and in the meantime, we revised and polished the prototypes. The result is this book.

Introductory philosophy can be an exasperating experience for students because most philosophy texts include selections by philosophers writing *to one another*. Such texts are usually well beyond the comprehension of a first-time philosophy student. Students may read and reread the assignment but still have little idea what it is about, and little hope of improving by sheer effort alone. In class discussions, the all-too-common nervous silence in response to the instructor's questions only makes the matter more urgent—a text is needed that speaks *to the student*. Of course, this is not to say that this text is the only one that introduces philosophy to the introductory student, nor that this volume will solve the problem once and for all. There are many other factors beyond the selection of the texts that contribute to the difficulty of a first-time philosophy course, but at least this book was written with the problem in mind. Whether it succeeds or not, time will tell.

The challenge of this approach is to engage the introductory student by discussing, in accessible fashion, subjects in the core areas of the discipline that are of interest to "professional" philosophers. Most of the essays in this volume include a survey of a particular territory, but the keen reader will note each author's intention to lead students through some specific position. Questions on the essay and suggestions for further reading are included at the end of each chapter to focus students' reading of the material, to stimulate class discussion, and to assist students with topics not developed in detail in the text.

The individual chapters of this book can be assigned with a number of primary sources or with readings in an anthology of primary and secondary sources. While the order of the topics seemed most natural to us, some instructors may prefer to begin with later chapters or avoid some altogether. The chapters are sufficiently self-contained to allow the instructor to skip around the book and take up the issues that best suit the interests of the students and the selection of primary sources.

Because this text is a collective effort, thanks are due first and foremost to each of the contributors. We are particularly indebted to William H. Brenner for the original idea for such a collection of essays. To Don Reisman and Frances Jones of St. Martin's Press, special thanks are due for their early support of the project and countless helpful suggestions along the way. William R. Connolly, University of Evansville; Peter Dalton, Florida State University; Albert Flores, California State University—Fullerton; Jasper Hopkins, University of Minnesota; Chin-Tai Kim, Case Western Reserve University; Derk Pereboom, University of Vermont; and Stephen Satris, Clemson University, provided valuable criticisms of several chapters. These critical reports were especially helpful in the revision stage. Our thanks are due to Denise Quirk for her acute eye in copyediting the manuscript and to Emily Berleth of St. Martin's Press. David Marlow of Wittenberg University also gave sterling assistance in the completion of this project. Finally, the Provost's Office at Central Michigan University very kindly provided financial support for expenses incurred in producing the manuscript, and for this we owe thanks to Robert Franke.

I..B.M.

F.R.A.

CONTENTS

■ CHAPTER THREE

Metaphysics, LEEMON MCHENRY   35

■ CHAPTER FOUR

Epistemology, FREDERICK ADAMS   53

■ CHAPTER FIVE

Ethics, JOYCE HENRICKS   69

■ CHAPTER NINE
Personal Identity, GARY FULLER   145

■ CHAPTER TEN
Philosophy of Mind, JOHN HEIL   165

■ CHAPTER ELEVEN
Cognitive Science, KENNETH AIZAWA   187

■ APPENDIX
Writing Philosophical Papers, LEEMON MCHENRY   205

■ CHAPTER ONE

Introduction

LEEMON McHENRY

■ AIM OF THIS BOOK

For the student, philosophy can be bizarre and somewhat frustrating because it proceeds in a way unlike most other academic subjects and deals with questions that are extremely difficult to answer. This does not mean that mathematics, physics, and other subjects do not have questions that are extremely difficult to answer, but that such questions become apparent in these other subjects only at the most advanced levels of study. Although philosophy does require the ability to master central principles and concepts, as well as the ability to remember who said what and in what order, it typically goes further: It demands that students learn to think for themselves—to do philosophy. In this respect, one must understand that philosophical problems are, by their very nature, controversial and open to a continuous process of argument, rejoinder, and reevaluation. The student of philosophy is thus invited to join in the twenty-five-hundred-year-old tradition and grapple with some of the most profound and perplexing questions confronting human existence.

We prepared this collection of essays with the conviction that philosophy is an activity that one learns only by actually doing it, rather than by just memorizing what the great historical figures have said along with the standard objections to these views. Of course, these essays are no substitute for reading the classic texts of philosophy; they are rather a supplement to such texts and are written to stimulate lively debate and discussion of contemporary philosophical problems. Much of what follows originates with the great philosophers of the past. Instead of an historical or chronological method, however, our approach is problems oriented and aims to encourage the development of a philosophical frame of mind and a reflective attitude of critical analysis.

■ RATIONALE FOR SELECTION OF TOPICS

Each of the ten chapters that follow introduces a major branch of philosophical inquiry or a special area of philosophic concern and its central problems. The topics of Chapters 2 through 7 cover the main branches of philosophy usually discussed in introductory courses—logic, metaphysics, epistemology, ethics, political philosophy, and aesthetics. We begin with logic as the indispensable tool of analysis necessary for evaluating arguments and further exploring philosophical issues. The chapter on logic also introduces some crucial philosophical terminology used in subsequent chapters. Chapters on metaphysics and epistemology follow and address problems concerning the nature of reality and the conditions by which we can acquire knowledge. Chapters on ethics, political philosophy, and aesthetics fall under the general area of philosophy known as *axiology*, or value theory. Ethics—or moral philosophy—is concerned with the standards for judging the correctness of human behavior. Political philosophy addresses the issue of just distribution of wealth by the state. Aesthetics focuses attention on the definition of art and problems of judging artistic value.

Chapters 8 and 9, on the philosophy of religion and personal identity, cover additional issues usually raised in a first philosophy course. Finally, Chapters 10 and 11, on philosophy of mind and cognitive science, while slightly more challenging for the introductory level, are included for the broad interdisciplinary interest these topics have sparked in our time. While problems of the nature of mind and artificial intelligence have their origin in the philosophies of the seventeenth century, they have certainly become more acute in the twentieth century with the arrival of computers.

Although the authors of each of the ten chapters are specialists in their respective fields, they have intentionally simplified the issues discussed to accommodate the student. In the interests of clarity, we have omitted some of the more complex topics and disputes that engage philosophers in these fields. Each contributor takes up only a few of the central problems and attempts to work through them in a clear and elementary manner. We have sought to avoid the method of laying out five or six competing theories and giving the impression that all are equally good and that nothing could ever be resolved in philosophy. Our approach encourages students to become acquainted with the ways in which contemporary philosophers formulate and attempt to solve problems, but we also invite students to evaluate critically the solutions offered and to advance their own views.

It should be noted that while we have attempted to give these chapters an overall coherence, each, to some extent, introduces its own method and approach. So, the approach to aesthetics will be rather different from the approach to metaphysics or the philosophy of religion. In an effort to keep the topics current, all of the contributors have tried to communicate some of the most recent work in these areas.

■ WHAT IS PHILOSOPHY?

The very attempt to say what philosophy is itself raises a philosophical problem. This is because the whole enterprise of providing definitions inevitably involves us in the activity of doing philosophy. So, from the start we find ourselves embroiled in controversy. Philosophy is not as easily defined as, say biology, where "the science of life and life processes" will more or less serve as an adequate starting point. That is, biologists are unlikely to see this definition as problematic and would much rather get down to the business of studying the function, structure, and evolution of living organisms than trouble over whether the definition of the field precisely captures what the science is about. Most philosophers, however, will take the very definition of their subject as open to discussion. Let us investigate some of the reasons why philosophy is difficult to define, and then, in spite of the difficulty, offer a working definition.

If we turn to the dictionary for our answer, we are likely to find straightforward etymology from two Greek words, *philein*, "to love," and *sophia*, "wisdom." Thus, philosophy is the "love of wisdom." Although this stresses the point that philosophy is a kind of attitude or frame of mind rather than a specific body of knowledge acquired, it remains dreadfully uninformative. Besides, most philosophers today would agree that, perhaps unfortunately, much of what goes on in the philosophical world would hardly count as wisdom. If there is something in this traditional definition that captures the essence of philosophy, it needs further clarification and explanation well beyond mere etymology.

But now suppose we turn to someone who counts himself or herself a philosopher, and pose the question. Whether we choose historical figures or living, practicing philosophers, we are likely to find that our definition multiplies with the number of philosophers we consult. Each philosopher may define the subject according to some particular manner of doing philosophy or some specific conception of worth in philosophy. So, any single definition advanced will not be satisfactory to all philosophers because the very definition is part of the rivalry between different schools of thought or different traditions of philosophy. We might then, at this point, conclude that philosophy is defined by each individual who engages in the activity. But now we are left with a state of chaos with respect to our original task. Is there anything that ties this philosophical activity together in such a way as to arrive at a general, all-encompassing definition?

In a certain sense, each of the ten essays in this book gives an explication of philosophy from the standpoint of some particular area. Philosophy is founded on the problems that essentially drive the philosophical endeavor—problems of how we gain knowledge, how we conceive of the nature of reality and of right and wrong behavior, and how we understand the nature of mind, self, state, religion, or art. I think it is true to say, in addition, at least for this collection of essays, that philosophy is a *rational* discipline that attempts to articulate and solve these problems. This is our first important characteristic of philosophy. Fundamentally, philosophy is an intellectual activity that attempts to arrive at sound knowledge through the use of reason. What usually passes for knowledge in ordinary social intercourse is often vague, lazy, unfounded, or dogmatic; philosophers are typically more obstinate about what will serve as a satisfactory account of some claim to know something, and criticism lies at the heart of their quest.

How you *feel* about a philosophical issue or problem, without any further justification, hardly counts at all. Opinions based on purely emotional responses do not score high points in philosophy. Feelings are just that—feelings; but reasons can be criticized or praised; they can be judged to be good or bad, plausible or implausible, strong or weak. Indeed, it is the job of *reason* to control or keep in check the emotions—to stop the murder by the jealous lover, repudiate the bigot's opinions, or hold back the fanatical zealot.

Hearsay or appeals to authority figures—religious and moral leaders, parents or teachers—do not count for much in philosophy either. The response "Well, *they* say . . ." is a common appeal to the unknown scientific authority that supposedly settles the issue at hand. Sometimes such appeals are warranted, but they are all too often just poor and lazy substitutes for finding solid evidence. As noted at the outset of this chapter, we have to learn to think for ourselves about philosophical problems, and this involves using sound reasoning; clarifying the meanings of important or controversial terms; drawing out assumptions, presuppositions, and fallacies; and investigating the legitimacy of evidence used to support knowledge. In this respect, philosophy is much like science, especially the theoretical part of science—both seek truth about the world through the use of reason.

There are other important characteristics that shape the core of philosophical activity, many of which emerge in the essays in this book. For example, philosophy studies problems of an extreme generality in every area of human inquiry: science, religion, politics, morality, law, art, history, medicine. The problems that engage the philosopher's attention, however, are not the same as those of the scientist, historian, moralist, or artist. They are, rather, problems of a "higher order." Philosophy is not a specialized form of inquiry that provides particular information about our world. Although some areas of philosophy are indeed technical and detailed, the issues philosophers discuss arise from broad questions such as "What is knowledge?" "How do we justify a moral principle?" "What makes art valuable?" or "What is ultimately real?" Thus, the type of knowledge sought is of a general sort. Philosophy often asks questions of such a generality that it inevitably cuts across boundary lines that divide other subjects. So, to discuss the whole question of the nature of mind, the philosopher seeks knowledge of various fields ranging from neurology to psychology, and biology to computer science. Even knowledge of theology might be required if the discussion addresses the notion of the human soul. After all, these subjects are part of the evidence that is relevant for the evaluation of the theories discussed or the attempt to formulate a new theory. Solutions offered by the philosopher will, in turn, have important implications for each of the separate disciplines.

Finally, although information from the sciences is often relevant to discussing philosophical problems, the problems themselves are so general that they resist solutions by experiment and observation alone. Philosophical problems are unlikely to be settled finally by the methods of the special sciences such as physics, chemistry, biology, psychology, or sociology. Rather, philosophical problems gain some clarification and find some solution, however tentative, by the use of careful reasoning and critical reflection on the strong and weak points of various theories.

Let us say, then, that *philosophy is the rational, critical investigation of fundamental questions of an extreme generality that resist solutions by the empirical sciences.* Returning to the notion that philosophy is the "love of wisdom," we might find this idea acceptable if we clarify the meaning of *wisdom* such that we understand it to be a knowledge of the very broadest sort, a knowledge that addresses the most basic concerns of existence, of ourselves and our world. If we love wisdom, we cultivate in ourselves a persistent thirst for this knowledge. In this way, a lover of wisdom is one who seeks truth in the service of living well. For having obtained truth about ourselves and our world, we would live a more enlightened and orderly life, and happiness would be the ultimate result. This squares with what most of the early philosophers in both the Eastern and Western traditions believed to be the essence of philosophy; and our formidable list includes such figures as Pythagoras, Socrates, Plato, Aristotle, Epictetus, Sextus Empiricus, St. Augustine, Confucius, Lao Tzu, Buddha, Nāgārjuna, and many others.

Whether the above definition is satisfactory, I shall leave for the reader to decide. Undoubtedly there are characteristics of philosophy I have left out; the definition is general but tentative. It is our hope that the following chapters will serve the reader in the task of deciding whether this definition is adequate. Perhaps we might make considerable progress here if we establish what philosophy is *not*.

■ SOME MISCONCEPTIONS ABOUT PHILOSOPHY

Since philosophy is seldom taught outside of the college setting, students come to an introductory course with many misconceptions about the subject. This is not to say that the only place one will learn about philosophy is at a college or a university; but granted that this is where most philosophers happen to congregate, it is where one is more than likely to encounter the subject in a serious context. Popular culture often conveys impressions about philosophy that are caricatures, misleading, or just plain false. We will need to eliminate these misconceptions before we proceed any further.

1. *Philosophy is what a guru does on a mountaintop.* The picture of an old man with a long beard meditating on some remote, isolated mountaintop captures one popular idea of a philosopher. Perhaps this idea comes from the notion that philosophers are deep thinkers who must escape from the "real world" to arrive at truth.

Certain religious traditions do promote the idea that we must remove ourselves from society to find our true spiritual selves, and there might very well be something in this recommendation that is agreeable to philosophers in that they generally reject superficial, frivolous, and flashy ideas that surface in contemporary society and clutter the mind. The overall impression, however, is not very accurate. Philosophers generally work in a context in which ideas and theories are advanced and criticized. This means that they learn from one another by vigorously debating one another's ideas. So, for the most part, philosophers aim to work in and with the world to improve our knowledge and our behavior toward one another. Historically, philosophers have made profound contributions to the shape of political and social institutions, public policy, law, science, mathematics, and literature.

2. *Philosophy is one's view on life or other matters.* In popular parlance, the term *philosophy* is used in a loose and misleading way. We find football coaches explaining their "defensive philosophies" before the game or grandfathers telling grandchildren about their "philosophies of life." And sometimes we find witty lines or sayings, for example in Chinese fortune cookies, that pass for "a philosophy." This will not do. Philosophical views are often carefully worked out, and emerge only after criticism, revision, and years of study. Truth does not come easily; so, it is unlikely to be captured in some simplistic or haphazard fashion. We all live in the world and operate with a set of beliefs about it, but the continual quest to challenge those beliefs and improve them is something that requires a particular kind of dedication that few are willing to undertake.

3. *Philosophy is psychiatry or psychoanalysis.* Only a little needs to be said to clear up this misunderstanding. Philosophy may, in fact, afford a type of therapy that one practices on oneself. Indeed, if the point of philosophy is to discover truth in the service of living well, it is an edifying experience that one practices for life. Socrates held the view that the "unexamined life is not worth living." For him, philosophy was a type of cure for the soul because one continually confronts oneself with the truth. Philosophy, however, is not the practice of psychiatry wherein a patient's psychological problems are examined and diagnosed in a clinical setting. The theories of psychoanalysis originated in the writings of philosophers, but this is another matter.

4. *Philosophy is* just *personal opinion.* This claim is related to the kind of misunderstanding examined in point 2, but the idea here is rather different. After examining some of the controversy that lies at the core of philosophical debate, some students will throw up their hands in frustration and conclude that it is all *just* opinion, and nobody knows any more than anybody else.

To the student, philosophy often does seem to go around in circles; or even worse, it appears that the argument amounts to little more than people exercising their tonsils with no practical results. Depending on the one to whom we are listening, this may or may not be an accurate assessment. To the ear untrained in argumentative techniques, philosophy can often give this impression. But this just means that the answers to the problems are difficult to acquire, and patience is required to make progress.

Although there often appears to be little or no agreement on a given philosophical topic, it does not follow either that there is no truth to the matter or that any view is just as good as any other. Clearly, some opinions are blatantly false because they are based on misinformation, incomplete evidence, or logical fallacies. Consider, for example, Adolf Hitler's opinion that Jews are inferior to Aryans and his actions (based on this opinion) that resulted in the Holocaust. If philosophy is *just* personal opinion, it seems that all are entitled to their opinions, Hitler included. If we are a bit more critical about particular opinions, however, we find that some are seriously flawed. Hitler's view in *Mein Kampf*, for example, is based on confusions about superior and inferior races—in this case, that Aryans are superior, and Jews and other races are inferior. But neither the Aryans nor the Jews are a *race*. Anthropologists identify races according to classifications such as Caucasians, Mongolians, and so on. Aryans and Jews, however, are ethnic groups. Even if, by some extremely charitable interpretation, we grant Hitler the issue of race, we still have to demand some solid answers to the question of criteria for establishing the alleged superiority of the Aryans. This means that his simplistic notions about blond hair and military force as the basis for superiority are thrown into serious question. In the end, Hitler's definitions turn out not to be, strictly speaking, biological or anthropological. They are manipulated for a narrow political purpose, which at the time was largely a matter of economic advantage for the Germans.

Of course, the case of Hitler is an extreme one, and the problem of racism (and other pressing issues of social and moral concern) strike us as having an urgency that is lacking in purely abstract problems of epistemology, philosophy of mind, or metaphysics. But the example certainly exposes the naïveté behind the charge that "philosophy is *just* personal opinion." Our task in philosophy is largely a matter of sorting out which opinions are supported by good reasons and which are not. Philosophy is an intellectual challenge. To dismiss it all as "*just* personal opinion" is in effect to withdraw from some of the most important questions human beings face.

5. *Philosophy does not make real progress like the sciences.* This is a common charge against philosophy. One hears, for example, "We are still very much struggling with the same problems that originated with Plato and Aristotle, and today, over two thousand years later, we still have not definitely answered the questions they raised. But physics, chemistry, and biology have made profound advances in the last two hundred years." This misconception can be approached from two different angles.

First, the question of progress in science is a deep and hotly debated issue. When we get down to it, the whole idea of what counts as progress turns out to be one of enormous philosophical significance and involves our getting clear about what is ultimately valuable. Progress can only gain some meaning with respect to our goals, and our goals only become meaningful with respect to what we determine to be valuable. The science and technology that have given us nuclear weapons would hardly count as progress given that our goal is a world safe from their potential destruction. After all, if we destroy all human life on the planet, what good will it have done that science "progressed" to this state of affairs?

Second, philosophy and science share a common historical origin. From the early Greek philosophers on up well beyond the times of Sir Isaac Newton, science was simply "natural philosophy," the attempt to discover truth about the physical world. It is only fairly recently that we have come to see science as detached from the parent discipline of philosophy, largely because of the intense specialization of science in the twentieth century. The great scientists of the past—Aristotle, Galileo, Newton, Einstein, and Bohr, to name a handful—all thought of themselves as philosophers. Science seems to advance much more quickly by the use of scientific method, by observation and experiment, and the immediate result is often of significant practical value. But this only applies to its testable content. The theoretical content of science, in contrast, is more difficult to evaluate. Here advance is made in much the same way as it is in philosophy.

Sometimes, progress is a simple matter of clarification of a problem or the more precise formulation of the theory that attempts to solve the problem. At other times, progress is measured by subdividing problems and by distinguishing different questions and issues such that we can attempt to analyze them separately and attempt to solve them. Furthermore, progress is sometimes made when total abandonment of some problem or theory occurs. In this respect, philosophy and science may progress in a curiously negative manner: we abandon that which we believe to be false, inconsistent, contradictory, or simply useless in advancing our understanding of the world.

Progress by elimination, however, does not tell us that we have the truth. It tells us only what is ruled out. Theories are evaluated in terms of their explanatory power and their comprehensive ability to account for the facts. One theory may be rejected in favor of another if it is clearly inferior in this way; such a move yields more fruitful results in the long run, and in this respect both philosophy and science are in the same boat.

■ CONCLUSION

In summary, then, having now come to some understanding about what philosophy is and what it is not, we conclude with a few remarks about what philosophy attempts to achieve: (1) philosophy is an intellectual challenge that sharpens the wits by a relentless use of reason; (2) it liberates us from dogmas and forces us to examine beliefs held without good reason; (3) it opens us to a diversity of views and issues never before contemplated; (4) it develops our capacity for constructive critical thinking; (5) it demands consistency about our various beliefs and encourages us to develop a coherent worldview; but ultimately, (6) philosophy seeks wisdom as a broad type of knowledge and understanding about issues of fundamental concern.

■ QUESTIONS

1. Examine the characteristics of philosophy given in this chapter, and compare them with the view of philosophy most often given by the proverbial man-on-the-street. Has your view of philosophy changed after reading this chapter?

2. Consider the difference between someone you might call "wise" and someone you might call "knowledgeable." What is the difference between knowledge and wisdom? Is wisdom a broad kind of knowledge or something altogether different?

3. Philosophy is often charged with lack of progress in comparison to science. Can you think of any examples of what was thought to be scientific progress in the past but is now believed to be otherwise? How might these examples challenge your current view of scientific progress?

4. Thomas Carlyle once said, "What is philosophy but a continual battle against custom; an ever-renewed effort to transcend the sphere of blind custom?" Explain what this means and how it characterizes philosophy. Does it address some aspect of philosophy discussed above? ■

■ FOR FURTHER READING

General Reference
Edwards, Paul, ed. *The Encyclopedia of Philosophy*. 8 vols. New York: Macmillan, 1967.
Lacey, A. R. *A Dictionary of Philosophy*. New York: Scribner's, 1976.

History of Philosophy
Copleston, F. C. *A History of Philosophy*. 9 vols. London: Burns, Oates and Washbourne, 1946–1975.
Hamlyn, D. W. *A History of Western Philosophy*. Harmondsworth, Eng.: Penguin, 1987.
Jones, W. T. *History of Western Philosophy*. 4 vols. New York: Harper and Row, 1976.
Russell, Bertrand. *A History of Western Philosophy*. London: Allen and Unwin, 1961.

■ CHAPTER TWO

Logic

WILLIAM H. BRENNER

Logic is about reasoning, and reasoning takes a variety of forms. This chapter emphasizes that variety and also the connection between logic and other parts of the enterprise that began in ancient Greece and was called *philosophy*.

■ DEDUCTIVE ARGUMENTS

In the sixth century B.C., Thales of Miletus claimed that everything is made of the same thing, namely *hydor*—water. His fellow Milesian Anaximander criticized this view, reasoning that nothing made of fire could be made of water, because all things made of water are essentially wet and cool, while nothing made of fire is essentially wet and cool. Anaximander proceeded to propose his own theory, which one can read about in any history of early Greek thought. Suffice it to say here that Thales and Anaximander between them initiated a tradition of systematic reasoning about the fundamental principles of nature, a tradition that, in the fifth century B.C., gave us the famous "atomism" of Democritus:

> By convention there is sweet, by convention there is bitter, by convention hot and cold, by convention color; but in reality there are only atoms and the void.[1]

Also in the fifth century B.C., an Athenian Greek by the name of Socrates argued that there is a radical difference between the physical causes put forward by the "natural philosophers" from Thales to Democritus and the moral ideals that can move human beings to action. He then initiated a tradition of systematic reasoning about such "moral principles."

In the fourth century B.C., Plato wrote the dialogues that were to make Socrates famous. He also founded the first university, the Academy, which endured for over nine hundred years. Plato's outstanding student was Aristotle, who along with (and sometimes in opposition to) his master, developed the inquiries begun by Socrates and the earlier philosophers. He also invented a new discipline—the systematic inquiry into the principles of reasoning, known as *logic*.

Looking back at the inquiries of his predecessors from Thales on down, Aristotle saw that they not only stated opinions about various subjects, but also reasoned about them; he saw further that their reasoning could be analyzed into "units of reasoning" that he termed *arguments*. An argument is composed of at least two statements, one of which (the *conclusion*) is claimed to follow from the other statement or statements (the *premise* or *premises*). Thus, from the premises

No things made of water are essentially hot and dry.
All things made of fire are essentially hot and dry.

Anaximander had drawn the conclusion

Nothing made of fire is made of water.

And from the premises

No material things are eternal and unchanging.
All moral ideals are eternal and unchanging.

Socrates had concluded

No moral ideals are material things.

The preceding arguments are deductive: in a *deductive argument*, the conclusion is claimed to follow *necessarily* from its premises. The preceding arguments are also valid: in a *valid deductive argument*, the conclusion *does* follow necessarily from the premises, as claimed. (Nondeductive arguments will be discussed later in this chapter.)

Characteristically, the validity of deductive arguments is determined by *logical form*. Aristotle was the first to perceive and develop this point. For example, he saw that, although the preceding two arguments differ radically in subject matter, they have the same logical form, namely:

No P are M.
All S are M.
∴ No S are P.

(The symbol ∴ stands for "therefore," "thus," or "consequently." M, P, and S are variables that can be filled in with any terms [*things made of water, gods,* and the like].)

The preceding logical form can be represented in a diagram such as the following:

Explanation: Because nothing in M is in P, and everything in S is in M, nothing in S can be in P.

Both Anaximander's and Socrates' arguments are valid because they embody this form. Any argument of the same form will be valid, no matter what terms are substituted for *P*, *M*, and *S*. Therefore, the following argument is valid:

No cats are meat-eaters.
All tigers are meat-eaters.
∴ No tigers are cats.

Of course, we do not accept both of its premises. But *if* we did, then (to be consistent) we would have to accept the conclusion as well. *If* we start with true premises, then we are bound to get a true conclusion. By definition, *valid deduction preserves truth*. This means that a valid deduction cannot possibly have all true premises and a false conclusion.

Although the preceding argument is valid, it is not, for all that, a good argument. A good argument has to be "sound." A *sound argument* has *true premises* (only true premises), as well as *validity* (that is, logical connection between premises and conclusion). Thus, in evaluating reasoning we need to remember that there are two different questions to ask, one about whether the premises are true, the other about whether the conclusion follows from the premises. If the answer to both questions is "yes," then the argument is sound.

Note that the "sound/unsound," "valid/invalid" distinctions are to be applied only to *arguments*—not to premises, conclusions, or other statements; the "true/false" distinction is to be applied only to *statements*, not to arguments.

■ MORE DEDUCTIVE ARGUMENTS

The Stoic philosophers of late Greek antiquity supplemented Aristotle's contribution to logic with (among other things) an analysis of *conditional (if/then) arguments*. In this section, we shall take a look at a few such arguments, reviewing in the process the important distinction between valid and invalid deduction.

Consider first the following two valid arguments:

If that's a metal, it conducts electricity.
That's a metal.
Therefore, it conducts electricity.

If that's a metal, it conducts electricity.
It does not conduct electricity.
Therefore, it's not a metal.

The first is an instance of the form

If p, then q.
p.
∴ q.

and is known as *modus ponens* ("mode of affirming"). The second is an instance of the form

> If *p*, then *q*.
> not *q*.
> ∴ not *p*.

and is known as *modus tollens* ("mode of denying"). Whatever statements are substituted for the *p* and *q* in these formulas, the resulting arguments will be valid.[2]

Modus ponens and *modus tollens* are among the most common forms of reasoning. Almost as common are the two corresponding *invalid* forms:

> If *p*, then *q*.
> *q*.
> ∴ *p*.

known as *fallacy of affirming the consequent*, and

> If *p*, then *q*.
> not *p*.
> ∴ not *q*.

known as *fallacy of denying the antecedent*. (*Antecedent* refers to the *if*, and *consequent* to the *then*, components of an *if/then* sentence.)

That the preceding two argument forms fail as "truth preservers" can be demonstrated by giving clear *examples* of them in which false statements are concluded from true premises. Thus, the following example demonstrates the invalidity of affirming the consequent:

> If she's a senator, she's a citizen.
> She's a citizen.
> Therefore, she's a senator.   (Madonna is a citizen but not a senator.)

And the following demonstrates the invalidity of denying the antecedent:

> If it's purple, it's a mixed color.
> It's not purple.
> Therefore, it's not a mixed color.   (Orange is not purple but is a mixed color.)

Compare the preceding argument with the following:

> If Ted Kennedy is president, then he lives in the White House.
> Ted Kennedy is not president.
> Therefore, he doesn't live in the White House.

The first instance of denying the antecedent had true premises and a false conclusion; this one has true premises and a true conclusion. An invalid form of reasoning may indeed happen to have true premises and a true conclusion; what makes it invalid is that it is also *possible* for it to have true premises but a false conclusion.

Demonstrating invalidity is a matter of producing a clear illustration of that possibility.

■ INDUCTIVE ARGUMENTS

Valid deduction "preserves truth." This means that if the premises of a deductive argument are true, its conclusion *must* also be true. This *must* signifies logical necessity. To say that a proposition is *logically necessary* means that it cannot be denied without contradiction. Logical necessity arises either from (1) logical form or (2) the meaning of terms. For example: (1) "If I'm supposed to take a pill at breakfast and a pill at dinner, then I'm supposed to take a pill at dinner" has the form "If p and q, then q"; denying any statement of that form would yield a contradiction of the form "q and not q"; (2) "If you're a sister, then you're a female" is true because of what the word *sister* means; denying it would yield the contradiction "Some female sibling is not female."

What logical necessity is to deduction, *probability* is to induction. In an *inductive argument*, it is claimed, on the basis of evidence drawn from past experience, that *probably* the conclusion is true. For example, on the basis of what has been seen of ravens, it has been concluded that probably all ravens are black. In the light of that evidence, the negation of "All ravens are black" is judged improbable. Whether this reasoning is acceptable cannot be decided merely by analyzing logical form or the meaning of terms, as in the case of deductive arguments. Its acceptability depends on whether there is reason to think that past experience furnishes us with a "representative sample," and that depends on whether we have observed a sufficient number and variety of ravens. If we have failed to observe a sufficient *number* of instances, we commit the *fallacy of hasty induction*; if we have failed to observe sufficient *variety* (for example, females as well as males), we commit the *fallacy of forgetful induction*. But when are the variety and number sufficient? The answer cannot be calculated on the basis of a formula; it is a judgment made in the light of a whole range of background information and general knowledge. This background information includes, in the raven case, facts such as birds of the same species tend to have similar coloration; in the light of *this*, we have some reason to regard a few well-chosen examples as representative of the whole population. If they are not well-chosen, so as to take into account factors such as sex, which past inductions have shown to be relevant, then there is a fallacy of forgetful induction.

The conclusion of an inductive argument is *always empirical*: it claims to describe how things happen to be in the world, based on "the evidence of the senses" (observation or experiment). An empirical proposition is always open in principle to confirmation or disconfirmation by future experience. For example, the generalization about all ravens being black would be disconfirmed (indeed refuted) should a strain of green ravens be observed in the future. Another example: In the past I have had many pairs of Grungie shoes, each of which lasted at least a year without falling apart; from this I infer that my new pair will also hold up at least that long, because they're similar to my past shoes in being made of the same materials and by the same company. Although my inference is a prediction in which I rightly have confidence, future experience may possibly falsify it.[3]

The importance of inductive reasoning, and the radical, irreducible difference between it and deduction, has been an important theme in "modern" (postmedieval) philosophy, beginning with the English politician and philosopher Sir Francis Bacon.[4] In his *Novum Organum (New Organon)*, published in 1620, Bacon argued that Aristotle and his medieval followers had slighted inductive logic, thereby ignoring the very instrument (Greek *organon*) we need for enlarging our store of information about the world.

Some famous images from Bacon help convey the essential difference between deductive and inductive reasoning. Deduction is like the work of the *spider*; induction, like the work of the *bee*. As the spider spins her web from what is already in her belly, so a (valid) deduction "draws out the implications" of its own premises—that is, makes explicit in the conclusion what is already contained in the premises. And as (cooperating with its fellow workers) the bee ventures forth to gather new materials for the sustenance and increase of the hive, so an inductive argument (supported by previous related inductions) ventures beyond the data contained in its premises—that is, it "extrapolates" a conclusion which (if true) adds to our store of information about the world. We need them both: inductive logic guides us in our efforts to add new truths to our store of empirical knowledge; deductive logic enables us to maintain consistency through time in the various statements we make, and to "preserve the truth" of what we have already learned.

Different as they are in function and appropriate mode of assessment, induction and deduction remain closely related. They are both concerned with truth: induction with gathering it, deduction with clarifying and preserving it. Moreover (and relatedly), serious inductive research requires systematic—deductively structured—observations or experiments.[5] Without these, the work of induction no longer resembles the activity the bee, but of the *ant*—who, according to Bacon, forages without method and accumulates without discrimination.

Accumulating many and varied confirming instances does not by itself produce a valid inductive basis for believing a given generalization; one must also continue to regard the generalization as an *empirical* proposition—one that may need to be changed in the light of fresh observation and experiment. So, one is obliged to be alert for, and to deal fairly with, any data that may appear to *disconfirm* the (perhaps cherished) conclusions of one's past generalizations. Failure to meet this obligation is known as *neglect of negative instances*.

One "neglects negative instances" when one presents cases that seem to support a favorite inductive generalization while "turning a blind eye to" those that seem to undermine it. Bacon maintained that this is the basis of superstition. Think of the belief that a black cat crossing our path leads to bad luck: the instances reinforcing it tend to be dramatic and memorable—something that makes us neglect or forget the many instances of black cats crossing our path without incident. Bacon tells of how a certain sceptical individual in ancient times was shown (on the wall of a temple) a painting of people who had escaped shipwreck after having "paid their vows"; this was supposed to demonstrate the power of the gods. In the following famous passage from *Novum Organum*, Bacon approvingly quotes the ancient sceptic's response, then defines the error against which he was responding:

> "Aye," asked he, "but where are they painted that were drowned, after their vows?" And such is the way of all superstition, whether in astrology, dreams, . . . or the like; wherein men, having a delight in such vanities, mark the events where they are fulfilled, but where they fail, though this happens much oftener, neglect and pass them by.[6]

Suppose someone continues firmly to believe in the power of the gods after becoming fully aware of the sort of negative instances Bacon was talking about. Is he being unreasonable? If he continues to claim that his belief is an inductively ("scientifically") validated empirical proposition, then he is being unreasonable and "pseudo-scientific"; for if the belief has the inductive status he claims for it, he *ought* to be worried about the negative instances. If, however, he gives up that claim, nothing unreasonable may remain about his belief in the power of the gods. It may now be a pure, unsuperstitious expression of a wholesome attitude of religious serenity—an attitude *we* might call "being in the hands of the Almighty."

Here is a different but related example. Some of us claim to believe that all people are always selfish. If we present this belief as an empirical proposition solidly grounded in inductive reasoning and yet neglect (or dogmatically dismiss) proposed counterexamples (such as Mother Teresa), then we are being unreasonable. But if we give up the claim that our belief has inductive status (admitting, perhaps, that it is really nothing more than the expression of a certain cynical attitude), then we are no longer committing the fallacy of neglect of negative instances—we are no longer being unreasonable, at least in *that* way.

■ NONINDUCTIVE REASONING BY ANALOGY

Some philosophers recognize a third main category of argument: *noninductive reasoning by analogy*.[7] Reasoning by analogy is reasoning by appeal to analogous (parallel or similar) cases. *Inductive* reasoning by analogy is a matter of formulating an empirical hypothesis about one case based on past experience with analogous cases. *Noninductive* reasoning by analogy is reasoning by analogy in which the conclusion is *not* an empirical hypothesis—not a proposition subject to confirmation or refutation by evidence drawn from sense experience. Noninductive arguments by analogy are also nondeductive: one does not determine their validity by appealing to established definitions or formal principles (such as *modus ponens*).

A certain logic student claims that "Only virtuous people are lovers of angling" is logically equivalent to "All virtuous people are lovers of angling." He can be refuted by giving parallel, analogous, sentences that clearly are *not* equivalent: "Only females are bearers of children" and "All females are bearers of children," for instance. Our conclusion—that his claim to logical equivalence is false—is not an empirical truth open to confirmation or disconfirmation by sense experience; we are not, then, dealing with an inductive argument. Nor is the validity of our reasoning to be determined by reference to an established formal principle or definition;[8] so we are not dealing with a deductive argument.

Consider now a case from the history of mathematics. Long ago "numbers" were just "integers or fractions of integers." Then one day some followers of Pythagoras investigated the "unit square." Reasoning, in accordance with the Pythagorean theorem, that the square on its diagonal is equal to the sum of two unit squares, they proceeded to the question "If the root (side) of the unit square (its square root) is 1, what is the root of the square on the diagonal?"

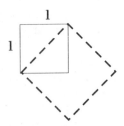

Disturbed to find that the answer could not be expressed as an integer or fraction of integers, they wondered whether to admit it among the ranks of numbers at all, in view of the great dis-analogy between it and standard numbers. They finally decided to say that it *is* a kind of number (an "irrational number"), presumably because they judged the analogy to be of greater significance than the dis-analogy—the analogy being (roughly) that the root of the diagonal square is, like a "standard, rational number," a quantity related to figures and figuring. In concluding that "the irrationals" are numbers, the Pythagoreans were not formulating an empirical hypothesis (as in inductive reasoning), nor were they dealing with an inference that could be assessed by standard definitions or formulas (as in deduction). Using noninductive reasoning by analogy, they were expanding the boundaries of a mathematical concept. And mathematicians have continued to extend the concept of number ever since—as in spinning a thread a spinster twists fiber on fiber.

Consider now two examples from the sphere of ethics, both taken from the abortion controversy, both addressing the question of whether to call the human embryo a human being. The first argument compares the embryo to the foundation of a house: just as stopping the construction of a house with the foundation is not destroying a house, so stopping a pregnancy at the embryo stage is not destroying a human being. This analogy, however, is *strained*, because there is a significant dissimilarity between the terms compared: The one is the product of a construction that could be stopped now and resumed later; the other, a natural process of generation that, once stopped, cannot be restarted. This strain is not present in the second argument, where the embryo is compared with a germinating acorn: just as grinding up the acorn is not "oakicide" (killing an oak tree), so aborting an embryo is not homicide (killing a human being).[9]

Arguments of this sort figure importantly in meaningful discussions of controversial issues, where often the disagreement cannot be resolved either by empirical investigation and inductive inference or through deduction from mutually accepted principles. Participants in such discussions want to present coherent and compelling views, not simply to express personal preferences. And so they offer arguments by analogy, test each other's arguments for "strains," develop new analogies, and so on. Of course, the disagreement may persist no matter how long the discussion continues. But the main point of the discussion may not be to overcome disagreement; it may be to clarify and develop the discussants' positions and to further their mutual understanding and respect.

■ FALLACIES

Suppose I present the following argument to persuade someone of the immorality of abortion:

> All murders are wrong.
> All abortions are murders.
> ∴ So, all abortions are wrong.

I am supposed to be leading someone to accept a proposition she now rejects, but in my argument I assume that she already accepts it: if she accepts that all abortions are murders, then she already accepts the conclusion, because *by definition* all murders are *wrongful* killings; thus I am assuming what I am supposed to be proving. This type of illogical thinking is called *begging the question* (or *petitio principii*). A classic example of this fallacy takes the form of a dialogue:

> "Why do you believe what the Bible says?"
> "Because it is the Word of God."
> "What makes you think so?"
> "Because the Bible, in several verses, speaks of itself as the Word of God."

Begging the question is one of the three main categories of *fallacies*, that is, *logical errors*. The second main category is called *inconsistency*, which means that there is a contradiction in the premises of one's thinking. For example:

> John, sixty-five years old, was convicted of using illegal drugs. Arguing for a light sentence, he told the judge that his drug habit was harmless, as he was too old to do any useful work. Asked how he lived, he replied, "On the wages of my twin brother."

The third, and largest, category of fallacy is *non sequitur,* where the conclusion of the argument does not follow from the premises. *Invalidity* is another name for this fallacy. To call an argument invalid is *not* just another way of saying that it commits a fallacy: it is to say that it commits a specific type of fallacy—*non sequitur.*[10]

We have already encountered the names of some special forms of *non sequitur: hasty induction* and *forgetful induction,* which are *non sequiturs* that only inductive arguments can commit, and *strained analogy,* which pertains to non-inductive reasoning from analogy. The following, known as *formal fallacies,* are peculiar to deductive reasoning:

1. *Illicit conversion* (three forms). (a) "If *p,* then *q,* so if *q,* then *p.*" (For example: "If you're a communist, then you're a socialist, so if you're a socialist, then you're a communist.") (b) "All *S* are *P*; thus, all *P* are *S.*" (For example: "All sound arguments are valid; thus, all valid arguments are sound.") (c) "Some *S* are not *P*; consequently, some *P* are not *S.*" (For example: "Some intoxicants are not alcoholic beverages; consequently, some alcoholic beverages are not intoxicants.")
2. *Affirming the consequent.* "If *p,* then *q*; *q*; thus, *p.*" (For example: "If the miners; are alive, then there is oxygen in the mine; there is oxygen down there; thus, the miners are alive.")
3. *Denying the antecedent.* "If *p,* then *q*; not *p*; thus, not *q.*" (For example: "If you're a communist, then you're a socialist; I see you're not a communist; thus, you can't be a socialist.")

You can justify a charge of formal fallacy if you can show that an argument deserves one of the above three names. But most formal fallacies are nameless. In such cases, we demonstrate the invalidity by using a formal technique (such as a logic diagram), or by using a parallel example (see p. 14).

Some arguments that may seem to commit fallacies of *non sequitur* should be regarded instead as enthymemes. An *enthymeme* is an argument with one or more assumed but unstated premises. "Some gloves are not flammable, because some gloves are made of asbestos," for example, should be regarded as a valid argument with the unstated assumption "No articles made of asbestos are flammable." "Socrates is a man; therefore, Socrates is mortal" is the classic example of an enthymeme. Adding the obvious unstated premise, we get the valid argument: "All men are mortal. Socrates is a man. Thus, Socrates is mortal."

"Some lovers of virtue are not lovers of angling; therefore, some lovers of angling are not lovers of virtue." Is *this* an enthymeme? No: it already fits a familiar argument pattern—illicit conversion; nothing would be clarified by adding another premise.

Enthymeme comes from a Greek word meaning "have in mind." Assumptions that we have in mind but leave unstated often influence our thought and action. If they are innocent pieces of common knowledge ("Men are mortal," for example), they may best be left unstated. But if they are dubious, harmful, or unhealthy (as are, for example, racial prejudices or paranoid attitudes), then they should be made explicit and challenged.

■ MORE FALLACIES

Of the many general forms of *non sequitur*, the following are among the most common:

1. *Equivocation*. Mistaking an invalid inference for a valid one because of an ambiguity in some word or phrase in the argument. For example: "We want our children to be normal. Now, normal children are always fighting with each other. So, we don't want our children to stop fighting." (*Normal* in the sense of "average" is confused with *normal* in the sense of "desirable.") Another example: "God is love, and love is blind; therefore God is blind."

2. *Composition*. Inferring that something can be truly said of a collection simply because it is truly said of the parts of that collection. For example, the nineteenth-century English philosopher John Stuart Mill argued that because each person's happiness is a good to that person, it must follow that the general happiness is a good to the aggregate of persons. Another example: "Atoms are not solid; they're mostly empty space. Therefore, the floor, which is made of atoms, can't really be solid either!" Beware of confusing a fallacy of composition, such as

   The sentences in his poem are well-constructed.
   Therefore, the poem is well-constructed.

   with an inductive generalization, such as

   Those sentences of his are well-constructed.
   Therefore, probably all of his sentences will be well-constructed.

3. *Division*. Inferring that something is true of the parts of a collection simply because it is true of that collection. For example, the seventeenth-century philosopher Gottfried Leibniz inferred that each of the tiny water particles in the surf must make a (tiny) noise from the fact that the surf (a collection of water particles) makes a noise. Another example: "That hunk of coal is black; therefore, the molecules making it up must be black."

4. *Black-and-white thinking*. Inferring that because one extreme is false, the opposite extreme is true. "You don't love us? Then you must hate us!" Another example: "Life's not a bed of roses, so it's a crock of manure."

5. *Irrelevant* ad hominem. Seeking to discredit what somebody says by citing an irrelevant fact about his or her background, circumstances, personality, or character. For example, Richard Wagner dismissed a certain music critic's negative assessment of his compositions with the argument "He's Jewish!" Another example: "Wife: 'You're spending too much money on golf.' Husband: 'You sound just like your mother—a nag!'" (That the wife has faults too does nothing to invalidate her criticism.)

6. *Irrelevant appeal to authority*. "Justifying" a claim by appealing to the word of someone whose say-so carries no special weight in the matter at hand. For example: "Franz, an expert etymologist, told me that some beetles are three feet long and talk. So, there exist some really amazing beetles in the world!" Now, even enlightened people who think for themselves base *some* of their beliefs on the say-so of "eyewitnesses" and "experts"; but they make sure both *who* their "authorities" are and that *what* they are claiming makes sense in the light of common knowledge.

7. *Irrelevant appeal to pity*. Citing facts that are calculated to arouse sympathy but that have no logical bearing on the question at issue. For example: "I deserve a

higher grade in philosophy, because if I don't get one, I won't graduate." Another appeal to pity would be a convicted criminal's plea to the judge for mercy on the grounds of a miserable childhood. Although the grounds adduced by the criminal may be insufficient or false, they are not logically irrelevant. Therefore, unlike the student, the criminal is not guilty of a *fallacious* appeal to pity.

8. *Irrelevance.* When there is nothing more specific to call an invalid argument, it may be labeled *irrelevant.* For example: A student trying to answer an essay question will sometimes resort to filling the page with miscellaneous information that has little or nothing to do with the question at issue, hoping thereby to "snow" the teacher.

Outline of Fallacies

    I. Begging the question (*petitio prinicipii*)

   II. Inconsistency

  III. *Non sequitur* (invalidity)

      A. Special (pertain to a specific type of reasoning)

        1. Formal fallacies: illicit conversion, affirming the consequent, denying the antecedent (pertain to deduction)

        2. Hasty induction and forgetful induction (pertain to inductive reasoning)

        3. Strained analogy (pertains to reasoning by analogy)

      B. General

        1. Equivocation

        2. Composition

        3. Division

        4. Black-and-white thinking

        5. Irrelevant *ad hominem*

        6. Irrelevant appeal to authority

        7. Irrelevant appeal to pity

        8. Irrelevance

■ A SHORT SERMON

The Sophists of ancient Greece were itinerant speech teachers and self-proclaimed "wisdom experts." Socrates fought against them, arguing that they taught not love of wisdom ("philosophy") but only tricks for scoring debating points. *Sophistry* is named after them—as is *sophism*, another name for *fallacy.*

It would be better not to learn fallacy labels at all than to develop an "uncritically critical" attitude about their application. So, we should cultivate the habit of carefully justifying our critical judgments, learning to regard fallacy terminology (and other concepts of logic) as tools for uncovering truth, rather than as weapons for winning debates. We will then be walking the path of philosophy rather than of sophistry.

■ NOTES

1. Philip Wheelwright, trans., *The Presocratics* (New York: Odyssey, 1966), 183. *Atom* comes from Greek roots meaning "what cannot be cut." The atoms of Democritus were indivisible particles characterized by size, shape, and position in "the void" (space).

2. *Modus ponens* and *modus tollens* are related to the important concepts of *sufficient condition* and *necessary condition*, respectively. "If the mouse in the jar is alive (A), then there is oxygen in the jar (O)" says that A is a *sufficient* condition for O—that is, says that seeing the mouse "alive and kicking" is sufficient for concluding that there is oxygen in the jar. Thus:

If A, then O.
A.
∴ O.   (Given what's sufficient for O, you get O.)

"If A, then O" is equivalent to "O is a *necessary* condition for A." This means that if the oxygen is sucked out of the jar, then the mouse will die. Thus:

If A, then O
not O.
∴ not A.   (Removing what's necessary for A removes A.)

3. The conclusion of the second example is *singular*—that is, about a single case (the new pair of Grungies). Such an argument is sometimes called *an inductive analogy*. The first example had a *universal* conclusion—a conclusion about *all* ravens. It is called *an inductive generalization*. (So, the common dictionary definition of induction as "reasoning from individual cases to a general conclusion" is too narrow.)

4. For more on the difference between induction and deduction see Brian Skyrms, *Choice and Chance* (Belmont, Ca: Dickenson, 1966).

5. Review question 6e (p. 26) to see how deductive reasoning, in the form of *modus tollens*, structured Lavoisier's famous anti-phlogiston experiment. For other examples, and to go more deeply into inductive logic and philosophy of science, see the excellent book by Carl G. Hempel, *Philosophy of Natural Science* (Englewood Cliffs, NJ: Prentice-Hall, 1966).

6. From *Novum Organum*, "Aphorisms concerning the Interpretation of Nature and the Kingdom of Man," no. 46.

7. I take this term from Stephen F. Barker, *The Elements of Logic*, 5th ed. (New York: McGraw-Hill, 1989), 225 ff. What Barker and I say about noninductive reasoning by analogy is indebted to John Wisdom's notion of a "case-by-case procedure." See his *Proof and Explanation: The Virginia Lectures* (Lanham, MD: Univ. Press of America, 1991). Although noninductive reasoning by analogy is more controversial than anything else in this chapter, I believe that it has considerable philosophical relevance and merits study.

8. The argument under discussion could not be reduced to a deduction such as

No sentence of the form "Only S are P" is equivalent to a sentence of the form "All S are P."

"Only the virtuous are lovers of angling" is a sentence of the form "Only S are P."
Therefore, "Only the virtuous are lovers of angling" is not equivalent to "All the
virtuous are lovers of angling."

Why accept the formal principle expressed in its first premise? Its truth is less evident than
that of the conclusion, while the truth of the "parallel case" in the original analogy is more
evident.

9. These arguments concern how human embryos *ought* to be classified and treated.
They are not inductive arguments because their conclusions are not empirical hypotheses—not conjectures about the world that are confirmed or refuted on the basis of observation and experiment. "My new car won't break down for at least a year" is empirical and
predictive. "The human embryo shouldn't be called a human being" is normative and
prescriptive. (There is more to say about these matters, but this is not the place for it.)

10. My treatment of fallacies owes a lot to Barker's *Elements of Logic*. For somewhat
different approaches to the topic, consult the logic texts mentioned under For Further
Reading.

■ QUESTIONS

Deductive Arguments*
1. For each of the following, ask: Is it an argument? If so, indicate the conclusion and
premise(s). If not, explain why not.
   *a. Since all Christmases are legal holidays, and no legal holidays are banking days,
no Christmases are banking days.
   b. Since the First World War, America has been deeply involved in European affairs.
   *c. Today is Monday; therefore, tomorrow is Tuesday.
   *d. If today is Monday, then tomorrow is Tuesday.
   e. The streets are wet; therefore, it must have rained.
   f. Sharma was a Hindu, so probably he was a vegetarian.
   g. If by *whiskey* you mean the devil's brew, that evil concoction that lures men away
from their families, ruins their health, and undermines the very structure of society, then
I'm against it. On the other hand, if by *whiskey* you mean that warm liquid that puts some
life into a gentleman on a cold winter's day, that oil of social intercourse and good fellow-
ship, that drink that puts much-needed tax dollars into the state treasury, then I am for it.
That, sir, is my stand on whiskey.

   *2. Correct or Incorrect?
   a. Every argument with true premises and a true conclusion is valid.
   b. Every argument with true premises and a true conclusion is sound.
   c. All valid arguments are sound.
   d. All sound arguments are valid.
   e. Some arguments are true.
   f. Some conclusions are true.
   g. Some statements are valid.

* An asterisk (*) denotes questions whose solutions are given on pp. 31–32. (See "Answers
to Selected Questions.")

h. A valid argument has to have a true conclusion.

i. A valid argument has to have true premises.

3. For each of the following: Is it *sound* or *unsound*? Explain.

*a. All animals are mammals; all dolphin are animals; therefore, all dolphin are mammals.

*b. All mammals are animals; all dolphin are animals; therefore, all dolphin are mammals.

*4. Explain the difference in *logical form* between (a) and (b) in question 3.

5. Are the following arguments *valid* or *invalid*?

a. All crafts are capacities for opposites. No virtues are capacities for opposites. Therefore, no virtues are crafts.

b. All virtuous people are patient; all good anglers are patient; consequently, all good anglers are virtuous.

*c. Some good Buddhists are not believers in God or gods; all good Buddhists are religious people; so some religious people are not believers in God or gods.

More Deductive Arguments*

*1. (a) Is every deductive argument with true premises and a false conclusion invalid? (b) Is every invalid deductive argument an argument with true premises and a false conclusion?

2. State an example that clearly demonstrates the invalidity of *affirming the consequent*.

3. For each of the following, formulate an *example* that demonstrates its invalidity:

*a. Followers of Rawls aren't socialists. Libertarians aren't socialists. So, Libertarians are followers of Rawls.

b. All religious believers are believers in a higher power; therefore, all believers in a higher power are religious people.

c. We never get both steak and lobster. We're not getting steak. So, we must be getting lobster.

4. The following additional valid arguments are well worth learning:

contraposition
> If *p*, then *q*.
> ∴ If not *q*, then not *p*.

chain argument
> If *p*, then *q*.
> If *q*, then *r*.
> ∴ If *p*, then *r*.

simplification (two forms)
> *p* and *q*.   *p* and *q*.
> ∴ *p*.   ∴ *q*.

Give a *sound* example of each of the above forms.

5. For each of the following common invalid forms, give a clear instance in which a false conclusion follows from a true premise or premises:

---

* See p. 32 for answers to exercises marked with an asterisk (*).

"*pseudo-contraposition*"
  If p, then q.
  ∴ If not p, then not q.
"*pseudo-chain*"
  If p, then q.
  If r, then q.
  ∴ If p, then r.
illicit conversion
  If p, then q.
  ∴ If q, then p.

6. For each of the following, say whether it is valid or invalid, and justify your answer. (Hint: Identify the argument as a *modus ponens*, fallacy of affirming the consequent, chain argument, or some other form.)

*a. If the rod is copper, then it conducts electricity; it conducts electricity; therefore, it is copper.

b. If the rod is copper, then it conducts electricity; it's not copper; therefore, it doesn't conduct electricity.

*c. If natural occurrences aren't coincidental, they're purposive. They're not coincidental. So, they're purposive.

*d. If that mark is a word, then it has a meaning. If it has a meaning, then it has a use that can be taught and learned. Consequently, if that mark is a word, it has a use that can be taught and learned.

*e. If burning is a matter of a substance giving off something, "phlogiston," then every substance is lighter after it's transformed by burning than before. But not every substance *is* lighter after burning. Therefore, burning is not a matter of a substance giving off phlogiston. (Lavoisier's argument against the medieval "phlogiston theory" of burning.)

*f. Unless you have a ticket, you will not be admitted. Therefore, if you have a ticket, you will be admitted.

*g. He's a senator only if he's not a convicted felon. He's not a convicted felon. Therefore, he's a senator.

*h. She's a citizen, if she's a senator. She's not a senator. Therefore, she's not a citizen.

*7. Use the *necessary/sufficient condition* terminology described in note 2 to explain why affirming the consequent and denying the antecedent are invalid. (Suggestion: In giving your explanation, modify the "mouse in the jar" examples of note 2.)

8. The expression *if and only if* is used to express the concept of *necessary and sufficient condition*. Thus, "So-and-so is president of the United States (P) if and only if So-and-so is commander-in-chief of the United States armed forces (C)" says that being commander-in-chief is both sufficient and necessary for being president—so that if you know C is true, then you can conclude P, and if you know P is true, then you can conclude C. Give two more illustrations of this concept.

Inductive Arguments*
1. "We should be careful to get out of an experience only the wisdom that is in it—and stay there, lest we be like the cat that sits down on a hot stove-lid. She will never sit

---

* See p. 32 for answers to exercises marked with an asterisk (*).

down on a hot stove-lid again—and that is well; but also she will never sit down on a cold one anymore." —Mark Twain, *Following the Equator*. What fallacy does the cat commit?

2. Evaluate the following arguments, saying what fallacy, if any, is committed. Explain your answers.

*a. I've talked to half a dozen people from Richmond, and they've all been weird. So, probably most people from Richmond are weird.

b. The drop of blood taken from the patient contains too few red blood cells; therefore, the patient probably has anemia.

*c. A whole bunch of us scanned the skies every morning and afternoon for bats, without sighting a single one. We conclude that probably there are no bats living around here.

d. Paraphrased from the report of a poll conducted by the *Literary Digest* during the depression:

> Choosing, at random, many telephone numbers of voters throughout the country, we asked whom they were going to vote for in the upcoming Presidential race. The great majority said they would vote for the Republican candidate, Alf M. Landon. Therefore, probably, Landon will win the election.

*e. From C. J. Jung, *Memories, Dreams, Reflections*:

> The unconscious . . . has . . . ways . . . of informing us of things which by all logic we could not possibly know. . . . I recall one time during World War II when I was returning home from Bollingen. . . . The moment the train started to move I was overpowered by the image of someone drowning. This was the memory of an accident that had happened while I was on military service. . . . I got out at Erlenbach and walked home. . . . Adrian, then the youngest of the boys, had fallen into the water at the bathhouse. It is quite deep there, and since he could not really swim he had almost drowned. . . . This had taken place at exactly the time I had been assailed by that memory in the train. The unconscious had given me a hint. †

3. A *paradox* has the form "That must be true—but it *can't* be true!" The following, known as *the paradox of the raven*, provides an interesting and instructive topic for discussion:

> If I brought you two black ravens, that would count as evidence for the generalization that all ravens are black. Similarly, if I brought two green shoes, that should count as evidence in support of the generalization that all non-black things are non-ravens. Now "All non-black things are non-ravens" is equivalent (by contraposition) to "All ravens are black."†† Therefore, what counts as evidence in support of the first, one should count as evidence in support of the second. Therefore, the two green shoes (as two instances of non-black non-ravens) should count as evidence for "All ravens are black."—But they don't!

This argument originated with the German-American philosopher Carl Hempel. Try to figure out for yourself how to avoid the absurd conclusion that green shoes support the generalization about ravens. (Hint: Ask whether green shoes would really be evidence for "All non-black things are non-ravens" in the way black ravens would be evidence for "All ravens are black." If not, why not?)

4. For each of the following propositions, say whether it is *logically necessary* or not.

*a. If no dogs devour glass, then no devourers of glass are dogs.

† For this and some other quotations used in the exercises, I am indebted to Barker.

†† Just as "If p, then q" is equivalent to "If not q, then not p," so "All S are P" is equivalent to "All non-P are non-S." Both transformations are called *contraposition*.

*b. No dogs devour glass.

c. You die if you fall to the ground from a twenty-story building.

d. Jon's car is larger than Ken's.

e. Anne has yellow hair.

f. Yellow is a color.

5. Earlier in this chapter (see note 2), we encountered the term *necessary condition*. We can now distinguish *logically necessary conditions* from those that are not. Being an animal is a *logically* necessary condition for being a cat; in other words, "If it's a cat, it's an animal" is a logically necessary statement. Being susceptible to many diseases is a necessary condition for being a cat, given the way the world is; in other words, "If it's an animal, it's susceptible to many diseases" is a true empirical statement. For each of the following, is a *logically* necessary condition being expressed?

*a. If a plant is uprooted, it must wither and die.

*b. If you're a bachelor, you're not married!

c. If that animal has given birth to a kitten, it must be a cat.

d. If Jon's car is larger than Ken's, and Ken's car is larger than Lou's, then Jon's car is larger than Lou's.

e. All mammals are animals.

Noninductive Reasoning by Analogy*

1. For each of the following noninductive arguments from analogy, *first* indicate the analogy employed, *then* evaluate it, probing for significant strains in the analogy.

*a. You should know what you want to be before you go to college, just as a builder should know what the house is to look like before he or she starts laying the foundation. For a college education is the foundation of one's career.

b. Just as we fire a coach who doesn't produce winning teams, so we should fire a teacher who doesn't produce classes that rank high in academic achievement tests.

c. Just as the ordinary person knows about ordinary, empirical facts (that the cat is on the mat, and so on) through "the evidence of the senses," so the mystic may know about extraordinary, "mystical" facts (that the individual ego is unreal, and so on) through the "sixth sense" of mystical experience.

d. Taxing earned income to support the needy is comparable to forced labor. So, it's wrong.

e. Based on Judith Jarvis Thomson, "A Defense of Abortion":†

Imagine that you are kidnapped in a remote and backward part of the world, and forcibly connected to a man with kidney failure. Until a kidney dialysis machine can be found, your body will serve as his life-support system. Just as it would be morally permissible for you to break the connection and escape, so it would be morally permissible for a woman to terminate a pregnancy that was the result of rape.

2. Are the following arguments from analogy noninductive?

*a. Nicotine extract produces tumors when smeared on the tender ears of mice.

---

* See p. 32 for answers to exercises marked with an asterisk (*).

† In *Philosophy and Public Affairs*, 1, no. 1 (1971). For another point of view, see Philip W. Bennett's "A Question for Judith Jarvis Thomson," *Philosophical Investigations*, 5, no. 2 (1982).

Therefore probably, because lung tissue is similar to ear tissue, nicotine extract applied to the lungs of mice would also produce tumors.

*b. No one knows that the human embryo *isn't* a human being. So you have no more moral right to abort it than a hunter has a right to shoot a creature in the bushes that he doesn't *know* to be nonhuman.

c. The universe is like an intricately designed clock. And as a clock implies a clock maker, so the universe implies a world maker.

Fallacies*

*1. Correct or Incorrect?

a. All invalid arguments are *non sequiturs*.

b. All *non sequiturs* are invalid.

c. All fallacious arguments are invalid arguments.

d. All invalid arguments are fallacious arguments.

e. If an argument begs the question, it is an invalid argument.

2. What type of fallacy, if any, is being committed in each of the following cases. Explain or justify your answers.

*a. The salesman says he likes me. And I believe him because I don't think he'd lie to someone he likes.

b. If Jon stays, Kim leaves; so, if Kim leaves, Jon stays.

*c. No generalizations are true; therefore, *your* generalization about my race is not true.

*d. All mammals are animals; all bats are animals; so, all bats are mammals.

e. To call them animals is to speak the truth. To call them pigs is to call them animals. Therefore, to call them pigs is to speak the truth.

*f. Only cocker spaniels chew ice cubes. Martha chews ice cubes. Therefore, Martha is a cocker spaniel.

g. I know that all tracks like these in the mud are made by muskrats, for my field guide, *Mammals of the Northeast*, says that a muskrats *always* makes tracks just like these.

3. Which of the following should be regarded as enthymemes? Identify unstated assumptions, where there are any.

*a. Mary went to school; therefore, her lamb went to school.

b. No one smiles at me. They must all hate me.

*c. Death is nothing to be feared, for good and evil imply consciousness, and death is the lack of consciousness.

d. All Virginians are Americans and all Londoners are Britons; therefore, no Londoners are Virginians.

*e. No sports cars are trucks; all sports cars are fast; so no trucks are fast.

f. We noticed no moths by the light in our backyard for thirty nights in a row. So probably the moths are not active in our backyard at this time of year.

More Fallacies**

1. What fallacy, if any, is committed? Be prepared to justify all answers.

---

* See pp. 32–33 for answers to exercises marked with an asterisk (*).

** See p. 33 for answers to exercises marked with an asterisk (*).

   *a. You can't believe what Socrates said about money not being the greatest good! He was a poor man and must have been envious of the rich.

   b. Her life was tragic. Therefore, each incident of her life must have been tragic.

   *c. What the distributors of pornography are engaged in is organized and it's criminal. Therefore, they must be mobsters engaged in organized crime.

   d. You're not a feminist? Then you must be a male chauvinist!

   *e. Stepping on my diseased toes makes them hurt *very* much, so you should be extra careful not to step on them.

   f. Officer, I didn't steal that whiskey. It'll kill my mother if you arrest me!

   *g. No one who loves God loves money. Marty hates money. So he must love God.

   h. The colors in the painting are beautiful. Therefore, the painting is beautiful.

   *i. Since no religious teachings are scientific hypotheses, it follows that all of them are *un*scientific hypotheses.

   j. Most members of our organization, the National Teachers Association, favor increasing taxes to support education; therefore, probably the public at large would support such a tax increase.

   *k. Everything in the universe—everything from you and me to stars and galaxies—has a cause. Therefore, the universe itself must have a cause.

   l. How do I know that Jesus loves me? The Bible tells me so!

   m. George Washington said that we should not get involved in foreign alliances. Therefore, President Bush made a mistake when he made all those alliances with Arab and European powers.

   n. Phil is an excellent lawyer. Phil is a human being. Therefore, Phil is an excellent human being.

   o. Inductive reasoning has worked in the past; therefore, probably it will work in the future.

   p. Printed under the picture of a naked hitchhiker in an advertisement for clothes: "Nothing is better than Land Lubber Clothes."

   2. Name the fallacy committed, if any, in each of the following. Justify your answers.
   a. From St. Thomas Aquinas (thirteenth century), *Summa Theologica*:

   > Everything that is in motion must be moved by something else. If therefore the thing which causes it to move be in motion, this too must be moved by something else, and so on. But we cannot proceed to infinity in this way, because in that case there would be no first mover, and in consequence neither would there be any other mover; for secondary movers do not cause movement except they be moved by a first mover, as, for example, a stick cannot cause movement unless it is moved by the hand. Therefore it is necessary to stop at some first mover which is moved by nothing else. And this is what we all understand God to be.

This is St. Thomas's *argument from motion*, the first of his "five ways" of proving the existence of God. As a first step in analyzing it, focus on the conclusion that it is necessary to stop at some first mover. Then carefully review each line that led up to it.

   b. From *New York* magazine (an instance of the kind of thinking the author calls "fascism of the left"):

   > Debate, and the analytic thinking it requires is oppressive. . . . It forces people to make distinctions, and since racism is the result of distinctions, it should be discouraged.

   *c. Extracted and paraphrased from G. K. Chesterton, "The Ethics of Elfland," in *Orthodoxy*:

Life is a gift.
All gifts have a giver.
Therefore, there is a Giver of Life.

The world is magic.
Magic implies a magician.
Therefore, the world implies a magician.

3. Using examples, explain why the following are not always invalid: appeal to pity, *ad hominem*, and appeal to authority.

*4. "I will die, because I am human and all humans die" is a valid deductive inference from a "whole" (humans) to a "part" (*this* human, me). Explain how this sort of inference from whole to part differs from a fallacy of division. ■

■ ANSWERS TO SELECTED QUESTIONS

Deductive Arguments

1. a. Argument. Premises in the first two clauses, conclusion in the third. **c.** Argument. Premise: "Today is Monday." **d.** A single *if/then* statement. An argument requires at least two statements.

2. a. I; **b.** I; **c.** I; **d.** C; **e.** I; **f.** C; **g.** I; **h.** I; **i.** I.

3. a. Unsound because a premise is false. **b.** Unsound because invalid. Even though every dolphin is a mammal, this does not follow from the given premises. (See answer to 4b.)

4. The logical form of question a is clarified through the use of symbols. A diagram also helps:

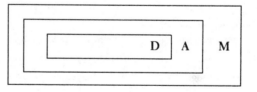

All A are M.
All D are A.
So, all D are M.

Compare with the following for (b):

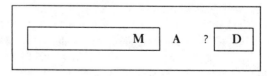

All M are A.
All D are A.
So, all D are M.

Here the premises don't determine the whereabouts of D: it *could* be entirely outside of the M box.

5. c. Valid. Can be diagrammed as follows, where "*" = "someone who's *not* a believer in God or gods":

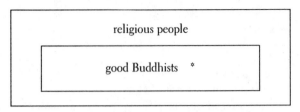

Explanation: Every good Buddhist is in the *religious people* box, and at least one person who is not a believer in God is in the *good Buddhist* box. Consequently, there must also be at least one person in the *religious person* box who is not a believer in God.

More Deductive Arguments
1. a. Yes, because—by definition—valid deduction "preserves truth." **b.** No. If your deductive reasoning is invalid, there is no *guarantee* that you will get a true conclusion even when all of your premises are true. But you might still "luck out" and get a true conclusion.

3. a. Followers of Jesus aren't atheists. Muslims aren't atheists. So Muslims are followers of Jesus.

6. a. Invalid, affirming the consequent; **c.** Valid, *modus ponens*; **d.** Valid, chain; **e.** Valid, *modus tollens*; **f.** Invalid, "pseudo-contraposition" (NOTE: "Unless" = "if not"); **g.** Invalid, affirming the consequent (NOTE: "*p* only if *q*" = "If *p*, then *q*"); **h.** Invalid, denying the antecedent (NOTE: "*p* if *q*" = "If *q*, then *p*").

7. "If the mouse is alive (A), then it has oxygen to breathe (O)." "If A, then O" says (or implies) that O is necessary for A—not that it's sufficient. So, A doesn't follow from O. Similarly, "If A, then O" says that A is sufficient for O—not that it's necessary. So, *not* O doesn't follow from *not* A. (In both cases, cyanide gas could have been mixed with the oxygen!)

Inductive Arguments
2. a. Hasty induction; **c.** Forgetful induction; **e.** Neglect of negative instances.

4. a. Logically necessary; **b.** Not logically necessary.

5. a. Not logically necessary; **b.** Logically necessary.

Noninductive Reasoning by Analogy
1. a. College : one's life :: a foundation : house (college *is to* one's life *as* . . .). Strained analogy. One point is that, unlike job training, a college education is meant to provide the foundations for many possible structures, not for one fixed structure.

2. a. No, it is inductive argument by analogy. Note that the conclusion is an empirical prediction. **b.** Yes, it is noninductive. To say that the creature in the bushes is a deer is an empirical prediction; to say that the embryo in the womb is a human being is not.

Fallacies
1. a. C; **b.** C; **c.** I; **d.** C; **e.** I.

2. a. Begging the question. The customer is taking the affection of the salesman for granted—the point he's supposed to be establishing. **c.** Inconsistency. The premise "No generalizations are true" implies its own falsity. **d.** Formal fallacy of *non sequitur*. (The invalidity of a similar argument is demonstrated in the diagram for answer 4b under "Deductive Arguments.") **f.** Although the first premise happens to be false, no *logical* error (fallacy) is committed.

3. **a.** Everywhere that Mary went, her lamb was sure to go. **c.** Whatever is to be feared is something involving good and evil. **e.** Formal fallacy of *non sequitur*. Compare: "No dogs are cats; all dogs are mammals; so, no cats are mammals."

More Fallacies

1. **a.** Irrelevant *ad hominem*. **c.** Equivocation on "organized crime." **e.** An appeal to pity, but not a fallacious one. For surely the premise is relevant to the conclusion. **g.** Fallacy of affirming the consequent. "If he loves God, he doesn't love money; he doesn't love money; thus, he loves God." **i.** Black-and-white thinking: that religious belief isn't a scientific hypothesis (one extreme) doesn't imply that it is an unscientific hypothesis (the other extreme); a religious belief may be no kind of hypothesis at all, whether scientific or unscientific. **k.** Fallacy of composition.

2. **c.** Nobody who doubted the conclusions of these two arguments would agree to the first premises. Thus, if meant to *prove* their conclusions (that is, to "refute the atheist"), they would be question-begging and unsuccessful. But these arguments do not sound like attempted proofs. When read in context, it is quite clear that Chesterton is using these arguments for the purpose of *elucidating* the idea of "God as Giver of Life and Cosmic Magician," not for the purpose of proving the existence of something. (In general: it is important to remember *first* that the fallacy of begging the question can be committed *only* by arguments intended to prove [or make probable] their conclusions, and *second* that not all arguments are intended in that way.)

4. In the valid deduction, *whole* is to *part* as *species* is to *its members*; in fallacy of division, *whole* is to *part* as an *ensemble or collection* is to *the elements composing it*. What is true of a species is true of it "distributively"—that is, of each and every example of it; what is true of an ensemble or collection is true of it "collectively"—but not necessarily of the elements composing it.

■ FOR FURTHER READING

Ackrill, J. L. *Aristotle the Philosopher*. New York: Oxford Univ. Press, 1981.

Barker, Stephen F. *The Elements of Logic*. 5th ed. New York: McGraw-Hill, 1989.

Brenner, William H. *Logic and Philosophy: An Integrated Introduction*. Notre Dame, IN: Univ. of Notre Dame Press, 1993.

Churchill, Robert Paul. *Logic: An Introduction*. New York: St. Martin's, 1990.

Fisher, Alec. *The Logic of Real Arguments*. New York: Cambridge Univ. Press, 1988.

Hempel, Carl G. *Philosophy of Natural Science*. Englewood Cliffs, NJ: Prentice-Hall, 1966.

Kelley, David. *The Art of Reasoning*. New York: W.W. Norton, 1990.

Radner, Daisie, and Michael Radner. *Science and Unreason*. Belmont, CA: Wadsworth, 1982.

Skyrms, Brian. *Choice and Chance*. Belmont, CA: Dickenson, 1966.

Wisdom, John. *Proof and Explanation: The Virginia Lectures*. Lanham, MD: Univ. Press of America, 1991.

CHAPTER THREE

Metaphysics

LEEMON McHENRY

There is a science . . . that studies Being qua Being, together with those properties which belong to it by reason of its essential nature. This science is quite distinct from what we may call the special sciences, none of which investigates Being in its purely general aspect as Being, but each of which rather cuts off some partial aspect of Being and studies the set of properties belonging to that partial aspect: as do the mathematical sciences. But it is first principles and the highest reasons that we are seeking, and clearly these must constitute a subject- matter with a nature of its own.[1]
ARISTOTLE

■ INTRODUCTION

It is widely agreed by historians of philosophy that Western philosophy began with metaphysics. Philosophers before Socrates, the "pre-Socratics" (roughly 625–371 B.C.), were essentially concerned with the nature of ultimate reality. Thinkers such as Thales, Anaximander, Pythagoras, Parmenides, and Heraclitus sought what might be called "first principles" of reality, and thus they established metaphysics and natural science in one shot. Perhaps the most important discovery of this period was not so much the *answers* they gave us but rather the *questions* they asked, for the whole context in which they raised their questions presupposed a *naturalistic*—as opposed to a *supernaturalistic*—answer. In this respect, the pre-Socratics broke with the strong mythological character of the thought of their predecessors. Instead of giving explanations of humans and the world in terms of the worldviews of Homer and Hesiod—that is, the struggles between the gods, and their various dealing with mortals—the pre-Socratics introduced metaphysical concepts such as "substance," "form," "permanence," and "change" into the basic framework of thought about our world. Pre-Socratic metaphysics thus takes as its ultimate conviction the idea that the universe is a natural entity that is comprehensible by rational thought.

Aside from tributes to the ancient Greeks for the origins of metaphysics, and of philosophy as a whole, anyone who has asked basic questions such as "Who or what am I?" or "What is my place in the scheme of things?" or "What is ultimately real?" has unwittingly taken the plunge into metaphysics. It is at such times of solemn introspection coupled with profound curiosity about ourselves and the nature of the universe that we discover *wonder* and its infinite territory. The need to question and the uncertainty or incompleteness of the answers linger just beyond the veneer of our everyday existence.

■ WHAT IS METAPHYSICS?

Before we embark on more specific investigations into the metaphysical issues raised above, we need to make some attempt at a more precise characterization of *metaphysics*. This is especially important since misconceptions of the subject are widespread in popular culture. For example, one popular understanding (or misunderstanding) of metaphysics places it wholly within the context of spiritualism; or worse, the occult; or still worse, pseudoscience. It may very well be the case that the world's great religions implicitly convey a metaphysical view about the nature of reality as ultimately spiritual, but this is another matter. The type of misuse of the term *metaphysics* I have in mind is current among practitioners of New Age spirituality. This is a poor substitute for the philosophical, critical, and systematic inquiry into the nature and structure of reality.

As the traditional story goes, the term *metaphysics* comes from Aristotle's editor, Andronicus of Rhodes, who in the first century B.C. classified and cataloged Aristotle's works. Andronicus took the writings Aristotle called "first philosophy" and placed them after his treatise on physics.[2] Metaphysics, from the Greek *ta meta ta physika*, literally means "those things after the physics." But this historical origin of the term is purely accidental. Metaphysics is better understood as the systematic investigation of the most general principles of reality, or, as Aristotle himself said, it is "a science that studies Being qua Being." In Aristotle's sense, the metaphysician seeks principles that are prior to or beyond any investigation in the special sciences. A chemist, for example, may explain the particular molecular composition of a substance, but the question "What is substance in general?" is of no interest to his or her investigations. Similarly, a physicist will explain particular causes in material bodies from the effects of magnetism, electricity, light, and so on, but the attempt to understand the very notion of causation falls outside his or her area of concern. Such issues do, however, lie at the center of the metaphysician's quest.

Insofar as metaphysics does not proceed as one of the special sciences, the results of direct observation and experimentation are not the primary means of constructing first principles, albeit such results will have some place within the scheme of principles, given that the metaphysician seeks a system that is consistent with current science. The evidence of sense perception has usually taken a back seat to the attempt to construct principles of the universe by means of logical investigation—that is, of reasoning *a priori*. In this respect, the metaphysician does not need a laboratory or high-tech instruments to do the necessary work. The metaphysician's procedure in attempting to discover the fundamental features of reality is more akin to that of the mathematician or the theoretical physicist. The main tool is logic, but intuition and insight are equally, if not more, important.

The great metaphysicians of the past have always had a vision of the essence of reality, and the picture they paint is always fascinating, if not mind-boggling. I need only mention the likes of Plato, Aristotle, Descartes, Spinoza, Leibniz, Hegel, and Whitehead as typical examples of metaphysical vision in the Western tradition. But their particular views of reality are very different, and on many points they directly contradict one another. The attempt to decide whose vision is right is a matter of extreme difficulty, and the criteria for deciding whose vision comes closest to the truth seems to elude our grasp forever. But one thing is sure— a view that is supported by precise and rigorous argumentation can only gain the attention and respect of those who are seriously engaged in the pursuit of truth.

Some philosophers see metaphysics as a *superscience* because to do it at all adequately, one must attempt to grasp the essential nature of the universe, not in some fragmentary or piecemeal fashion, but as a whole. The principles put forth therefore have a universal character in the sense that they attempt to give a general account of everything in the universe, including the actual and the possible. Such principles then serve as foundations from which reasoning in the special sciences proceeds. Metaphysical principles are the most basic and most general principles of reality.

We can thus provide an abstract characterization of metaphysics, though it is only by examining specific metaphysical problems that we can come to a real understanding of the subject. Let us now proceed to consider the branch of metaphysics called *ontology*. In the course of exploring the issues in this area, we discover some of the most perplexing yet compelling problems of metaphysics.

■ ONTOLOGY

Questions regarding ontology lie at the heart of metaphysics. Ontology attempts to determine what *is*; thus, philosophers who are concerned with this area are especially interested in questions such as "What sorts of things exist?" "Are existence and being the same?" "What is the status of various types of entities?" and "Do some entities depend on others?"

Let us speculate for the moment about what sorts of things are real, or exist. An initial list might include entities as diverse as people, animals, and other material objects such as trees, houses, cars, books, bicycles, computers, and coffee cups. But someone might disagree from the start that the list is too narrow and that entities such as minds, ideas, numbers, sets, geometrical figures, and God and the angels must be included. Still someone else might find this survey lacking and might wish to include fictional entities such as unicorns, mermaids, leprechauns, the Greek and Roman gods, and extraterrestrials. After all, granted that ideas are real, the content of our ideas must have some sort of reality as well.

Now our universe is starting to get *very* populated, and for some, much too cluttered. How, then, shall we decide what to include? An appeal to direct observation will not help us much here because that would rule out not only God, minds, ideas, and numbers but also the subatomic world of physics, and to complicate matters even more, the past and future, because strictly speaking we only observe the content of the present. Common sense does not fare much better as the final arbiter because it is notoriously defective. What we would like to believe to be so common to ourselves is unfortunately uncommon to others. And if we appeal to science, we find that scientists themselves hardly agree about what is really real. Electrons, quarks, cosmic strings, and black holes are all plausible candidates, but none are firmly established beyond doubt.

Perhaps we can clarify things a bit by introducing a few metaphysical concepts and by distinguishing between actuality and possibility, concrete and abstract, and real and ideal. Armed with such distinctions we can move on to classify and categorize our ontological clutter. This prepares us for our real problem, which is to construct a theory that will commit us to what the universe actually contains—no more, no less. This is a formidable task that divides metaphysicians into two schools of thought: *analytic ontology*, which is a somewhat restrictive or conservative approach to determining what is real, and *speculative metaphysics*, which is a more expansive or liberal approach. Let us first take up the speculative approach and become deliberately expansive about our ontological theory; then let us raise questions from the point of view of analytic ontology.

If we begin with the sorts of things that are actual and concrete, our universe already contains a lot of "stuff." Sense perception informs us of broad outlines of order in the concrete, material world. Within this context we discern individuals—people, animals, houses, cars, plants, stones, and so on. These are *individual substances*, which Aristotle believed to be the concrete particulars that populate space and time. Individual substances are roughly identified by nouns that take an indefinite article—an apple, a man, a car. Proceeding in this manner, wood, steel, and clay do not pass for individual substances. These function as the *matter* of individual substances. For Aristotle, an individual substance is a particular combination of *matter* and *form*. Matter is what an individual substance is made of. Form is how the matter is structured.

Individual substances have two important characteristics: (1) they are self-same centers of change; that is, they endure throughout their changes as the same individuals, and (2) they are capable of independent existence. To grasp the point of this second characteristic, we must distinguish substances from *properties* or *qualities*—red, sweet, round, courageous. Qualities cannot exist independently.

They are, rather, dependent upon the individual substances that they qualify. We never find the quality *red* by itself, for example. It is always a property of some concrete individual thing like a car or an apple. Furthermore, qualities can exist in many different individuals. The quality *red*, for example, may characterize different individual things at the same time or at different times. My tie is the same shade of red as the apple in front of me and the car that was outside my window yesterday.

The subatomic world that lies at the base of this macroscopic world is constructed theoretically. Provided that our physical theory is correct, subatomic particles, atoms, and molecules are actual, concrete entities as well. These are not, however, individual substances. They are part of the theoretical framework of matter. We make sense of this world by describing individual things in terms of form, matter, and quality. The changes that these things undergo over time we call *events*. Furthermore, our discourse about concrete, actual things involves us in various attempts to explain causal interactions between them. This is the business of the special sciences: geology, biology, zoology, chemistry, subatomic physics, astrophysics, and so on.

Now, what about such things as sets, relations, numbers, and geometrical figures? These are abstract entities that some philosophers believe inhabit an eternal permanent world of their own. The entities of this world might be thought of as "ideal" because their perfect essences are never realized in our "real" world but only contemplated in thought or in theorems of mathematics and geometry. Plato is a major proponent of this sort of view. In fact, for him the immaterial mathematical entities occupy an intermediate position between the eternal "Forms" and the concrete particulars of sense experience.[3] This is the territory of the pure mathematician, where vast systems of abstract order are discovered.

Aside from the actual world and the abstract world of mathematics, we also discern *possible* worlds, and here our ontology multiplies to include infinities of worlds of a rather perverse sort. The worlds of possibilities include not only whatever fictional characters or entities we can dream up, but also histories that *might have been*, or what *could possibly be* in the future.[4] This we might call the worlds of "if," as in "if this world had been otherwise. . . ." Consider, for example, the counterfactual conditional "If Adolf Hitler had won the Second World War, the world would be ruled by Aryans." Whatever we might imagine for counterfactuals defines a possible world. Although these statements are counter to fact, we *can* imagine what the world would be like in many different ways if they were realized, and we have thereby defined those possible worlds.

Possibilities are what might be or what might have been. At each moment of the universe, possibilities become actualized. When some possibilities are actualized, infinitely many other possibilities are excluded from being actualized. For example, when I drove to the university this morning, I made actual a possible world from several other options I could have chosen, and in my own small way contributed to what is actual now and placed limitations on what will be in the future.

As mentioned above, other types of possible worlds include the worlds of fictional characters in novels, the bizarre creatures of science fiction, or even the dream worlds we presumably enter into every night when we go to sleep. Perhaps the only things that are ultimately excluded from these worlds are logical impossibilities such as the round square, the son of a barren woman, and the married bachelor. These are contradictions and, therefore, cannot become actual under any circumstances. Necessarily true propositions, on the other hand, are true for all possible worlds: for example, "Bachelors are unmarried men" or the truths of mathematics and geometry ($5 + 7 = 12$, or the Pythagorean theorem: If a and b are the lengths of a right triangle, and c is the length of the hypotenuse, then $a^2 + b^2 = c^2$).

The actual world—the world we happen to inhabit—is only one of many possible worlds. The German philosopher Gottfried Leibniz believed it to be "the best of all possible worlds" because God, being perfect, would not have made actual an inferior world. Most philosophers believe that nonactual possible worlds are merely conceptual and exist only in the mind or in the mind of God. No matter how sophisticated or advanced our space travel might become, we will never be able to travel to a nonactual possible world. They are only places in logical space where we can soar in the wings of imagination, but as high and as wildly as we like. Other philosophers disagree. Modal realists, for example, believe possible worlds are no less real than the actual world. By means of a high-powered and sophisticated modal logic, they argue their case for the existence of all possible worlds.[5] This does not mean that our world is in any way connected spatially or temporally with other worlds or that some sort of travel between them would be possible, but it does mean that there is nothing very special about *our* world other than the fact that we happen to inhabit it. Given this sort of outlook, the very distinction between the actual and possible seems to dissolve, because every way that a world could possibly be is a way that some world is.

Now to all of this ontology, if we include God and the angels, we see that they have rather a lot to look after.[6]

I am not forgetting minds and their ideas. But are these entities in their own right and part of the actual, concrete world? To answer this question, we might resort to the metaphysical concept of substance again. This time, however, we are not concerned so much with individual substances as with general *types* of substance.

Those who believe that there are two types of substance, mental and physical, are called *dualists*. Dualists claim that there are minds having *thought* as their essence and bodies having *extension*—spatial magnitude—as their essence. A view of this sort is implicit in the religious doctrines many of us learned as children. Even if it is only held implicitly, however, it looms large in the background of our most basic thoughts about the world and beyond. The notion that a person has an immaterial soul that survives the death of the body is sharply contrasted with the material world of which the body has its being. Invariably this view runs into trouble when we ask bothersome questions about the relations between the immaterial world of minds or souls and the material world of bodies, as did the French philosopher René Descartes.[7] For example, how does one substance that is immaterial and unextended—namely, thought—interact with and influence another world of substance—namely, the material, extended world—and vice versa?

Look at it this way. We have some conception of what it is for one substance to interact with another of its own kind. So, we can make sense of physical things such as molecules interacting with other molecules and producing more complex molecular compounds. We can also make some sense of how ideas interact with one another in an individual's consciousness. But how is it that my idea of moving my fingers over the keyboard of the computer actually causes my fingers to move? Or how is it that the bowling ball that fell on my foot produced the mental event I so intimately know as a painful throbbing? The fact that these things happen is obvious. The question is, "How can we make sense of their happening?"[8]

Descartes thought that the two different substances do causally interact with each other through a small gland in the brain, the pineal gland, which he thought was the seat of the soul. But the gland itself is a *physical* thing, so this does not seem to get us anywhere. The idea of one substance interacting with another different kind of substance is obscure at best. Since Descartes defined the substances of mind and body as radically different and utterly distinct, it is difficult, if not impossible, to understand how to put them together in such a way as to get interaction.

Recognizing the inherent difficulties with metaphysical dualism, most philosophers have adopted some version of a monistic or pluralistic ontology. The ontology of two different types of substance is thus replaced by an ontology of only one substance or many substances of the *same* type. Perhaps there are just physical things after all, and minds are nothing more than brains. At the other extreme, it might be that physical things do not *really* exist but are only appearances of a more fundamental substance that is ultimately mental. Clearly, the battleground between physical, materialist ontologies and psychical, immaterialist ontologies results from an inability to solve the mind-body problem.[9] For myself, all this shows that the concept of substance is suspect and needs to be replaced with a different type of ontology altogether. This we shall explore in the following section.

Questions about the ontology of the world (or worlds) invariably lead us to much more than we ever thought possible. Thus far, however, we have only categorized and classified different types of entity that are discussed by metaphysicians. How do we decide what the world actually contains? The simple answer is everything; but what exactly constitutes everything is a complex problem.

For the sake of simplicity, let us take the world to contain those items mentioned earlier: quarks, electrons, atoms, molecules, material bodies, properties, events, sets, relations, numbers, geometrical figures, minds, ideas, God, angels, and possible worlds *ad infinitum*. With speculative metaphysics this is basically it, allowing for some variations here and there described by different philosophers.

Much of the controversy among different speculative systems stems from attempts to establish which class of entities is *basic* or fundamental and which of the other classes are derived from the basic class. Plato and Aristotle clashed on the issue of whether the concrete particulars (tables, chairs, trees) depend upon the abstract, mathematical entities, or vice versa. The three great continental rationalists—Descartes, Spinoza, and Leibniz—differed on whether everything depended upon two substances, one substance, or many substances of the same kind. Materialists argue that the world is fundamentally matter, while idealists argue that everything is fundamentally constructed out of mind. So, what we take to be the basic ontological entities determines the status of the other types of entities or whether certain types exist at all.

As I mentioned at the beginning of this section, one of the major issues that concerns philosophers of the analytic approach is a fear of overpopulation: We end up with more in our philosophy than that which actually exists in heaven and earth. The task of depopulation and the attempt to trim our picture of the world down to just the right size is more difficult than the ease with which we just populated it. As American philosopher W. V. Quine puts the point, the shaving of Plato's beard has proven tough and has frequently dulled the edge of Occam's Razor.[10] Occam's principle (known as "Occam's Razor"), "Do not multiply entities beyond necessity," tells us to postulate entities only to the extent that we are forced to do so in the course of explanation. Historically, Occam's Razor has always been a logical tool against ontological excess, but as Quine suggests, the shaving still proves to be a tough job.

As far as the difficulty of overpopulation is concerned, natural languages, such as English, are often the prime suspects mainly because they allow us to play fast and loose with vocabulary and construction, while at the same time they seem to commit us to the existence of whatever emerges in discourse. For example, we say that we do things for the sake of honor or love. But do *sakes* exist in addition to individual acts of honor and love? We speak of them in ordinary language, but perhaps this is just a "manner of speech" and nothing more. The question, however, is, "How much more of ordinary language is like this?"[11]

Where we can do with less in our ontology, to have more, according to Occam, is superfluous. Consider, for example, how much reduction occurs if we simply regard talk about possible worlds as logically consistent states of affairs instead of actual realities. In this way, the possible worlds of the Greek gods, Pegasus, Medusa, unicorns, and mermaids are simply regarded as talk about beings in stories or about what people once believed to be part of the real world.

Reduction of ontology is important to those philosophers who favor theoretical economy. Others favor all manner of entities provided that they serve some important function in theory. Just as pure mathematicians are inclined to believe in the existence of an infinite hierarchy of sets for the benefits it yields in terms of theoretical unity, some philosophers find the vast realms of possible worlds equally plausible.

■ EVENTS VERSUS SUBSTANCES

Now that we have discovered the task of ontology as well as the problems associated with this field, let us pursue one solution to the specific problem of determining which class of entity is basic, and proceed to depopulate our ontologically cluttered universe. Instead of viewing the world primarily in terms of the concept of substance, let us change the framework by regarding events as the primary entities, and eliminate substance altogether. We can then examine the results of this type of ontology in terms of theoretical economy and its compatibility with modern physics.

When we ordinarily think of events, we tend to view them as *happenings* or *changes* to individual substances. Our ordinary language certainly reinforces the picture that events have a kind of dependent existence on particular material things. If we say "Gary won the Boyne Mountain downhill race in record time" or "A 747 Jumbo Jet crashed at London's Heathrow Airport yesterday," we state some change to a substance, that Gary did this, or a Jumbo Jet did that. Individual substances are named by the grammatical subjects of the sentences, while events are described in terms of actions to such substances and appear in our language as verbs and adverbs. We can always change the subjects of our sentences and use nouns or noun phrases to talk about battles, explosions, performances, achievements, defeats, and the like, but these nouns are derived from verbs or verb phrases. For example, "The crashing of the jet resulted in a tragic loss of life." In this way, the very structure of our language provides us with a definite ontological picture that consists of the primary things, the individual substances, and the changes that occur to such substances over time. This is all fine and well taken at face value. But it appears that we may have put the cart before the horse by placing such faith in our ordinary language to do the work of ontological construction.

If we begin with our experience of the world, instead of the way we talk about the world, we first of all discover that we never actually experience substances. When I look about my desk, I perceive properties in various spatial relations—mainly colors, shapes, sizes, and shades of light and dark—but I never experience substance as that which upholds the properties.[12] What, then, is substance other than a nonempirical supposition I use to construct my world? Even if I now appeal to physics and chemistry to tell me the substance of objects, I am given explanations that involve refinements of properties down to the levels of molecules, atoms, and subatomic particles, but still the substances refuse to reveal themselves. What I do experience is transitions in time that involve changes of properties. In each moment of experience, I am aware of the passage of nature.

Instead of taking individual substances as the basic class of entity (which we never experience in the first place), let us focus attention on the temporal transitions that I now call *events*.[13] Within the duration of any experience, I discriminate constituent events. My typing this sentence contains my typing individual words, and my typing the individual words contains my typing the individual letters. Events therefore extend over one another in a four-dimensional array of whole-part relations, each having a definite volume and duration. Admittedly, we do not experience the most basic events as minimal occurrences. We must therefore postulate atomic events to prevent an infinite regress in nature. However, our experience does include transitions in time that make up various layers of events in nature.

Events happen only once; they are nonrepeatable particulars of space-time. Within these events, I also experience properties that give the events a definite structure. The properties are indeed repeatable. I notice, for example, how the color of the apple before me is the same as that of another apple I ate yesterday, or how the color of this apple continues to characterize it from yesterday to today. But now I have to admit that the apple itself is nothing more than a series of events, although compared with what I ordinarily call events, the apple's history is a series of events that is rather monotonous. That is, the apple before me is nothing more than the particular way that the events of this region of space-time continue to carry the pattern of properties that I call "the apple." Ordinary objects of perception seem to survive across time as stable substances, but it is only the repeatable patterns of properties that survive over a specific period of time, and the pattern is subject to change given a sufficient period.

From this point of view, the appearance of stability in objects is relative to the period of time under consideration. So, for example, the sequence of events that characterize the apple across time has a relatively short life span compared with the sequence of events that form the history of my body. My body has an extremely short life span compared with the history of planet Earth. From the point of view of astronomical time, the massive sequence of events that form a planet or a galaxy are relatively short-lived compared with the history of the universe. The point here is one that was clearly recognized by the ancient Greek Heraclitus—namely, everything changes. Apparent stability is simply a slower rate of change in an object where there is more similarity in the succession of events.

The results of an ontology of events involve us in a complete transformation of common sense.[14] The usual dependence of events upon particular substances is now reversed so that events become the basic entities on which we perceive the continuity of objects. Objects are now construed in terms of patterns of properties across time; so the very concept of substance as a self-same basis for the properties is superfluous. Substance is eliminated from our ontology. It no doubt continues to be indispensable for our ordinary ways of getting on in the world. For example, it is necessary for our habits of speech and for the marketplace, but metaphysically it appears to have outlived its usefulness.

From the perspective of theoretical economy, then, the theory of events has streamlined the ontological clutter of the foregoing categorization, because we no longer need substances for each and every type of entity in the world. The two basic types of entities—*events* and *properties*—provide a consistent framework for understanding objects as sequences of events structured by repeatable patterns of characters.

But what is it that we are committed to when we claim that events, and not substances, are the basic units of reality? One of the central issues at stake concerns what is to count as basic particulars, the most fundamental things that populate or make up the structure of space and time. In accepting the notion that events are the basic particulars, we are committed to the idea that dynamic happenings make up the fundamental reality of the world, and these basic entities form the basis for the stable structures discerned in our perceptual experience. The second important issue at stake concerns the notion of identity across time. With an ontology of substances, individuals allegedly retain their identity despite undergoing numerous changes of properties. Something, namely the substance, remains the same throughout change. With an ontology of events, however, the particulars have a momentary existence, and the identity of objects across time is construed as a matter of retention of certain properties in a sequence of events constituting the object. No object is entirely the same, because at each moment we have new events that make up the continuity of that object.

Strange as it may seem from the point of view of common sense, an ontology of events has definite advantages from the point of view of modern physics. With the introduction of quantum theory at the beginning of this century, the atomic theory of matter seemed to be challenged by a certain insubstantial and unthinglike behavior of elementary particles. According to quantum theory, energy of all types occurs in quanta or minimal packets, and atoms are to be understood in terms of waves of radiation that they can emit or absorb. On this view, then, we no longer have a simple, billiard-ball view of matter as our fundamental conception of nature, but rather energetic vibrations in an electromagnetic field. An ontology of events appears to be more consistent with the findings of this theory in at least two respects: (1) energy quanta fit snugly into the framework of events because particles are now understood in terms of dynamic occurrences of energy that do not remain identical throughout their changes, and (2) the quantum conception of the universe does not contain the old distinction between things and empty space, that is, atoms and the void. It rather proposes the notion that the field is fundamental and that particles are simply particular regions in the field that undergo all sorts of energy transformations. Thus, particles are no longer seen as having hard boundaries distinct from the surrounding space; rather, they have a wavelike presence in an ill-defined locality.

Also from the point of view of the theory of relativity, space and time become fused into space-time, and objects take on a strange character of four dimensions. Objects are not regarded as simply located in definite spatial regions at different times but rather exist as complex structures of space-time that form what we might call "space-time worms." The ontology of basic events takes this idea of the conjunction of space and time seriously because each event is essentially a fusion of space and time, and the resulting structure of space-time depends on the manner in which particular events are interrelated in nature. This means that we no longer regard space as a kind of container of things; rather, space-time is a four-dimensional character of events.

The detailed elaboration of the complexities of quantum physics and the theory of relativity obviously cannot be pursued in this introductory exposition. Suffice it to say that the ontology of events is a serious contender for the foundations of modern physics; however, it is by no means uncontroversial or unproblematic.

■ METAPHYSICS UNDER ATTACK

The case against metaphysics gains force from time to time. Historically, this usually happens as a result of a turn in philosophical fashion when intense analysis and adherence to method attempt to prune back the somewhat grandiose speculations of metaphysics. The British empiricists John Locke and David Hume, for example, reacted against the excessive metaphysical claims of the continental rationalists Descartes, Spinoza, and Leibniz by concentrating on the epistemological question "What are we capable of knowing?" Indeed, for Locke and Hume it seemed that the attempt to construct first principles *a priori* was a fundamental source of the trouble in our lack of progress in answering philosophical questions. In the twentieth century, the attacks against metaphysics have been renewed with increased vigor and have come from many different schools of thought: logical positivism, linguistic analysis, pragmatism, phenomenology, and deconstruction. I shall briefly discuss criticisms from logical positivism and from pragmatism, and then respond in defense of metaphysics in the conclusion of this chapter.

Logical positivists argue that there are two classes of statements that are meaningful. The first class is that of empirical statements, such as "There is a coffee cup in front of me," "Mt. Everest is the highest mountain in the world," or "Earth is the third planet from the sun." Such statements are shown to be true by observation. When we deny them, we utter false statements about the way the world is. The second class is that of logically necessary statements. They can be shown to be true by definition. For example, "All bachelors are unmarried" or "All bodies are extended." Such statements are tautologies; their truth is merely formal and abstract. When we deny these statements, we utter contradictions, that is, necessarily false statements.

According to this classification of meaningfulness, metaphysical utterances such as "God is the creator of the universe," "Events are the basic units of reality," or "Possible worlds exist" fail to be meaningful because they are neither empirically verifiable nor logically true. No experience would prove or disprove these claims, nor are they true by definition. Metaphysical utterances are, therefore, neither true nor false. They assert nothing, and contain neither knowledge nor error.

Positivists thus argue that metaphysics is a type of misplaced poetry that expresses emotion about the world, but when taken literally, it fails to be meaningful.[15] Furthermore, the metaphysician seems to be engaged in a type of propaganda for a given view of the universe, and like all forms of propaganda, the enterprise involves the exaggerated importance of one type of conceptual scheme. The real issue, however, is not the defense of one type of conceptual scheme over another but, rather, the type of *verification* we can get for statements. Positivists contend that once we recognize that metaphysical statements cannot, even in principle, be verified, we can dismiss the whole field of inquiry.

Pragmatists hold that the metaphysician attempts to view the universe from God's point of view. However, because this is quite impossible for finite beings, our persistent attempts suffer from a kind of megalomania. For a pragmatist, then, we must give up the attempt to discover absolute truth in metaphysical *foundations* and be content with a concept of truth in terms of usefulness.[16] Truth, according to this view, is good enough when it delivers results and cashes out in practical consequences. In no sense, though, do we justify the beliefs we have by appeal to the absolute certainty of a metaphysical principle. Pragmatists, therefore, discard the attempts of systems-building or the attempts to answer the more profound questions of philosophy because the answers make no practical difference to our lives. They indict metaphysics for sterility and argue that philosophers should concentrate their efforts on questions and problems that are more fruitful.

■ CONCLUSION AND REPLIES TO OBJECTIONS

Everything in metaphysics is controversial. The fact that an issue is controversial or a problem extremely difficult to solve, however, should not force us to see it as "meaningless" or "sterile," for the value of philosophy in many cases lies in the uncertainty of the *solutions* offered and the neverending task of criticism and revision. This is what confronts us in much of life's bigger problems anyway, whether we are talking of science, politics, morality, or religion.

One objection to positivism is well known. It involves turning the positivists' procedure on themselves. The very principle of verification that states "A sentence has literal meaning if and only if the proposition it expresses is either analytic or empirically verifiable"[17] is itself an unverifiable proposition. That is, the verification principle is neither true by definition nor true by observation. So, it seems that the positivist must be doing metaphysics in the course of demonstrating its meaninglessness, for the verification principle, like metaphysical principles, is theoretical and unverifiable even in principle.

But let us take the positivists' recommendation seriously for the moment and see where it leads. If we are to stick to what is observable, we seem to be restricted to saying things about the present, and the present only. Notice, for example, that we cannot make claims about history because we cannot observe the past. Even if we confine ourselves to the present, our interpretation of experience and our judgments about the world invariably involve us in the use of a language that is fully stocked with metaphysical concepts such as "change," "cause," "substance," "property," "event," "identity," and "individual." Our ordinary language and the logical form of statements already contain a metaphysics dating back all the way to the ancient Greeks—if not before. This involves critical reflection on metaphysics from the very start.

Furthermore, it is extremely difficult to understand what would become of science if we accepted the positivists' recommendation. It seems unlikely that we can have any science at all without the essentially unverifiable theories by which we understand the meaning of experimental results. Much of scientific theory involves metaphysical principles that are fundamental to such concepts as "matter," "space," "time," and "motion." Moreover, physical laws like Newton's laws of gravity and motion or the laws of quantum mechanics are more than just summaries of observations—they are meant to apply to the unobserved events of the future, which is the whole point of scientific prediction. No law is ever proved ultimately because we can never observe if it continues to hold in the future. Much of science, and the hypotheses that guide the direction of scientific inquiry, would be thrown out with metaphysics. So, it seems that the positivist has thrown the baby out with the bathwater. The two classes of statements necessarily exclude or eliminate metaphysical claims from meaningful discourse, but the positivists assume too quickly that the classification is complete and final. Both metaphysics and science seek theories that will promise deeper penetration into nature's secrets. Metaphysics is distinguished from science in the sense that it attempts to be a more comprehensive study of reality.

Now, as to the objections of the pragmatist, we might first ask just exactly what is meant by the concept of truth as *useful*. If an idea "works," then presumably there is some sense in which the idea grasps reality or an aspect thereof. Let us take a simple example from astronomy, Kepler's proposal that the planets mark their orbits around the sun in ellipses. This idea works better than Copernicus's idea that the planets travel in perfect circles. But why? The pragmatist would reply that Kepler's idea makes a *practical difference* in our attempts to calculate and predict the motions of the planets, so it is to be preferred to Copernicus's idea. But the metaphysician believes truth is more than just what is useful or practical—in this case, that Kepler's idea "works" because it is more accurate in its grasp of the structure of reality. Besides this, there are many intellectual pursuits that have no immediate practical use, but only come to be useful in a later time. Much of the research in pure mathematics or theoretical physics, I take it, falls roughly under this category, as well as the type of metaphysical issues I am presently defending.

The metaphysician seeks the ultimate truth of reality, yet the pragmatist contends that this is a hopeless struggle. But *seeking* the truth and claiming to *know* the truth are two entirely different things. On this score we must make concessions to the pragmatist, for human systems are never complete and final. This accounts for the on-going endeavor of criticism and revision in philosophy. Metaphysics is certainly no exception here, but neither is any other aspect of human inquiry. It very well may be that we never get there—that is, at the end of our search—but this does not mean that the journey is worthless. On this point, perhaps American philosopher George Santayana put it best when he said at the outset of his monumental *Realms of Being*: "Here is one more system of philosophy. If the reader is tempted to smile, I can assure him that I smile with him. . . ."[18]

Metaphysics is presupposed in much of our thinking about ourselves and our world. The question is not whether we are to do it at all, but whether we are to do it well and in full conscience of its place in the wider context of philosophy.[19]

■ NOTES

1. Aristotle, *The Metaphysics*, trans. Philip Wheelwright, *Aristotle* (Indianapolis: Bobbs-Merrill, 1977), 77.

2. Richard McKeon, *The Basic Works of Aristotle* (New York: Random House, 1941), xviii.

3. See, for example, Plato's theory of the divided line in his major work, *The Republic*, especially Books 6 and 7.

4. For a rather simple and entertaining explanation of possible worlds, see G. K. Chesterton, "The Ethics of Elfland," *Orthodoxy* (London: Bodley Head Library, 1941).

5. See, for example, David Lewis, *On the Plurality of Worlds* (Oxford: Basil Blackwell, 1986). While Lewis's view is ontologically very generous in that he believes that each world is actual, other modal realists, such as Alvin Plantinga, believe that possible worlds exist only in the abstract sense of numbers and sets.

6. For a discussion on the nature and existence of God, see Chapter 8, especially the section on metaphysics.

7. René Descartes, *Meditations on First Philosophy*. Many translations and editions since its appearance in 1641.

8. Princess Elizabeth of Bohemia was quite insistent on this point with her philosophical mentor, Descartes. See Godfrey Vesey, "The Princess and the Philosopher," *Philosophy in the Open*, ed. Godfrey Vesey (Milton Keynes, England: Open Univ. Press, 1974), for an amusing account of their exchange.

9. See Chapter 10 for a more detailed discussion.

10. W. V. Quine, "On What There Is," *From a Logical Point of View* (New York: Harper Torchbooks, 1963), 2.

11. An excellect discussion of the problem of ontological excess can be found in Keith Campbell, *Metaphysics: An Introduction* (Encino, CA: Dickenson, 1979). See especially Chapter 8.

12. In this connection, see especially John Locke, *An Essay concerning Human Understanding*, Book 2, Chapter 23. Many editions since its appearance in 1690.

13. For a more thorough exposition of the theory of events than explained here, see Bertrand Russell, *The Analysis of Matter* (New York: Dover, 1954), and Alfred North Whitehead, *The Concept of Nature* (Cambridge: Cambridge Univ. Press, 1920). The benefits of this theory have also been explored by W. V. Quine, *Word and Object* (Cambridge, MA: MIT Press, 1960), especially Chapter 5, Section 36, and "Whither Physical Objects?" *Boston Studies in the Philosophy of Science*, 39 (1976): 497–504.

14. For a defense of the ontology of material substance against an ontology of events, see P. F. Strawson, *Individuals: An Essay in Descriptive Metaphysics* (London: Methuen, 1971).

15. A. J. Ayer, *Language, Truth and Logic* (New York: Dover, 1952), 44.

16. Pragmatism is a twentieth-century American philosophical movement initiated by Charles Pierce and carried on by William James, John Dewey, C. I. Lewis, and more recently by Richard Rorty.

17. Ayer, *Language, Truth and Logic*, 5.

18. George Santayana, *Scepticism and Animal Faith* (New York: Dover, 1955), v.

19. Thanks are due to Frederick Adams, Dorothy Emmet, Gary Fuller, and John Heil for helpful suggestions.

▪ QUESTIONS

1. How are the investigations of the metaphysician different from those of the scientist? How are they similar?

2. Examine each of the following statements, and explain how the statement does or does not commit us to the existence of the entities introduced in the subject of the sentence.

a. A married bachelor lives next door.

b. The present king of France is bald.

c. Quadruplicity eats purple.

d. Unicorns are horses with horns.

e. Quarks and leptons are the fundamental atomic particles.

f. The average man has 2.5 cats.

3. What is a possible world? What are the minimal restrictions for defining a possible world? What kind of ontological status does a possible world have?

4. Explain how the following passage involves a metaphysical problem discussed in this chapter:

> "All right," said the Cat; and this time it vanished quite slowly, beginning with the end of the tail, and ending with the grin, which remained some time after the rest of it had gone.
>
> "Well! I've often seen a cat without a grin," thought Alice; "but a grin without a cat! It's the most curious thing I ever saw in all my life!"   —Lewis Carroll, *Alice's Adventures in Wonderland*

5. Identify and explain the different ways the concept of "substance" is used in this essay.

6. Aristotle gives several characterizations of substance. In one of these characterizations, he says that substance is what is capable of independent existence. Qualities are incapable of independent existence, whereas substances can exist independently. Explain what is wrong with this characterization. Consider what sort of things would count as independently existing individuals from the following list: human beings, trees, cars, houses, planets, solar systems, galaxies, clouds, rainbows, rivers, rocks, rays of light, molecules, atoms, electrons.

7. It is sometimes argued that an ontology of events cannot account for identification and re-identification of individual things over time, but an ontology of individual substances can serve this important function of language. If events are basic particulars and exist only momentarily, how could we re-identify an object like a cat as the same one encountered earlier? What is the cat in this theory?

8. If mind and body are construed as completely different substances, we find that their interaction is difficult, if not impossible, to explain. But if we begin with an ontology of events, we only have one kind of entity, namely, events or event-sequences. How would we explain consciousness on this account? Does this give us a more adequate basis for solving the mind-body problem, or does it simply raise new problems?

9. Which of the following statements would the positivist consider meaningful?
a. Grass is green.
b. Pericles was an Athenian general who lived from 495–429 B.C.
c. All sisters are females.
d. The universe is one substance.
e. Light is composed of electromagnetic waves.

10. Do you find that the defense of metaphysics in this chapter is successful against the antimetaphysicians? Why, or why not? ■

■ **FOR FURTHER READING**

Brenner, William H. *Elements of Modern Philosophy: Descartes through Kant*. Englewood Cliffs, NJ: Prentice-Hall, 1989.
Campbell, Keith. *Metaphysics: An Introduction*. Encino, CA: Dickenson, 1976.
Carter, W. R. *The Elements of Metaphysics*. New York: McGraw-Hill, 1990.
Loux, Michael J., ed. *The Actual and the Possible*. Ithaca: Cornell Univ. Press, 1979.
Moser, Paul K., ed. *Reality in Focus: Contemporary Readings in Metaphysics*. Englewood Cliffs, NJ: Prentice-Hall, 1990.
Pears, D. F., ed. *The Nature of Metaphysics*. London: Macmillan, 1962.
Sprigge, T. L. S. *Theories of Existence*. Harmondsworth, Eng.: Penguin, 1984.
Walsh, W. H., and Roger Hancock. "Metaphysics, Nature of," and "Metaphysics, History of." *The Encyclopedia of Philosophy*. Vol. 5. New York: Macmillan, 1967.

■ CHAPTER FOUR

Epistemology

FREDERICK ADAMS

■ INTRODUCTION

Epistemology derives from the Greek *episteme* ("knowledge") and *logos* ("account or reason"). The study of epistemology is the attempt to give an account of the source and nature of knowledge.

Knowledge is a highly prized commodity. CIA and KGB agents kill to get it. Scientists spend billions of dollars trying to find a cure for cancer—to know *if* there is a cure and *what* the cure is. If you knew the winning numbers in the next state lottery drawing, you could become rich and maybe famous by purchasing a ticket with those very numbers.

We would like to know many things that we do not know. Is there life on other planets? Will computers someday actually be able to think? And there are many things that we know *now*. We know enough physics, engineering, and computer science to send people to the moon and return them to Earth safely. The knowledge that your instructors impart to you in four years at your college or university is, sadly, an incredibly small fraction of what is known. The quantity of knowledge is growing at exponential rates. Science, medicine, and all academic pursuits of knowledge have been paying high levels of return—in many cases faster than we can absorb fully. Pick up any encyclopedia or professional journal in the library and you will have a partial list of the many things that we now know.

What you will *not* find in an encyclopedia (except in the *Encyclopedia of Philosophy*), is an answer to the central question of epistemology: "What is it for a person to know something?" This question does not only ask things such as whether Tom *knows* that Joe uses drugs; more important, it asks *what is required* for Tom to know that Joe uses drugs. For example, how accurate must a drug test be to give knowledge that someone testing "positive" actually uses drugs—85 percent accurate? 95 percent? 98 percent? The answer can only be reached by examining the very process and *criteria* of knowing—not merely things that are known. To ask such questions is to turn the pursuit of knowledge inward upon itself. What have we said when we say that someone knows something? This is the sort of inquiry that philosophy, the parent discipline of epistemology, is all about—examining the foundations of all knowledge. Fundamental epistemology asks what knowledge *is*, not unlike fundamental chemistry's asking what water *is*. We knew that water was around long before we knew that water was H_2O. Similarly, we have a lot of knowledge long before we know what knowledge is.

A useful beginning to discovering what knowledge is involves distinguishing the kinds of things that a person *S* may be said to know. *S* may be said to know: (1) a *thing x* ("Bo knows football"), (2) *how to do* something *y* ("Colleen knows how to count in German"), or (3) *that p*—that a statement or sentence is true ("The governor knows that our school needs more money"). Consider knowing *things*. It is common to say that we know some *place*, such as Chicago; or that we know a *person*, Toni; or even a *language*, Spanish. Consider knowing *how*. We say things such as "I know how to speak French," or "Jean knows how to program in Basic," or "David knows how to get to John's house." Consider knowing *that*. Scientists talk about whether (or not) we know *that there is life on other planets*. Students say they know *that calculus is harder than geography*. In each of these cases, it may seem that because we are using the *same word, know*, we must be saying the *same thing* in saying that people know things. This is not obviously the case, however, as we will see.

Consider knowing things once again. A good case *can* be made that knowing some place, thing, or person, can be resolved into either *knowing how* or *knowing that*. On the one hand, when Gary says that he knows Chicago, he may mean only that he knows how to get around in Chicago when walking or driving. He can find Soldier Field, the Field Museum, the Shedd Aquarium, and a few restaurants. As it may happen, Gary's knowledge of Chicago may be this general *skill* at getting to and around town with very little detailed *propositional* knowledge of the town. On the other hand, Gary's knowledge of Chicago may be propositional; that is, Gary's head may be filled with facts about Chicago. He may know that the best way to get downtown is to approach from Lake Superior Drive to Michigan Avenue. He may know that the Palmer House is at the corner of State and Monroe. Gary may know that the Memories of China restaurant has excellent food and that it is located at 1050 N. State Street. Furthermore, Gary's knowledge of facts about Chicago may extend on and on. As is most likely, Gary's knowledge of Chicago will consist of a little of each, knowing how and knowing that. This tends to show that knowing things is *not* a separate *kind* or category of knowledge different from the other two. Similar things can be said about resolving knowledge of a person, Toni, or a language, Spanish, into knowing how or knowing that. This still leaves us, however, with *two kinds* of knowledge or uses of the word *know*, and it is not clear how they could be resolved into one.

Having skills (knowing how) seems quite different from knowing propositions to be true (knowing that). Skills are things like knowing how to ride a bicycle or knowing how to articulate the word *epistemology. Knowing that*, however, may involve detailed propositions about the forces exerted on the person riding a bicycle or on the muscles in face, throat, and mouth that are involved in articulating words. Even when we come to know the detailed propositions about these complex activities, if we were to concentrate too heavily on them, we probably could not ride or talk at all. To ride or talk smoothly, we must concentrate on where we want to go and on what we want to say, not on the theories that explain how we do what we do. When you ride a bicycle, you probably cannot say which kind of forces your body is compensating for at any given time. But your body *is doing this* if you have not fallen off. When you say *e, pis, te, mol, o, gy* in the act of articulating the title of this essay, you probably have no idea of the position of your tongue. Is it flat, against the teeth, away from the teeth? But you do *know how* to make these sounds. Thus, knowing how seems irreducibly distinct from knowing that. It is not that there are no propositions which, when known, will explain how we do the things that we know how to do (that explain our skills). Rather, it is that *in acquiring* these skills, we do not have to concentrate on the theories and descriptions of how we are able to do them.

■ THE ANALYSIS OF *KNOWING THAT*

We shall focus primarily upon *knowing that*. One reason knowing that is highly prized is that it is a kind of knowledge that links us with the world (reality). When we know that something is the case, we know that some propostion (sentence, statement, hypothesis, or theory) is *true*.[1] Since propositions are *about reality*, if we know they are true, we know something about reality. It seems, therefore, that for a person S to know *that p*, where *p* stands for some proposition, the proposition known must be true. *We cannot know something that is false*, but we can know *that proposition p is false*. For example, we can know *that it is false that the Earth is flat*. But if *p* is false, we cannot know *that p*. We cannot know *that the Earth is flat*.

   We can, I suppose, imagine someone protesting that we often say "I just knew the Pistons would win that game" when, in fact, they did not go on to win. This type of statement does not really show that we can know things that are false. It shows instead that we sometimes *say* things like this when we *mean only* "I really believed that the Pistons would win" or "I was just sure that they would win." The problem, of course, is that strong belief or high confidence *alone* does not ensure knowledge. We have all had experiences where our memories have played tricks on us. We were just sure that we left our keys somewhere, only to find that they were somewhere else.

   If you are not already convinced that knowing *that p* requires the truth of *p*, imagine the oddity of saying to the ticket taker at the racetrack "I know that Tag-a-long won in the fifth race," when it is false that Tag-a-long won. You may stand there until the track empties, but the ticket taker will not pay off on your ticket if it is false that Tag-a-long won in the fifth (Gumshoe did). She will insist, rightly, that you may *believe* that Tag-a-long won, but you do not *know* this, because it is *false*.

We have, then, an important ingredient of knowledge—*truth*. Truth seems to be a matter of correspondence with reality.[2] A statement is true if and only if it corresponds with reality, with the facts. "Tag-a-long won in the fifth" is true if and only if Tag-a-long *did win* in the fifth. It is false if he did not (if Gumshoe won). Therefore, S knows that *p* (for some person S and some proposition *p*) only if it is *true that p*. What other conditions (ingredients) go into *knowing that*?

A strong case can be made for claiming that *belief* is a necessary condition of knowing *that p*. To begin to see this, consider that knowledge is always *of* or *about* something. If we think of knowledge as a relation between a person and the world—the way that marriage is a relation between a person and another person—we can ask what relates a person epistemically to the world. What must happen to bring a person into the knowledge relation with reality (to make the person's knowledge *of* reality)? When one enters into a marital relation with another person there is usually a member of the clergy and a ceremony that includes the exchanging of vows and rings. Each married person acquires a ring, let us say, and its acquisition symbolizes one's entering into the marriage relation with one's spouse. But what happens to put a person into the knowledge relation with reality? There are no knowledge vows, or ceremonies, and there is no knowledge ring to symbolize that one has knowledge.

Still, something very important *does change* when one acquires knowledge that something is the case. When Sue comes to know *that she is pregnant*, she acquires a *belief* that she did not have previously. In her mind is a representation (a *thought*) of the world and her condition that was not there before. She may have wondered whether she was pregnant before, but she did not actually *think that* she was. Therefore, at least one of the things that is necessary for *Sue* to enter the *knowledge relation* with the *truth* that she is pregnant is for her to have the thought or *belief* that she is pregnant. Thoughts or beliefs are Sue's ways of representing the world—her ways of picturing the world or cognitively relating to the world. It is, then, fairly clear that one could not know that something is true if one had no thoughts at all about that thing. Sue could not know that she was pregnant if she had no thoughts about being pregnant—no beliefs about it one way or the other. It is equally clear that one could not know that something was the case if one believed the opposite. If Tom believes that Nixon *did not* resign from office, Tom certainly does *not know* that Nixon *did* resign. For these reasons, therefore, we can add *belief* and *truth* to our list of things necessary for S to know *that p*.

As before, we can find cases where Tom may say "I don't believe I'm hungry, I *know* I'm hungry!" But this does not show that belief is not required for knowledge. First, when Tom knows that he is hungry, Tom *does* believe he is hungry. Tom must have some way of representing his hunger to himself, and *belief* is the usual way. Second, when Tom says "I don't believe that *p*, I know that *p*," this is an elliptical or shorthand way of saying "I don't *merely* believe that I'm hungry, I'm positive that I'm hungry"—or something to that effect. Again, Tom's choice of wording does not show that belief is not necessary for knowledge. It is mainly for emphasis to contrast with cases where we *tend to* believe that something is the case, but we are not sure or not confident—such as "I'm not sure I'm going to the concert, but I believe that I am."

Our list of conditions that must be satisfied for one to know that something is the case now looks like this:

S knows *that p* only if:
1. *p* is true.
2. *S* believes that *p*.

Is that it? Are we done? We now have good reasons to think that these are *necessary* conditions for knowing (one could not know that *p* without these conditions being satisfied), but are they *sufficient*? That is, if satisfied, are they enough to allow one to know?[3] A necessary condition A for something else B is that without which B could not obtain. For example, it is necessary that one be admitted to this institution (A) in order to obtain a degree here (B). Admission is not sufficient for the degree, of course. A sufficient condition X for something Y is when X can ensure Y by X's occurrence. Thus, receiving a grade of *B* + (X) in this course is sufficient for passing the course (Y). Of course, it is not required to pass. Many other grades, A, *B* −, *C* +, would do.

It is fairly easy to show that conditions 1 and 2 are *not sufficient*. Suppose that I now believe that there is life on planets other than Earth. Suppose further that *there is* life on other planets. Then both of our conditions are satisfied. Let *p* be the proposition that there is life on other planets. *P* is true and I believe that *p*. But it can be made pretty clear that I *do not know* that *p*. I have had no contact with extraterrestrial life forms. I have no radio transmissions from outer space that I have decoded. No missions to space have brought back any evidence of life—and so on and so forth. Nor do I have any other evidence to support or justify my belief that *p*. Indeed, I have *no evidence* at all for the truth of *p*. I might just as well have flipped a coin. Heads, I believe that *p*; tails, I believe that not *p*. If the coin comes up heads I have a true belief, but it is *just dumb luck*. It could have come up tails—my belief would have been false, and I would have been none the wiser about the truth or falsity of my belief. The coin is *no guide to the truth of p*. It does not reliably indicate the presence of life on other planets and, therefore, cannot give me knowledge—nor can my just guessing, as above.

If you are not yet convinced, consider another example.[4] You are walking in the park one day and see what you take to be fresh deer tracks on the ground. On the basis of this, you come to believe that *p* (*p* = there was a deer nearby). Suppose that *p* is true—there were deer in the park—and you now believe that *p*. Do you *know* that *p*? If you say "yes," let me fill in the rest of the story. Your walk in the park is in November, during hunting season. I am an animal lover and hate for deer to be killed during hunting season. So, I have made a deer-track maker that imprints *fake* tracks indistinguishable from real deer tracks. If there were a real track adjacent to a fake, you could not tell them apart. Furthermore, I have been trying it out in the park *where you are walking*. For all you know, the very track you are looking at could be a fake. You would not know the difference. As it turns out, you are looking at a real track. But right next to it lies a fake. Now, p is still true, and you still believe that p is true because you did not hear my story and know nothing about my fake track maker. So, you satisfy conditions 1 and 2. But do you *know* that there is a deer nearby? Pretty clearly not, for it is pure luck that you are looking at a real track, not a fake. Had you seen only the fake, you would still have believed there was a deer nearby. You would have believed it even if no deer had been in the park—just me and my track maker. The fact that you are looking at a real track is just as much *luck* as if you had flipped a coin, as above. Your belief is true but so *accidentally true*, so *lucky*, that if you had just guessed whether or not p was true, you would have had as good a chance of being right.

These examples show that guessing or flipping a coin is not a good indicator or good evidence of truth. Something's looking like a deer track when local, fake tracks look just the same is not a good indicator of the presence of deer. It is not reliable evidence that deer are present. These examples show that what is lacking on our list of conditions for knowing is that one must have some reliable evidence or indication that p is true. Merely having a true belief is not enough, because a belief can be true by luck or accident. In addition to having a true belief, one's belief must be based on *reliable evidence* for the truth of p. Let us add that to our list and then try to say more about what makes evidence reliable.

Our revised (and final) list looks like this:

S knows *that p* if and only if:
1. p is true.
2. S believes that p.
3. S bases his or her belief on reliable evidence.

Does that do it? Is that the end of our list of conditions? I claim that it is. (For a full explanation of my claim, see my paper listed under For Further Reading.) Not everyone agrees, however. For example, Laurence Bonjour would add to the list a fourth condition; namely, that S's belief that p be *justified* (in the sense of being reasonable or responsibly formed). Much of contemporary epistemology is devoted primarily to analyzing what is required for a belief to be justified. There are many theories of justified belief (*foundationalism, coherentism, reliabilism*, and others), and they become complex very quickly. (For more information on the complexities of the theories of justification, see the works listed under For Further Reading.)

As it turns out, some theories of *justified belief* (*reliabilism*, for example) identify a belief's being justified with its being based on reliable evidence. These theories may not differ from our theory that identifies *knowing that p* with true belief based on reliable evidence. Other theories do *not* identify a belief's being justified with its being based on reliable evidence alone. For example, coherentism identifies a belief's being justified with its cohering (fitting together consistently) with one's other beliefs. These theories of justified belief turn out to be significantly different than ours in that they require that one's belief be justified (or epistemically responsible) *in addition to* its being based on reliable evidence. So, why deny that justified belief (of this sort) is necessary for knowledge? Let me give a brief example to explain, and then we will proceed.

Suppose that Ken is a clairvoyant, but does not know this. Because Ken is a clairvoyant, when an idea pops into his head, seemingly from nowhere, it is reliably true. Ken's reliable mechanism is his clairvoyance itself. His reliable evidence is an idea's popping into his head itself. Suppose, however, that Ken does not know that he is a clairvoyant, does not know that an idea's popping into his head is reliable evidence of its truth. Furthermore, he has good reason to think that clairvoyants do not exist (as do we). So, when an idea pops into Ken's head, he has no more justification for believing it than we would if it happened to us—at least as far as Ken knows. Those who argue for a fourth condition on knowledge want to say that if it pops into Ken's head that Mount St. Helens will erupt next Thursday, Ken does not know that it will—even though it is true that it will erupt next Thursday. For he would be unjustified or irrational to believe it based only upon his shoddy evidence (this thought's popping into his head). Having something pop into one's head is usually not good evidence of its truth, and Ken knows this.

Notice that our three conditions alone would suggest that Ken *does know* that Mount St. Helens will erupt on Thursday. We would be forced to admit this because an idea's popping into the head of a clairvoyant *is* reliable evidence for the truth of the idea. That is what it *means* to be clairvoyant. As long as Ken *believes* the ideas that clairvoyantly come to him (they are overpowering and he cannot resist believing them), then our three conditions would be satisfied, and we would attribute knowledge to Ken. Proponents of theories of knowledge requiring the fourth condition would be able to deny that Ken has knowledge, for Ken lacks a kind of justification for his belief—something that makes it rational or epistemically responsible for him to believe.

Although it is highly counterintuitive to some that Ken's clairvoyantly held beliefs are knowledge, his beliefs *are* nonaccidentally true. Ken will *never* make mistakes due to error of belief, if he acts on such beliefs. I cannot, therefore, find sufficient reason to deny that Ken knows in such cases. True, he does not know that he knows, for he does not know he is clairvoyant. It is also true that he is not epistemically responsible in having his belief about Mount St. Helens. Still, what would such responsibility add? It may be that Ken would never have the *confidence to act* on the basis of any of his clairvoyantly held beliefs because, from his point of view, they are not responsibly formed. This, however, is not in dispute. We all know many things that we are not now acting on and some things that we might lack confidence to act on in the future. Ken may know, on the basis of his very reliable X-rays from his dentist, that he has no cavities. But if asked to bet $10,000 on his not having a cavity, he may be unwilling to act on his knowledge. He may think he has good justification for his belief, but not enough to risk such a large sum of money. Thus, lack of confidence may influence Ken's actions, but it does not imply that Ken lacks knowledge. As long as the X-rays are reliable and Ken believes on the basis of them (not by having an idea pop into his head), Ken will know that he has no cavities—despite his reluctance to wager. Therefore, if the lack of justification or epistemic responsibility does not have a negative effect on the accuracy and reliability of one's beliefs, I see no overwhelming reason to make it a necessary condition for knowledge. For these reasons, we shall move on. Of course, what makes a belief justified is important in its own right, and the import of the existing theories is not diminished, even if justification—supposing that justification is something other than reliablility—is not necessary for knowledge.

■ RELIABLE EVIDENCE

In this section, we need to say something about what it is for evidence to be reliable. We also need to distinguish its *being* reliable from our *knowing* that it is reliable. As we shall see, the failure to make this distinction can take one down the expressway to scepticism. Scepticism is the view that we know nothing or almost nothing. It is a position that one should adopt only as a last resort. No one should start out being a sceptic, nor should one be led to it by bad arguments or by failure to draw important distinctions.

Reconsider our example about the fake deer tracks. What would it take for the fact that there is something that looks like a deer track in front of you to *mean* or *indicate reliably* that there are deer nearby (at least one)? That is, what would it take to screen off or eliminate the fakes? It would take the following: that no local track would look exactly as a deer track does unless it were made by a deer. If there would not be a track that looks *like that* in the park unless it were made by a deer, then the track would be reliable evidence of the presence of at least one deer.

Compare two more examples to help understand the concept of *reliability* that we are after. Our fingerprints and our genetic codes are unique to us as individuals. You alone have the fingerprint pattern of your right index finger. Also, you alone, unless you are an identical twin, have your genetic code. That is why fingerprinting is reliable evidence that Smith touched the gun, when we find his prints on it. He may not have killed Jones—he may have been framed. But he *did* touch the gun, if his prints are on it. As you probably know, genetic screening is fast replacing fingerprinting in solving some crimes for similar reasons—it provides us with nonfakable, reliable evidence. You alone (barring identical twins) have your genetic map.

So a piece of evidence *e* (deer tracks) is reliable evidence that *p* (that there were deer nearby), when the tracks would not be there unless they were made by a deer. Stated more generally, evidence *e* is reliable for the truth of proposition *p*, if *e* would not exist unless *p* were true. E's presence, under these conditions, guarantees the truth of *p*.

We have, then, a definition of reliable evidence. But now we must address an important complication. In our earlier example, we used a case where I made a fake deer-track maker. If *I* could *do that*, will it *ever* be true that a track that looks like a deer track would not be in the park *unless it were made by a deer*? Could it not *always* be the case that the track *might* have been made by a fake track maker? If this is always possible in some sense, then, does that not mean that we can never know that there are deer by seeing tracks? Will one ever have reliable evidence for the presence of deer in the park—or reliable evidence of anything, for that matter?

The answer is "yes." You will have evidence that reliably indicates that certain things are true. We must not confuse knowledge with truth. It could be *true* that we had evidence that is reliable, even if we did *not know* that we had it (did not know that it was true that we had it). You need not know that the evidence is reliable for it to be true that it is reliable. Just as you need not know that there is life on other planets for it to be true that there is life on other planets. All it takes is for life to be there. And all it takes for you to have reliable evidence that deer are nearby is that no one is actually going around with a fake deer-track maker.[5] Thus, all it takes for you to know that there are deer is for you to believe it because you see a track that is reliable. You do not have to know or be able *to tell* that the track is reliable. It just has to *be reliable*.

I suppose that one must *believe* that a set of tracks is reliable in order to *muster up the belief* that there are deer. For example, if you did not *believe* your friend was a reliable source of information, you probably would not believe her when she tells you that your lover has been unfaithful to you. Still, you do not have to *know* that she is reliable in order to *learn* the distressing news. If somehow you *did* believe her, and if she *was* reliable, then you *would know* that your lover was unfaithful—no matter how much you might not want to know this. For, being reliable, she would not say this unless it were true—by definition of *reliable*. You do not have to know that you have knowledge in order to have it—just as you do not have to know that you have a disease in order to have the disease. We will return to the distinction between knowing that *p* and *knowing that you know*. For now, we simply note that there is such a distinction.

Remember also that my example was fictitious. I do not (nor does anyone I have ever met) have a fake deer-track maker. The mere fact that there *could be* one—that someone could make one—does not mean that there *is* one. Many things *could* happen that *do not* or *will not* happen. Your mother *could lie* to you when you ask her age. That does not mean that she *would lie*. It does not mean that you cannot trust her or that she is not a reliable source of information about her age. In the example, I asked you to imagine that I actually had a fake track maker and used it. In the world that we live in, I do not have one, nor, let us suppose, does anyone in or near your present location. Let us call the condition of the world that we actually live in condition *NFT* ("no fake track makers"). Then, in the world we live in, in condition *NFT*, deer tracks (things that look like them) *are reliable evidence* for the presence of deer—even if we cannot prove it. To prove it, for example, we would have to check every house in or near our current location to see if there were a fake track maker there. Surely, we could not do this within practical limitations. But we *do not have to prove* that our world is in condition *NFT* for it to be *in NFT*.

If the world were different (not in state *NFT*), if there were practical jokers on the loose with fake track makers, then we would all be *robbed of knowledge* of the presence of deer by *seeing only tracks*. We would occasionally have beliefs that were true by luck, but, as we have seen, true belief is not sufficient for knowledge.

Fortunately, the world is not like that, so we *do* get reliable evidence when we see the tracks.

As you should have noticed, this means that we are at the mercy of the world. The world must be in conditions comparable to *NFT*—that is, depending on what we want to know, there must be nothing fake to spoil our evidence. If the world is arranged properly, then we can get reliable evidence for the things that we want to know. If the world does not cooperate, we may think that we have reliable evidence, but not really have it. When you need to check the pressure in your tires, you grab the pressure gauge in your glove compartment. If it is a reliable gauge, it would not read "32 lb./sq. in." unless that much pressure were in the tire. But is it a reliable gauge? On our theory thus far, we can say this much: If the gauge is reliable, and you believe what the gauge says, then you know the pressure is 32 lb./sq. in. The world might not cooperate, however. The gauge may be defective, and you would not be able to tell just by looking at it. Of course, it may be *close enough* that you can tell the tire is sufficiently inflated, even if the gauge is not exactly accurate. That is, you may know that the tire is inflated enough to drive the car safely, but if the gauge is faulty, you would not know that the pressure of the tire is *exactly* 32, rather than 30 or 34, lb./sq. in.

We are, then, at the mercy of the world in the sense that we must have a reliable gauge in order to know tire pressure. For that matter, we must have reliable instruments to know anything else: how much gas is in the tank, what the oil pressure is, what the engine temperature is, and so on. *Our senses*, the physiologists tell us, are like *instruments* or *gauges*. The eyes detect electromagnetic radiation, the ears detect acoustic wave forms, the tongue and nose detect chemical compounds, and the skin detects physical surfaces or perturbations of the air around us, as well as thermal or kinetic energy of air molecules. So, our senses must be reliably functioning for them to give us knowledge of the world around us.[6] We are at the mercy of our senses and the world to cooperate. If our senses were not conditionally reliable instruments, or if what they detect were not unique to them, we would not be able to gain knowledge via the senses. For example, if sodium chloride tastes just like potassium chloride (salt substitute), then *by taste alone* we cannot know that it is salt (NaCl) that we are tasting. Our senses must cooperate (taste buds not on the blink), and the world must cooperate (no joker puts salt substitute in the salt shaker) for our senses to inform us reliably of the world around us. Radio, television, and newspapers must be reliable for us to learn anything from them. Our friends and teachers must be reliable sources of information if we are to gain knowledge from them. As long as the world cooperates and makes available to us reliable sources of information, we will have knowledge.

■ KNOWING THAT WE KNOW

Many want *more than knowledge*. They not only want to have it, they want to *know that they have it*. This is understandable. One not only wants to know that the food one is about to eat is edible, one wants to know that one knows. We want to *be confident*, to *feel secure* in acting on the basis of our knowledge. We not only want a reliable instrument to tell us our temperature, we want to know that it is reliable—so that we know whether to trust it, whether to feel confident that our child's fever has come down. We not only want reliable news sources, we want to know that they are reliable, so that we know whether to believe them.

Although, understandably, we want these things, they are not necessary for knowledge. They are something more—not knowing *that p*, but *knowing that we know that p*. As is clear from the structure alone, knowing that we know is a second-order affair. It is knowledge *twice* or at a *second level*. It may seem that knowing that *p* is true and knowing that you know are the same, but they are not; there is an important difference. It may seem that having reliable evidence and knowing that you have it are the same thing, but they too are importantly different. If we confuse these things, we may begin to slide into scepticism. So, we should be very careful to keep them distinct. Fortunately, we can easily show that they are distinct.

The easiest way to see this distinction is to understand that animals or infants may lack an articulated concept of knowledge. Without a concept of what knowledge is, they cannot know that they know things. Yet a dog may know his master is home, or an infant may know its mother is holding it. Also, we saw earlier, for S to know that *p*, S must satisfy the three conditions on our list. So, let S be *Joyce*. Let *p* be the proposition *that the battery in Joyce's garage is a twelve-volt battery*. Then for Joyce to *know that p* is for the conditions on our list to be satisfied: (1) *p* must be true, (2) Joyce must believe that *p* is true, and (3) Joyce must have reliable evidence that *p* is true. Let us put aside whether Joyce really does know that *p*, for a moment, and consider what it would take for Joyce to know that she knows. For second-order knowledge has importantly different requirements.

For one thing, for Joyce to know that she *knows that p* is for her to know, not just the proposition *p*, but a new proposition *q*. Let *q* be the proposition *that Joyce knows that p*. Proposition *q* is clearly *not* the *same* proposition as *p*; proposition *q* refers to proposition *p* as part of its content, but proposition *p* alone does not refer to itself. Fully articulated, of course, proposition *q* is as follows: *that Joyce knows that the battery in Joyce's garage is a twelve-volt battery*. Proposition *q* is, at least in part, *about Joyce's knowledge*. Proposition *p* is not about this—it is *only about Joyce's battery*. So, we can be assured that *p* and *q* are *different propositions* because they are about different things.

For another thing, as different propositions, *p* and *q* should require different things to be known. It requires different evidence to know that your checkbook balances than to know that it is raining, because they are different propositions. Similarly, to know *p*, Joyce must have a reliable source of information *about the voltage in her battery*. But to know *q*, Joyce must have reliable evidence *about her source of information about the battery*. She must know that it is reliable. Suppose that the way Joyce comes to know that the battery in the garage is a twelve-volt battery is by using the new voltmeter she just bought. Then, to know that the battery is a twelve-volt battery requires (in addition to truth and belief) that the voltmeter be reliable. That is *all* that is required for Joyce to know that *p*. If the meter is reliable and reads "12 V," and this is why Joyce believes the battery to be a twelve-volt battery, then she knows it is one. But suppose that Larry, her neighbor, asks whether Joyce knows that she knows it is a twelve-volt battery. Now to satisfy Larry, Joyce would have to *know that her new voltmeter is reliable*—that it was checked by the quality-control people at the factory, and so on. In addition to using the reliable meter to gain information about the voltage in the battery, Joyce would have to have some source of information about the voltmeter itself—reliable information that the meter is reliable. She cannot gain this information just by hooking the voltmeter up to the battery. So, to know *q* requires *more* and *different* information than to know *p*.

■ SCEPTICISM

Finally, we can discuss scepticism. *Scepticism* is the view that we know almost nothing. Sceptics grant that we believe that we have knowledge and that we may have many merely true beliefs, but they contend that we lack genuine knowledge. The expressway to scepticism is to accept the following argument:

1. To know that p, one must know that one knows that p.
2. One can never know that one knows that p.
3. Therefore, one can never know that p.

When we realize that almost any proposition at all can be substituted for p, we see how serious is the challenge the sceptic offers. I shall claim in this section that there is a way out of the sceptic's argument, but first let us see why it is so powerful.

Let us fill in the outline with the example of Joyce. The sceptic would say that Joyce cannot know that her battery is a twelve-volt battery unless she knows that she knows that it is one. As we have seen, to know this she must know that her voltmeter is reliable. But how can she know that? Not by measuring the voltage of the battery itself, for she does not yet know that it *is* a twelve-volt battery. Not by using some *other* voltmeter, because to use another meter to check this one's reliability, she would have to know that the *new* meter is reliable. But how will she know this? For any new meter she gets, she must know that *it* is reliable. But how? She cannot just go to the store and get a *new battery* marked "twelve volts" and then see if the new meter and old one read "12 V." For how did the store or battery factory *know* that it is a twelve-volt battery? Will not someone have to use a *voltmeter* to know that this battery or this type of battery made by the battery factory is a *twelve-volt battery*? And how will *they* know this? Will it not be by using *some* voltmeter? But how will they know *that* voltmeter (the one they use at the factory) is reliable? The circle of evidence turns back on itself. You see the problem. If the sceptic's argument is right, Joyce (or anyone) can never know of any battery that it is a twelve-volt battery.

As you may realize, this would not be such a problem if we were only talking about batteries. For, if you put the battery in Joyce's car and it *runs*, that may satisfy Joyce. The sceptic's challenge is only a problem because, as we noted earlier, *all of our knowledge* of the world relies on *instruments* (meters, gauges, our senses) of some type. The eyes, the ears, the sense of touch, the phone, the newspaper, the television—all these, even people—can be seen as sources of information. If they cannot be known to be reliable sources, then, by the above argument, we can not know anything by consulting them. But if true, we could know almost nothing. Perhaps we could know that we exist and know what we think, but not much more.

Fortunately, the sceptic is wrong to think that the argument is conclusive. As should be clear by now, at the very least we have proved that knowing that *p* is *not the same* as knowing that we know that *p*. So, for the sceptic to be right, he or she must prove that knowing *that p requires* knowing *that we know that p*. If these are not the same, *why should* knowing the one require knowing the other? That is, the sceptic must prove to us that step 1 of his or her argument is true. Any argument is only as good as its weakest link. If one of the steps is false, the conclusion may be false too. I see no reason to think that step 1 is true. Indeed, I have tried to give good reasons to think that it is *not true*. Since knowing something and knowing that you know it are different things, they require different things to be known and should be kept distinct. If your parents *are reliable sources* of information and they tell you that you were born in the evening, then you can know this by believing their testimony. Whereas, to *know that they are reliable* about the circumstances of your birth would take checking everything they have ever told you about it in earnest—or told anyone about it in earnest, for that matter. This you *could not do*—at least, I don't think you could. But you do *not need* to do this to know that you were born in the evening. To think you must is to confuse knowing something with knowing that you know it.

Also, the sceptic must be able to show that step 2 is true. But to show this, he or she must show that there is *no way* of knowing that a reliable source of information is reliable. The sceptic may well be wrong about this claim too. Go back, for the last time, to the example of Joyce. What if, at the factory, we have reliable ways of knowing that the parts that go into a voltmeter are good ones—we have excellent quality control? Suppose that we also can tell by a reliable machine that all the connections inside the voltmeter are made correctly and are in working order. Then we should be able to deduce, given good parts and good connections and stable laws of electronics, that the voltmeter will be reliable when hooked up to a battery. Wouldn't *that* let us know that we have a reliable meter? And if *we know* that we have a reliable meter, could we not know, since our meter reads the same as hers, *that Joyce knows* that the battery in her garage is a twelve-volt battery? Surely, if *we* can know that Joyce knows this, *she* can know that she knows this too. So, step 2 may be false as well.

Naturally, the sceptic will say that we cannot know that the voltmeter is reliable unless we also know that our way of knowing that the parts are good is reliable. We must know that our machine that checks connections is reliable. We must know that the laws of electronics have not changed, and so on. So, the sceptic will not be impressed, but consider what the sceptic is demanding. We must know all of these *other things* just to know that Joyce's battery is a twelve-volt battery. If we *tried* to know all of these other things, we would be led to *more* things and even more in the background that the sceptic would claim we must know to check the reliability of our knowledge of the parts and connections and laws of electronics, and so on. We would have to *know* practically *everything* just to be able to know something about Joyce's battery. Shouldn't we reply to the sceptic that these demands on knowledge are *too high*—unrealistically high? Surely we do not need to know everything that can be known just to know that Joyce's battery has twelve volts!

■ CONCLUSION

We have distinguished ways in which we use the word *know* and focused our attention on knowing that something is the case. Further, we have a list of conditions that one must satisfy in order to know that something is true. If we are right, one of the important ingredients of knowledge is reliable evidence. Reliable evidence is what *guarantees* that the truth of one's belief is no accident. It is this guarantee that is supposed to distinguish merely true belief from genuine knowledge.

Although we have an analysis of propositional knowledge, we have stressed that, in a certain respect, we are at the world's mercy. For if the world does not cooperate in such a way that it makes reliable evidence available to us, then we would not acquire knowledge—even if we held true beliefs some or all of the time. The lesson the sceptic wants to draw from this is not that the analysis of knowing that *p* is incorrect; the sceptic can accept our analysis. By accepting it, he or she wants to claim that we know nothing. He or she claims that we can only acquire knowledge if we can eliminate all uncertainty. We must, the sceptic would claim, knowingly eliminate the respect in which we are at the mercy of the world, or we can never know anything. The sceptic's recipe for eliminating this uncertainty is to make knowledge its own prerequisite. That is, to know that *p*, we must know that we know.

Resisting scepticism, I have maintained that the sceptic either confuses having knowledge with knowing that one has it or asks too much of knowledge—more than it requires to attain. In either case, the sceptic's argument is inconclusive as it stands. It takes more to show that we do not have knowledge.[7]

■ NOTES

1. Strictly speaking, a proposition is not the same thing as a sentence. We know this because "It is raining" and *"Il pleut"* are definitely not the same sentences—they have different numbers of letters in them and are in different languages (one English, one

French). But they express the same meaning or proposition. The distinction between sentences and propositions is important for logic and the philosophy of language. For our purposes, we shall avoid cases where the differences between sentences and propositions might have an impact on epistemology.

2. The correspondence theory of truth is one of many theories of truth. A full account of knowledge that incorporates this theory of truth would need to justify selecting it, as opposed to selecting one of the other theories of truth. This can be done, but it would take us on a very long digression.

3. This issue is central to Plato's theory of knowledge in his *Theaetetus*. See For Further Reading.

4. This example is similar in spirit to ones made famous by Edmund Gettier in "Is Justified True Belief Knowledge?" *Analysis* 23 (1963): 121–23, in which he was able to show that not only isn't true belief sufficient for knowledge, but even justified true belief is not sufficient for knowledge. The job of figuring out how to give an analysis of what it is to know that handles examples like this has been the main task of epistemology since Gettier's landmark paper appeared. Also see the readings in George Pappas and Marshall Swain, eds., *Essays on Knowledge and Justification* (Ithaca: Cornell Univ. Press, 1978).

5. Of course, there must not be anything *else* besides the fake deer-track maker that would make a track that looks like a deer track—no strange animals, bugs, falling rocks, and so on. I did not say that, but it should be understood to be a necessary condition of reliability.

6. Historically, this is the very problem that led Descartes (the father of modern philosophy) to seek a solution in his *Meditations on First Philosophy* (*The Philosophical Works of Descartes*, vol. 1, eds. Elizabeth Haldane and G. R. T. Ross [Cambridge: Cambridge Univ. Press, 1969]). It also led to some very unusual metaphysics. See also Chapter 3 and Chapter 10, especially the discussion of idealism, in this book.

7. This essay is written from the perspective of one who accepts what has come to be known as *reliabilism* (and *externalism*) in the theory of knowledge. Not all would agree with this approach. If by "justified," one means more than having a belief based on reliable evidence, I do not agree that more is required to know. Furthermore, I have yet to see a convincing argument for adding another condition to the analysis of knowledge. To fight this battle, however, would take us into territory appropriate for a course devoted solely to the subject of epistemology. We have also limited our account to empirical knowledge. A full account of knowledge, including knowledge of logical truths or mathematical truths, would introduce complications beyond the scope of the present essay. Please see For Further Reading (especially Chapter 7 of Robert Audi, *Belief, Justification, and Knowledge* [Belmont, CA: Wadsworth, 1988]). I would like to thank John Barker, Kevin Possin, and Leemon McHenry for helpful comments on earlier drafts. I would also like to thank Robert Audi, John Barker, and Fred Dretske for introducing me to epistemology.

■ QUESTIONS

1. What are the three different ways in which we use the word *know*? Explain how one of these can be resolved into the other two.

2. What does it mean to say that truth and belief are necessary for knowing that *p*, but are not sufficient?

3. Give some examples of reliable evidence for something, and explain what makes the evidence reliable.

4. What is the philosophical position called *scepticism*? Why is it a problem? How would a sceptic argue against the theory of knowledge presented here?

5. Could scepticism turn out to be true? How does the author respond to the challenge of scepticism? Do you tend to agree more with the author or with the sceptic? Explain. ■

■ FOR FURTHER READING

Adams, Frederick. "The Function of Epistemic Justification." *Canadian Journal of Philosophy* 16 (1986): 465–92.

Alston, William. *Epistemic Justification: Essays in the Theory of Knowledge*. Ithaca: Cornell Univ. Press, 1989.

Audi, Robert. *Belief, Justification, and Knowledge*. Belmont, CA: Wadsworth, 1988.

Bonjour, Laurence. "Externalist Theories of Empirical Knowledge." *Midwest Studies in Philosophy* 5 (1980): 53–73.

Chisholm, Roderick. *Theory of Knowledge*. Englewood Cliffs, NJ: Prentice-Hall, 1966.

Descartes, René. *Meditations on First Philosophy. The Philosophical Works of Descartes.* Vol. 1. Eds. Elizabeth Haldane and G. R. T. Ross. Cambridge: Cambridge Univ. Press, 1969.

Dretske, Fred. *Knowledge and the Flow of Information*. Cambridge, MA: Bradford/MIT Press, 1981.

Gettier, Edmund. "Is Justified True Belief Knowledge?" *Analysis* 23 (1963): 121–23.

Hamlyn, D. W. "Epistemology, History of." *The Encyclopedia of Philosophy*. Vol. 3. New York: Macmillan, 1967.

Lehrer, Keith. *Theory of Knowledge*. Boulder, CO: Westview, 1990.

Pappas, George, and Marshall Swain, eds. *Essays on Knowledge and Justification*. Ithaca: Cornell Univ. Press, 1978.

Plato. "Theaetetus." *Plato: Collected Dialogues*. Eds. Edith Hamilton and Huntington Cairns. Princeton: Princeton Univ. Press, 1961.

■ CHAPTER FIVE

Ethics

JOYCE HENRICKS

■ INTRODUCTION

It is impossible to read today's newspapers or watch the nightly news on television without thinking about such questions as "Should the state have the right to prevent a woman from having an abortion?" "Is it morally wrong to end the life of a person who is terminally ill?" "Do we have a responsibility to help the homeless in our own country or the starving in other countries?" "Is it ever morally right to discriminate on the grounds of race or sex?" Some questions come from one's own personal experiences, some from the experience of others. To think about these questions in a critical and systematic way is to engage in moral philosophy, or ethics.

We can distinguish three different types of questions within ethics. The first type is concerned with *normative* issues and asks such questions as "What kind of persons should we become?" "What things are worth pursuing?" "What kind of life is worth living?" "What are our obligations?" The second type is concerned with *meta-ethical* questions, such as "What is the meaning of terms like *right, good,* and so on?" "Can moral judgments be justified, and, if so, how?" Answering this type of question takes us into the areas of semantics, logic, and epistemology. The third type is concerned with *empirical* questions, such as "Is there a common human nature for all humans?" "Is there agreement between societies on basic standards of morality?" "What motivates people to be moral?" Answering this type of question involves using evidence provided by historians, psychologists, anthropologists, and sociologists.

There is obviously a connection between the normative views one advocates and the presuppositions one makes about meta-ethical and empirical matters. If one believes that there is moral knowledge and that reason is sufficient to attain this knowledge, one will most likely hold that moral standards should be the same for all human beings. If one believes that there is no common human nature and that different people truly differ in what they desire, one will most likely advocate different moral standards for different individuals or societies. And so on.

It is important to realize that morality is *practical* in the sense that it is an activity that aims to guide and influence action. Even those philosophers who emphasize the development of character in people as the basic goal in ethics would agree that closely tied to the kinds of actions one *does* is the kind of person one *is*. Aristotle, for example, emphasizes the importance of developing habits of behavior. Virtues are character traits. One is not an honest person until it becomes one's second nature to act honestly. One may tell the truth and yet not be honest, for being honest requires having developed a habit or "fixed disposition" of one's character to tell the truth. Thus, it was important to Aristotle to educate young people to *become* virtuous—that is, to develop habits to *behave* in certain ways considered virtuous. Even here, though, morality is ultimately tied to guiding and influencing actions. One of the jobs of ethics is to examine and evaluate these action-guides.

■ GROUND RULES

Let us first set out certain ground rules for doing ethics. Perhaps the most essential is to accept that in philosophy, one must have reasons for one's beliefs. In the next section, we will discuss various ethical theories, or proposed action-guides. While these theories differ in significant ways—some, for example, stressing rationality, others emotions, as the grounds on which we make our moral judgments—they agree that we must have *reasons* for our judgments. In studying ethics, we must include at least some of the following activities:

1. We must determine the factors that are relevant to our moral decisions about what kinds of actions we should perform and what kinds of persons we should become. (For example: Are the experiences of pleasure and pain relevant? Is a person's choosing for himself or herself relevant? Are dignity, honor, and justice relevant? Is acquiring knowledge relevant?)
2. We must consider analogous situations. (For example: Are we judging adultery to be wrong when someone else does it but permissible when we do it? Is there a good reason why we are making apparently inconsistent judgments here?)
3. We must attempt to get the facts straight to predict the consequences of our actions. (For example: Will our actions do more harm than good? Will our actions violate the dignity of anyone? Will our actions interfere with our becoming the sort of person we want to be?)

All this involves thinking, not emotion, and shows ethical reflection to be a reason-based process. We do not look for absolute certainty in ethics any more than we do in science or everyday life; we strive for reasonableness. As Aristotle said:

Our discussion will be adequate if it has as much clearness as the subject-matter admits of, for precision is not to be sought for alike in all discussions, anymore than in all the products of the crafts.[1]

Stressing the importance of our use of reason does not mean that we should not use information or facts obtained by others; we are always, at least in our youth, influenced by the judgments of others. It does mean, however, that as adults, we should not appeal blindly to authorities. In ethics, as in philosophy in general, it is not acceptable to respond to the question "Why is racial discrimination morally wrong?" with the answer "Because the law says so" unless one goes on to give reasons why the law is morally correct.

This point can be generalized to the following schema:

Why is X wrong?
Because A says so.

A can be any authority, whether parents, the law, religion, or even society at large, and X can be any action. There may be reasons why it is practical to do X (one doesn't want to get into trouble, be considered odd, and so on), but they are not relevant to why X is morally wrong. This same point can be made for such judgments as "You have a moral obligation to do X," "He is immoral," "It is morally permissible to do X," and the like.

Perhaps a few words on two of these authoritative sources especially is in order here. I assume that most of us reach a point where what our parents say no longer has the compelling force it had when we were children. Similarly, most of us, as we become aware of how our legal system works, no longer see laws as infallible sources of morality. Religion and custom, however, seem to have stronger holds on us than these first two sources of authority, but all appeals to authority must be supported with reasons.

■ Divine Command Theory

To many people, "Because God says so" seems not only an appropriate response to the question "why," it seems a definitive one. This approach has a long history and is called the *divine command theory*.[2] Plato, in his famous dialogue *Euthyphro*, asks the question "What is piety?"[3] In attempting to give a definition of piety, Euthyphro claims that piety is what is pleasing to the gods. Socrates, Plato's spokesperson in the dialogue, then asks Euthyphro, "Is something pious because it pleases the gods, or does it please the gods because it is pious?" Socrates, through some grammatical gymnastics, arrives at the answer that it pleases the gods because it is pious. He argues that if one accepted the other view—that is, that it is pious because it pleases the gods—we would not have been told what piety really is, and, therefore, the original question would not have been answered. The astute reader will note that Socrates' answer also does not tell us what piety is. What it does, however, is point us in the appropriate direction—toward the nature of piety itself.

For our purposes, the question raised in the *Euthyphro* becomes "Is something morally right because God commands it, or does God command it because it is morally right?" Socrates' answer would be "God commands it because it is morally right." In other words, morality is logically independent of God's will. To accept the other formulation would lead to the conclusion that we could not make moral judgments about God. We could not claim that God is morally good or that God's commandments are morally right. Because God determines what is morally right, or good, by an act of will, by simply deciding, there is no further standard by which we can evaluate God's decisions or actions. In other words, determining what is morally right is for humans a discovery, but for God, a decision.

Many people will perhaps claim that I have missed the point here, that my characterization of their position that X is right because God says so is unfair. They mean something like: We ought to follow God's commands because they are correct, and we know they are correct because God is all-knowing and can, therefore, know what is morally right in a way we, as humans, cannot.

This view, while perhaps more defensible than the divine command theory, still shows the logical independence of morality from religion as there is an independent standard of morality that God knows or discovers. In addition, there seems to be no *a priori* reason why we could not discover this same standard of morality for ourselves.

■ Ethical Relativism

The other appeal to authority—appeal to custom or society—is a popular approach called *relativism*. We must, however, distinguish here between the descriptive form and the normative form of this approach. The descriptive form of relativism, also called *cultural relativism*, simply says that different cultures (or societies) have different moral beliefs; that is, they have different beliefs about what is morally right or wrong. For example, Society A believes that abortion is morally wrong, whereas Society B believes that abortion is not morally wrong. Notice we have not indicated whether we approve or disapprove of abortion, whether we think abortion is morally permissible, morally obligatory, or morally forbidden. In other words, we have said nothing about the morality of abortion, only that Society A and Society B have different beliefs *about* the morality of abortion. To determine whether this claim is true or false, we would need to get the "facts" about Societies A and B. We would have to know their general cultures, their religious beliefs, their states of knowledge, their environmental/geographic conditions, and so on. Sometimes, for example, what appears to be a difference in morality is a difference in environmental conditions, as in the case of Inuits (central Alaskan Eskimos) leaving their aged parents to die of exposure, rather than take them along on their journey to new homes; or a difference in knowledge, as in the case of schools not allowing children with AIDS to attend school because they believe that the disease is spread by casual contact.

The normative form of relativism, called *ethical relativism*, says something very different. The most popular formulation of it, although perhaps the most simpleminded, is "Whatever a culture (or society) believes is morally right (or wrong) *is* morally right (or wrong)." Notice one can accept the descriptive form of relativism without accepting the normative form. One can agree that Societies A and B disagree on, for example, the morality of abortion, without also saying that both of them are right. Usually, however, someone who accepts the normative form will also accept the descriptive form; it would be quite strange to accept ethical relativism and yet deny that cultures do, in fact, differ.

The formulation of ethical relativism that we are discussing here fits into our scheme of appealing to authority: "Why is X wrong?" "Because A says so." Here the authority (A) appealed to is the society or culture.[4]

These forms of the divine command theory and ethical relativism get their force from the influence of general culture, including religion, on an individual's development. We all learn them from external sources in our lives—parents, teachers, the media, peers, social institutions, and society at large. Unless one is aware of plausible alternatives to general cultural influences, it is not surprising that the way things are done in one's society seems "natural" or "right." It is often difficult to imagine that these could be wrong, or even that there could be alternatives. For this reason, the appeals to the authorities of religion and society seem acceptable to many people. They are not accepted by most philosophers, however, and are regarded by many as examples of fallacious reasoning.

In the next section, we will examine some of the major ethical theories held by philosophers today. These theories are intended to be universal—that is, to provide us with correct moral standards for all people at all times. Let us turn to these theories and see if there *are* any that withstand criticisms and seem promising as candidates for a universal morality.

■ ETHICAL THEORIES

You have been assigned a paper on "the epistemological foundations of phenomenology." You have investigated the matter and found that you are the only one in your university to be working on the German philosopher Edmund Husserl. You find that there is only one book in the library on Husserl's philosophy and that book is at the reserve desk and cannot be checked out. Now, you want to write a good paper; you cannot work well in a library setting; you could do a much better job on the paper if you could take the book home for a longer period of time. What is also important, you know a foolproof way of getting the book out of the library without the librarian catching you. Should you "borrow" the book?

Ethical theories are attempts to give answers to such questions, but they do more than this. They provide us with general principles that can then be applied to particular instances such as the one discussed above. They are attempts to give answers to general questions such as "What kind of persons should we be?" "How should we live our lives?" "What is the right thing to do?" and so on.

Whether we think of the basic ethical questions in terms of character traits or actions, ethical theories can be thought of as proposed action-guides. Even if one focuses on the question "What kind of person ought I be?" eventually the question will include an action-guide, an answer to the questions "What ought I do?" "What is the right thing to do?" For our purposes in discussing ethical theories, I will focus on the latter questions, bringing in the former when appropriate.

■ Consequentialism

Consequentialist theories claim that the consequences are the only relevant factors to take into account when determining what is the morally right thing to do. There are many forms of consequentialism depending on both content and scope. When we consider content, we ask, "Which consequences are relevant—physical pain or pleasure? economic gain or loss? emotional well-being?" When we consider scope, we ask, "Consequences for whom—oneself? one's group? all humans? all living things?" The most widely held form of consequentialism is utilitarianism.

Utilitarianism was developed by the nineteenth-century British philosophers Jeremy Bentham and John Stuart Mill.[5] Briefly stated, utilitarianism claims that one ought to do that which will produce the greatest general good—that is, the greatest balance of good over bad consequences for the greatest number of people. Notice that this does not tell us what to do in a particular instance; in order to apply this principle to a particular instance, we need to have enough information about the particular instance and its context to know what the likely consequences of the various alternative courses of action will be. The principle can then be applied in choosing the course of action that will most likely produce the greatest general good. Two major formulations of utilitarianism merit our attention here:

> *Act Utilitarianism.* The right thing to do in any particular case is to do the act that produces the greatest balance of good over bad for all concerned in that particular case.
> *Rule Utilitarianism.* The right thing to do in any particular case is to follow the rule that produces the greatest balance of good over bad for all concerned.

Act utilitarianism looks at each case individually and is concerned solely with the consequences resulting from acting in that particular case. Rule utilitarianism looks at each case as an instance of a *type* of case and is concerned with the consequences resulting from everyone acting according to a rule that covers all cases of this type.

Let us return to the question raised at the beginning of this section: Should you "borrow" the book from the library? Or would that be morally wrong?

What would you have to consider if you were an act utilitarian? Well, you would have to consider all the people who might be affected by your taking the book and the likely consequences for these people. To make the distinction between the two types of utilitarianism clear, let us stipulate that no one else will be affected, negatively or positively; that no one will even know the book is missing—you intend to return it after you are finished with it; and that using the book at home will most likely allow you to write a paper that will earn you an A, whereas using it in the library for such limited periods of time will result in an inferior paper. Surely, it seems that taking the book will result in the greatest balance of good over bad consequences for everyone concerned, that is, you will be greatly helped, and no one will be harmed or even inconvenienced. In other words, you ought to take the book. But, you might feel a reluctance to reach this conclusion because, after all, taking the book is against the rules. In fact, some might even consider this stealing. An act utilitarian, however, would say if all the above assumptions are accurate, then you ought to "borrow" the book.

Many people who are attracted to utilitarianism find this conclusion objectionable. After all, if we can justify stealing in a case like this, surely we can find cases where we can justify killing innocent people. These people find the position of rule utilitarianism more attractive. Rule utilitarianism would claim that in determining whether an act is right or wrong we do not look at the consequences of doing the act, but we look instead to a generalization. For example, we do not ask, "Would stealing this particular book in this particular situation be right?" We ask, instead, "Would stealing, *in general*, be right?" In other words, we appeal to a generalized rule covering all cases of this type, not just the particular case in question. Because, in general, stealing would not produce the best consequences for everyone concerned, stealing in this particular case is wrong—even though, in this particular case, it might produce the best consequences. In other words, in rule utilitarianism one ought to do the act that follows a rule that will produce the best consequences.

Many people criticize both versions of utilitarianism as essentially claiming "the end justifies the means." A utilitarian would, however, dismiss this criticism with a bewildered "Of course! What else could possibly justify our actions?" A more serious criticism raised against utilitarianism concerns the issue of *justice*. For example, if more good can be produced by giving 10 percent of the population extra benefits (without their deserving these extra benefits in any way) while taking away some benefits from the rest of the population (again, without their deserving this loss in any way), it seems that the utilitarian is committed to the conclusion that one ought to do so anyway. And yet to many critics this seems unfair, or unjust. For many philosophers, an ethical theory that does not speak to the issue of justice is at best incomplete, at worst, inadequate.[6]

Utilitarians are also criticized for allowing, at least in principle, the possibility of violating some of our most cherished moral beliefs, for example, killing an innocent person or violating a person's rights, if doing so will produce more good for everyone. While some utilitarians claim we must then change our basic moral beliefs because they reflect our cultural teachings, which are often based on religion and superstition, others take these criticisms seriously and try to show how utilitarianism can be consistent with our basic moral beliefs. Whether these attempts succeed or not is open to debate. In any event, they have not satisfied many of the critics of utilitarian theories.

In the formulations of utilitarianism, I have not indicated which consequences are to be considered good. Many candidates for the good have been proposed, such as happiness, health, knowledge, dignity, autonomy, economic well-being, power, and so forth. Some philosophers have claimed that there is not just one thing that is "the good," but many things that are good. Obviously, depending on what one takes as good, different formulations of consequentialist theories will result.

■ *Non-Consequentialism*

Non-consequentialism is basically a catchall category for theories that deny that consequences are the only things that count. Depending on the type of non-consequentialism, such things as rules, motives, feelings, and so forth, count as relevant.[7]

■ KANT'S THEORY: CATEGORICAL IMPERATIVE

To Immanuel Kant, one of the best-known non-consequentialist German philosophers, motives as well as duties are essential for morality. A person's actions have true moral value only to the extent that they are done from duty. He distinguishes between acting *in accordance with* duty and acting *for the sake of* duty. Acting in accordance with duty is simply doing the right act, doing what duty requires. Acting for the sake of duty is doing the right act, not because you enjoy the act, or because it will get you something you want, but *because* it is your duty. For Kant, only this latter motive for doing your duty has any moral worth. That is not to say that any other motive necessarily makes your act immoral; it just does not give that act true moral value.

Consider the following situation: You are on line in a supermarket, and you hand the clerk a ten-dollar bill to pay for an item that costs five dollars. The clerk hands you back fifteen dollars in change, clearly having mistaken your ten-dollar bill for a twenty. Let us grant that the right thing to do in this situation, your duty, is to return the extra ten dollars to the clerk. Now, if you return the ten dollars because you are afraid you will be embarrassed if someone behind you notices the error, or because you are just an honest person and you automatically call the mistake to the clerk's attention, or even because it gives you satisfaction to do the right thing, your act, while the right act, has no true moral worth. Only if you return the money to the clerk because it is the right thing to do, because it is your duty, does your act have moral worth for Kant. Being motivated by duty involves having respect for moral principles that we think all persons ought to live up to, even if they have no desire to do so.

Perhaps explaining Kant's distinction between types of duties will help to clarify his position. Kant distinguishes between *categorical imperatives* and *hypothetical imperatives*. An imperative is simply a command; a hypothetical command is a conditional command, a statement of the form "If . . . , then. . .": If (you have certain desires or want to achieve some specific goals), then (do X). A categorical imperative is an unconditional command; it does not matter what desires or goals you have: "Do X. Your duty is your duty." For Kant, only duties in the form of categorical imperatives capture the importance of morality. Your moral obligations are unconditional; you ought to do X because it is your duty. Therefore, the motive behind the act is important. You are acting for the sake of duty when you do things that you believe are required by moral principles that everyone ought to follow.

To underscore the unconditional nature of morality, Kant calls the general principle by which we determine our duties the "categorical imperative."[8] This categorical imperative requires us to act so that the maxim of our action can consistently be willed to be a universal law. A *maxim* is the principle on which a person is acting, or, more specifically, a statement of our intent to act in a certain way along with a reason for that action. A universal law is a rule that applies to everyone. Take the example of the maxim "I can have something to drink when I am thirsty." Clearly, we can consistently—that is, without contradiction—apply this to everyone: "Everyone can have something to drink when they are thirsty." Now consider the example Kant gives: "Make a promise and break it if it is inconvenient to you." If we will this maxim to be a universal law, we want people to be able to make promises and want people to break promises when it is inconvenient for them to keep them. This involves an inconsistency: you cannot have the practice of making promises if everyone can break them when inconvenient. Would you accept my promise to repay the hundred dollars I borrow from you if you knew that I would not keep the promise if I did not want to? (If you're extremely generous, you might *give* me the money, but you surely would not *loan* it to me under these circumstances.) In somewhat oversimplified terms, what Kant is saying in the first formulation of the categorical imperative is "Be consistent—do not make exceptions for anyone, including yourself. If it is right for you to do it, it must be right for everyone, in relevantly similar circumstances, to do it."

To say that we should act only on those principles we are willing to have everyone follow is to say that we should treat all rational beings as having equal intrinsic value. Rational beings should never be treated as mere means for satisfying our desires. This leads to the second formulation of the categorical imperative.[9] It requires us to treat all rational beings, including humans, as ends, never merely as a means to an end. In other words, human beings, because they are rational beings, deserve to be treated as having value in themselves, not merely as a means to something else that has value. Again, in somewhat simplified terms, this comes down to saying "Do not *use* people."

To Kant, a non-consequentialist, the actual consequences of an act make no difference. "Borrowing" the book from the library would be stealing, and would therefore be morally wrong. Again, to Kant a lie is always wrong, even when it is the only way to save lives. While this view might be hard to accept in cases of stealing and lying, Kant's position, when applied to such instances as torturing innocent people to save the lives of others or testing medical drugs on human beings without their consent, is more plausible and worthy of further consideration, because we regard the individuals on whom the tests or torture is inflicted as ends in themselves, or persons.

Kant has been criticized on many grounds; one criticism focuses on the role of motive in his system. Many people believe that there can be more than one consideration motivating you to do an action; they find Kant's requirement that your only motive be to act for the sake of duty unnecessarily restrictive and therefore unreasonable. If you keep a promise to your sick grandmother because it is the right thing to do, your act has moral value; if you keep a promise to visit her because you enjoy doing so, your act does not have true moral value. Isn't it possible for both motives to be present? If so, would your act have moral value or not?

Perhaps the most crucial criticism for our purpose is one that pertains to the categorical imperative. First, Kant does not distinguish between making an exception to a rule and the rule's having exceptions. Consider traffic rules. If the rule prohibits parking on the street, then it is a violation of the rule to allow anyone to park on that street. To do so would be to make an exception to the rule. If the rule however, prohibits parking on the street from 8 A.M. to 5 P.M., then to park on the street from 8 P.M. to 10 P.M. is not a violation of the rule. In other words, rules can be "absolute" with no exceptions for any reasons allowed; or the rules themselves can have exceptions built into them. Notice the exceptions built into them will apply to everyone, so the rules are still universal. Kant does not seem to consider this distinction. For example, the rule "Keep your promise, unless keeping your promise will bring about extreme harm to an innocent person" would allow occasions when it would be permissible to break your promise. There is nothing inconsistent in allowing the maxim in this rule to become a universal law.

■ ROSS'S THEORY: *PRIMA FACIE* DUTIES

Another version of non-consequentialism that has gained considerable attention is that of the early twentieth-century British moral philosopher W. D. Ross.[10] Ross, while a non-consequentialist himself, tries to bridge the gap between Kant's extreme non-consequentialism and Mill's utilitarianism. He claims: (1) that there is more to morality than simply producing the greatest general good, and (2) that while rules are important, rules are not the absolute rules that Kant proposes. As a moderate non-consequentialist, he claims that rules should be looked at as *prima facie* rules, as rules that apply in general. All things being equal, for example, keeping your promise is right. In other words, unless there is some overriding consideration to cancel out the rightness of keeping your promise, you should keep your promise. For example, lying is *prima facie* wrong; it shows disrespect for the person being lied to, and it usually produces undesirable consequences. If one lies, he or she is doing something wrong *unless* the action can be defended by claiming, for example, that lying was necessary to avoid serious harm to someone. Then the *prima facie* rule to tell the truth is overridden by the *prima facie* rule to not harm others.

Moderate non-consequentialism thus avoids the criticisms that have been made against utilitarianism and Kantianism. It, too, however, has its critics. For example, some claim it is not clear how we determine what the *prima facie* rules are. Even more serious is the charge that this position gives us no way to resolve conflicts between *prima facie* rules. For example, if we can help many needy people by hurting one person, what should we do? There seem to be two rules here: Help others in need and do not hurt anyone. Which one takes precedence in this situation? The theory does not give us an answer.

Ross's own answer is to bring in a form of *intuitionism* whereby we all have a "moral faculty" that allows us to *know*, or *intuit*, what the *prima facie* rules (or duties) are, and which ones are more important or of a higher order than others. As Ross explains it:

> I should make it plain at this stage that I am assuming the correctness of some of our main convictions as to *prima facie* duties, or, more strictly, am claiming that we know them to be true. To me it seems as self-evident as anything could be, that to make a promise, for instance, is to create a moral claim on us in someone else. Many readers will perhaps say that they do not know this to be true. If so, I certainly cannot prove it to them; I can only ask them to reflect again, in the hope that they will ultimately agree that they also know it to be true. The main moral convictions of the plain man seem to me to be, not opinions which it is for philosophy to prove or disprove, but knowledge from the start, and in my own case I seem to find little difficulty in distinguishing these essential convictions from other moral convictions which I also have, which are merely fallible opinions based on an imperfect study of the working for good or evil of certain institutions or types of actions.[11]

■ Justification

This brings us to, perhaps, the most crucial issue in the field of ethics, namely, how do we justify our basic moral standards. This is one of the main questions discussed in meta-ethics. Unfortunately, this is an issue to which there is no present resolution. To discuss this issue would require an examination of moral language, moral reasoning, relationships between moral concepts, and so on. Some moral philosophers are working in the area of *deontic logic*, which is the logic of obligation. Whether the development of this branch of logic will shed light on what constitutes a justification in ethics remains to be seen.

But there is another way to approach this issue. In each of the views we have discussed so far, there has been a presumption on the part of the philosophers that we would find their positions plausible and that we would agree with them once we properly understood them. Mill spends a considerable amount of time trying to show that utilitarianism simply provides us with a more coherent, empirically based standard, which if adhered to will give a grounding for our basic moral convictions; further, that utilitarianism is not incompatible with Christian ethics; and that it embodies the best of all that Western civilization has to offer. Kant appeals to our beliefs about what reason would dictate, and Ross assumes a fundamental moral faculty common to all human beings. In all of these, there is a presumption that agreement will be forthcoming, and that there would be no further need to "justify" the basic moral standards.

What happens, however, when the expected agreement is not forthcoming? Utilitarians can revise their formulation of the theory to make it consistent with our moral convictions, as rule utilitarians do, or they can take a more extreme position, as act utilitarians do, and require us to revise our moral convictions to bring them in line with utilitarian theory. A Kantian can try to help us see more clearly what is involved in being a rational being, and that being a rational being commits one to accepting the categorical imperative. A more extreme Kantian might refuse to consider as rational someone who did not ultimately accept the categorical imperative. And a Rossian can claim that the person is not "seeing" the situation clearly, or requires more knowledge about the nature of the case, or is lacking or poorly using the moral faculty.[12]

■ THE CHALLENGE OF FEMINIST ETHICS

One recent challenge to this traditional approach to ethics is feminist ethics.[13] In 1977, the psychologist Carol Gilligan published *In a Different Voice*. In it, she attacked the findings of Lawrence Kohlberg on human moral development. Kohlberg, also a psychologist, had concluded from his studies that there were six developmental stages that human beings go through in becoming moral beings, from concern with one's immediate self-interest to an adherence to abstract formal principles. At these highest stages, one makes moral judgments independently of historical or social contexts and anchors one's morality in principles that are applied universally. In his studies, women rarely reached the highest stages of moral development, remaining instead locked into the less abstract, interrelational perspectives of the middle stages.[14]

Gilligan criticizes Kohlberg and other researchers, such as the famous French psychologist Jean Piaget, on the grounds that their research was conducted solely on male subjects. Once a profile of moral development was established for males, it was applied to females, who were found to be less morally mature.

Gilligan's research is of interest for philosophers because moral theories often presuppose empirical data about human behavior gathered by the various empirical sciences. It is also of interest because Kohlberg's conclusions seemed to provide the evidence to support views held by such famous thinkers as Aristotle, Aquinas, Kant, Hegel, Rousseau, and Freud, all of whom were convinced that women were deficient in moral reasoning.[15] They, too, used the male as the standard, attributing female *differences* to *deficiencies*.

Gilligan argues that the perspective of most moral philosophy is that of men, where abstract principles of justice and rights seem predominant. The concept of the self underlying this view is of an autonomous, independent individual, separated from others and from nature.

Women, because of their different life experiences, exhibit what Gilligan calls a "care perspective."[16] This perspective is grounded in a conception of self and others interdependent in social relations. One cannot ignore the historical and social contexts. In this perspective, responsibility, not rights, plays a central role in the morality. Using the example of the library book again, feminist ethics would ask a different question. It would not ask if the student was violating any rules, or if the student had the right to take the book, or even which course of action would provide the best consequences. It would ask, for example: "Why is the student in this situation? Are the library regulations reasonable? Could they be modified so as to allow this student, and others in similar situations, to take the book home? Is there a way that the interests of the library and the student could both be served?" This is not to say that the questions asked from the traditional perspectives of moral philosophy are inappropriate; only that there are other questions to be asked that, by asking, make possible different solutions.

These two perspectives have been compared by Gilligan to the duck-rabbit picture (the picture is drawn in such a way that one can view it as a duck or as a rabbit, depending on whether one "sees" an object in the picture as the open beak of a duck or the ears of a rabbit). It is not that one interpretation of the picture is correct; there is a tendency for an individual to perceive the picture more easily one way than the other, but the individual may change perceptions in different contexts. So it is with moral perspectives. Men tend to use the justice perspective, whereas women tend to use the care perspective more comfortably; each gender may change perspectives in different situations—for example, women who work outside the home tend to use the justice perspective at work and the care perspective at home, whereas men who are involved in child-rearing and the "helping professions" tend to use the care perspective in those situations. Again, the conclusion of many feminists is that neither perspective is *the* correct one, both may be.

We should note here that some feminists would disagree with this conclusion; they would claim that the care perspective is clearly the superior one and that the future of the world depends on everyone adopting the care perspective. Many feminists believe that the destruction that humans have visited on the planet and on each other is based on a male model of thinking and acting. When nature is conceived as separate from humans, it threatens to interfere with the fulfillment of human needs if not carefully controlled. On the other hand, conceiving of humans as part of nature allows for humans to cooperate with nature rather than strive to control it in order to fulfill their needs.[17]

The gender profiles established by Gilligan are based on North American college-educated men and women. We should not be surprised to find differences in moral thinking and worldviews from people who are engaged in different kinds of social activities in different kinds of situations. Can we assume that one's class and cultural background make no difference to one's moral perspective? More studies need to be conducted on a more diverse population before any conclusions can be reached about the differences between men's and women's moral perspectives. In fact, an examination of the moral views held by some native American nations and some African societies seems to indicate that men adopt the care perspective as frequently as women in those societies.[18] If this is so, the differences do not seem to be based on gender so much as on basic cultural differences.

Before going any further, let me caution the reader about an inappropriate use of empirical data in moral philosophy. We must be careful in reaching conclusions about what people *ought* to do based upon what they *do* do. This is not to say that the facts are irrelevant to moral philosophy, only that one cannot logically infer a normative conclusion from purely descriptive premises.

It is important to remember that raising objections to an opponent's position is not the same as defending your own. The fact that there are problems with most of the universalistic positions discussed earlier is not proof that feminist ethics is preferable. Feminist ethics has only recently appeared on the scene, challenging the established tenets of moral philosophy and asking philosophers to reexamine some of their most dearly held beliefs.[19] The direction it takes remains to be seen. It is already clear however, that, by its challenges, it is breathing fresh life into contemporary moral philosophy.

At present we are talking about an *approach* rather than a full-blown *theory*. This approach is not necessarily incompatible with a universalistic morality. To put this in the terminology we used at the beginning of this chapter, morality is considered to be important enough to keep on trying to convince others to agree with us. It is not like a disagreement on broccoli—I like it, you do not; it is just a matter of taste. Perhaps because we want to see the human in all of us, we refuse to admit that other humans would disagree on such important matters. On this reading, universalism becomes a matter of faith, a hope that if we try hard enough to understand each other's situation, we *would* agree in moral matters. Short of attaining this agreement, however, we still strive to understand other people and their different ways before making, and acting on, our moral judgments about them. Feminist ethics asks us to take seriously this attempt to understand the perspectives of others.

■ CONCLUSION

In light of our discussion, one might be inclined to abandon ethics altogether and just follow the rules of one's society or peers. This, however, would be overreacting. Again, paraphrasing Aristotle, in ethics as in most areas (except perhaps mathematics and logic), we must be content with less than absolute certainty.

Perhaps the most important lessons to be gained from this chapter are that: (1) we are ultimately on our own in deciding what to believe, and (2) making moral decisions is hard work with no guarantee of reaching certainty. For many of our moral decisions, decisive reasons can be given; and for the others, thinking through the issue as best we can will at least help us gain the clarity and focus necessary to make a reasonable and responsible decision.

I hope that after reflecting on some of the strongest attempts to state and defend ethical standards, and the critical evaluations of such standards, we will be less inclined to accept facile and dogmatic pronouncements on morality. If that is accomplished here, that is enough.

■ NOTES

1. Aristotle, *Nicomachean Ethics, The Basic Works of Aristotle*, ed. Richard McKeon (New York: Random House, 1941), 1. 3.1094b. 12–17.

2. This position is found in St. Augustine, *The City of God* and *The Morals of the Catholic Church*. It can also be found in the work of more contemporary writers, such as Emil Brunner.

3. Plato, *Euthyphro*. While *piety* has a religious overtone, the question Socrates is asking has more to do with moral than religious duties.

4. There are other formulations of ethical relativism that are more plausible. Because they are not as simple as the one discussed in the text, however, it would take more time than is available here to discuss these formulations adequately. Karl Marx proposes a form of ethical relativism based on one's class position in society, and Gilbert Harmon discusses a viable formulation of this position in *The Nature of Morality* (New York: Oxford Univ. Press, 1977).

5. Jeremy Bentham, *An Introduction to the Principles of Morals and Legislation* (New York: Hafner, 1948), and John Stuart Mill, *Utilitarianism* (Indianapolis: Bobbs-Merrill, 1971).

6. Mill handles the issue of justice by subsuming it under the broader category of utility. He argues that treating people justly will always produce more good than treating them unjustly. Whether this is a satisfactory resolution of the problem of justice for utilitarians I will leave to the reader to determine.

7. Two philosophers merit mention here. David Hume, *A Treatise of Human Nature* (Oxford: Clarendon Press, 1965), argues that morality is based on a "sentiment" of sympathy which we all share. In discussing the relationship of reason to emotion, he says: "Reason is . . . the slave of the passions." That is, reason can simply help us find the means to attain the goals, which are determined by our passions. Jean-Paul Sartre, an advocate of *existentialism*, claims that there can be no guidelines to help us make moral decisions because all situations are unique. The best one can do is *choose for oneself*.

8. Immanuel Kant, *Groundwork of the Metaphysics of Morals*, trans. H. J. Paton (London: Hutchinson Univ. Library, 1948). Kant sometimes writes as if there were one categorical imperative but three different formulations of it; at other times he writes as if there were three distinct categorical imperatives. I have chosen the first interpretation in what follows.

9. The third formulation deals with the autonomy of rational beings. It can be summarized as: "Always act on a maxim of your own choosing." Since it does not have the same function in Kant's system as do the first and second categorical imperatives, I have not discussed it in this chapter.

10. W. D. Ross, *The Right and the Good* (Oxford: Clarendon Press, 1930).

11. Ross, *The Right and the Good*, 20-21.

12. Another retort to a critic is to deny that the critic is taking "the moral point of view." This approach has problems, however, as it gives the definition of morality, or the moral point of view, a normative component, something that is usually to be avoided in definitions.

13. Other challenges come from existentialist and Marxist philosophers.

14. For a fuller account of Kohlberg's studies, see Lawrence Kohlberg, *Philosophy of Moral Development* (San Francisco: Harper and Row, 1981).

15. For representative passages from these and other thinkers, see Mary Mahowald, ed., *Philosophy of Woman* (Indianapolis: Hackett, 1983), and Rosemary Agonito, ed., *History of Ideas on Woman* (New York: Putnam, 1977).

16. There is another interpretation here—a psychoanalytic one—that I am overlooking for the sake of simplicity.

17. We cannot go into an examination of this more extreme feminist position. Ac-

cepting the care perspective as *the* correct one, the one to be universally applied, requires more of a defense than simply a strong statement of the position. The challenge to the care perspective is that by identifying with the group and its welfare the individual's needs are sometimes ignored. As many women have noted, being concerned with the needs of others often leads to a loss of self.

18. Sandra Harding, "The Curious Coincidence of Feminine and African Moralities: Challenges for Feminist Theory," *Women and Moral Philosophy*, eds. Eva F. Kittay and Diana T. Meyers (Totawa, NJ: Rowman and Littlefield, 1987).

19. Currently under debate is the notion that morality requires us to be impartial in our deliberations. Some philosophers are reexamining the view that we ought to give as much consideration to the welfare of strangers as to that of our loved ones.

■ QUESTIONS

1. Consider the following cases. Are they moral issues; that is, debatable in terms of right and wrong? Explain your answers.

a. A small town with a predominantly white population borders on a large city with a predominantly African-American population. Residents of the small town are issued passes for themselves and their guests to use the town's public parks. All others are barred from using the town's public parks.

b. In recent years, a number of cemeteries in the United States have allowed people to use the cemetery grounds for cycling, jogging, and even team sports.

2. Try to formulate a version of the divine command theory that avoids the criticisms raised in the text.

3. A tribe living in a remote jungle area shuns anyone who becomes seriously ill. Members of the tribe who become seriously ill cease to exist, in the tribe's view. They must leave the village and care for themselves. If they recover, however, they are restored to full tribal membership. Do you think that this shows that the tribe lacks compassion? Do examples like this prove that different cultures differ in their moral beliefs? Explain.

4. Do you believe that a person could have any moral duties or obligations if she or he were the only person living on a deserted island? Explain.

5. Utilitarianism can be understood to be composed of two parts: (1) maximize the amount of good produced, and (2) maximize the number of people who will receive this good. Do you see any problem with utilitarianism under this interpretation? If you had to choose which part was more important, which would you choose? Why?

6. Taking into account what Ross means by a *prima facie* duty, make a list of duties that you would consider to be *prima facie* duties. If you cannot do so, explain why.

In questions 7–10, consider how each of the theories we have discussed would go about answering the question. Then consider which of those responses, if any, comes closest to the way you would respond.

7. Mary's son, age twenty, is a junior in college. He decides to live off-campus with his girlfriend. Mary disapproves of this arrangement and tells him bluntly, "I won't continue to support you if you continue living with her." Is Mary's position morally justified? Would it make a difference if it were Mary's daughter who was living with a boyfriend?

8. The sponsors of television shows can exert influence over subjects and their treatments presented on television. In some cases, they may demand veto power over scripts, reasoning that because they are paying for the show and their product will be identified with it, they should have the final say about the show's content. Is it morally right for them to demand this veto power?

9. The artificial kidney machine is a rare and expensive machine. Very often a patient's life depends on the use of the machine. Unfortunately, there are not enough of these machines for all the people who need them. The choice of who should be given priority in the use of these machines can be an agonizing one. What factors do you consider to be the most important ones to consider in reaching such a decision? What is the relative importance of each of these factors?

10. In the 1940s, approximately four hundred women participated in a study to determine the effectiveness of the birth-control pill. Most of these women were poor Puerto Rican women who were seeking help in preventing further pregnancies. The women were divided into two groups, one group receiving oral contraceptives, the other group—the control group— receiving sugar pills with no birth-control chemical. None of the women were told about the sugar pills. As a result, six of the women in the control group became pregnant. Was this morally justified?

11. In questions 7–10, do you think the two perspectives discussed by Gilligan would give rise to different answers? Explain.   ∎

∎ FOR FURTHER READING

Agonito, Rosemary, ed. *History of Ideas on Woman*. New York: Putnam, 1977.

Aristotle. *Nicomachean Ethics*. *The Basic Works of Aristotle*. Ed. Richard McKeon. New York: Random House, 1941.

Bentham, Jeremy. *An Introduction to the Principles of Morals and Legislation*. New York: Hafner, 1948.

Brandt, Richard. *Ethical Theory*. Englewood Cliffs, NJ: Prentice-Hall, 1959.

Frankena, William. *Ethics*. Englewood Cliffs, NJ: Prentice-Hall, 1978.

Harding, Sandra. "The Curious Coincidence of Feminine and African Moralities: Challenges for Feminist Theory." *Women and Moral Theory*. Ed. Eva F. Kittay and Diana T. Meyers. Totawa, NJ: Rowman and Littlefield, 1987.

Harmon, Gilbert. *The Nature of Morality*. New York: Oxford Univ. Press, 1977.

Hume, David. *A Treatise of Human Nature*. Oxford: Clarendon Press, 1965.

Kant, Immanuel. *Groundwork of the Metaphysics of Morals*. Trans. H. J. Paton. London: Hutchinson Univ. Library, 1948.

Kohlberg, Lawrence. *Philosophy of Moral Development*. San Francisco: Harper and Row, 1981.

Mahowald, Mary, ed. *Philosophy of Woman*. Indianapolis: Hackett, 1983.

Mill, J. S. *Utilitarianism*. Indianapolis: Bobbs-Merrill, 1971.

Nietzsche, Friedrich. *Beyond Good and Evil*. Trans. Walter Kaufman. New York: Vintage, 1966.

Ross, W. D. *The Right and the Good*. Oxford: Clarendon Press, 1930.

■ CHAPTER SIX

Political Philosophy

BRAD HOOKER

■ INTRODUCTION

Some people have enough money for palaces, expensive delicacies, conspicuous consumption; others are too poor to afford enough to eat or a warm place to sleep. Governments can do something about the distribution of wealth. They can impose higher taxes on the rich and provide resources for the poor. They can influence unemployment rates, interest rates, and inflation rates. They can try to control wages and prices. But at what distribution of wealth should governments be aiming, if any at all? Presumably, they should aim at a *just* distribution. What is a just distribution of wealth? Let us refer to this as the question of *distributive justice.*

The just distribution of wealth is but one of many topics that comprise *political philosophy.* Much of political philosophy concerns the relation between the individual and the state, the government, and the law.[1] "What obligation do individuals have to the state?" "In particular, do they have a moral obligation to comply with the law?" "What could justify people's disobeying or revolting against the state?" "What ought the state do for its citizens?" "One thing a state should do is protect them from other states' aggression; is this the only defensible reason a state could have for declaring war?" "What other protections ought states provide their citizens?

Most of us agree that states should protect civil and political liberties. To be more specific, most of us accept that the law should accord citizens the rights to vote, to stand for office in free elections, to criticize the government, to own property, as well as the rights to religious freedom, to a fair trial, and to privacy. This consensus about rights, however, stops short of agreement about what justifies these rights. Some people argue that the rights are justified because on balance and in the long run, their establishment will promote human well-being. Others argue that they are justified because each of us would be willing to grant these rights to others in return for having them ourselves. There is also disagreement about how rights apply in certain circumstances. For example: "What circumstances warrant the suspension of free speech?" "Does the right to privacy go so far as to prevent the government from outlawing abortion or the recreational use of dangerous drugs?" "Should employers be allowed to hire or promote whomever they want, or can the state legitimately require racial diversity at all levels of the work force?"

All these questions are obviously important, but the central issue in contemporary political philosophy is the just distribution of wealth. Therefore, this chapter will focus on the question of distributive justice.

■ UTILITARIANISM

Consider the proposal that wealth should be distributed in whatever way will in the long run result in the greatest aggregate well-being. Aggregate well-being is everyone's well-being added together *impartially*—that is, without regard to race, religion, gender, social class, or the like. So, benefits to any one person are to count for just as much as the same size benefits to anyone else.

This proposal that the just distribution of wealth is whatever distribution maximizes aggregate well-being comes from a tradition of moral and political thought called *utilitarianism*. Utilitarians believe that the best distribution is the one that will in the long run maximize *utility*, and virtually all utilitarians conceive of utility as *well-being*.

But what is well-being? Earlier utilitarians (Jeremy Bentham, John Stuart Mill, Henry Sidgwick[2]) believed that well-being is purely a matter of happiness. Most present-day utilitarians have moved to the view that, although happiness is a major component of well-being, there are other components as well—that is, other things that can benefit people without increasing their happiness (even indirectly).[3] In any event, most of us share a rough intuitive grasp of what things count as benefits or harms, or, in other words, as increases or decreases to well-being. Let us assume for the sake of argument that we share enough common ground to allow us to talk intelligibly about aggregate well-being.

What particular distribution of goods, then, will result in the greatest aggregate well-being? Some utilitarians think the answer is a socialist economy that produces a *roughly equal* distribution of wealth. Other utilitarians think that the answer is a capitalistic economy with a *very unequal* distribution of wealth. Thus, while agreeing on the utilitarian account of distributive justice, utilitarians may disagree about economics in ways that lead them to disagree about what particular distribution utilitarianism endorses. Most contemporary utilitarians, however, acknowledge the fundamental importance of three considerations: the diminishing marginal utility of material goods, the need for individual material (more specificly, economic) incentives, and the corrupting influence of great disparities in wealth.[4]

The *diminishing marginal utility of material goods* is a fancy name for a familiar phenomenon. Examples of material goods are food, houses, clothes, cars, and money. To say that a material good has diminishing marginal utility is to say that the more of that material good I have, the less benefit I derive from a given amount of that good. Suppose I have no winter coat. If I then get a winter coat, my utility goes up dramatically. However, were I to have fifty winter coats, an additional one would benefit me little. Similarly, life was considerably more convenient for me after I got a car; but if I had eighty-six cars already, an additional car would probably not increase my well-being more than a tiny amount. Again, a hundred dollars might be the difference between starvation and survival to a desperately poor person, but a hundred dollars is unlikely to make much difference to a billionaire's well-being. Of course, there are cases in which material goods do *not* have diminishing marginal utility (for example, that eighty-seventh car might have won my collection some prize). Such cases are, however, exceptions. Normally, the more of a material good we have, the less any given amount of it benefits us.

That fact suggests that transferring some goods from the rich to the poor would harm the rich less than it would benefit the poor. So, the diminishing marginal utility of material goods gives utilitarians a reason for thinking that equalizing goods (and wealth) will increase aggregate well-being.

We can understand the diminishing marginal utility of material goods while thinking about distributions *statically*, that is, while thinking about distributions in the abstract and apart from their connections with past or future behavior. But, obviously, people's beliefs about how wealth will be distributed can influence their behavior. This influence raises the issue of material incentives.

A number of social institutions influence the distribution of goods and services—the market, taxation policies, public sector spending, and so on. Let us refer to these as *distributive institutions*. How distributive institutions are configured will influence material incentives. Let us refer to any particular configuration of distributive institutions as a *distributive system*. Here, then, is the utilitarian argument for thinking a distributive system should provide material incentives.

Often, you cannot be more productive (that is, produce more of what others value) without working longer or more intensely or both. Now, suppose you knew that each person would get an equal share of material goods, no matter how much he or she helped to produce what others valued. With everyone guaranteed an equal share, what incentive do you have for working hard? True, you would benefit greatly if many other people work hard, because then there would be a lot more goods to divide. But this fact is irrelevant when, as is often the case, you know that your working hard would have no significant influence on how hard others work. What of your own added productivity? Whether or not others work hard, your society may well have a larger stock of goods to divide into equal shares if you yourself work hard. Hence, your equal share would amount to more. Still, how hard you work is unlikely to make more than a small difference in your society's overall productivity. Except in the unlikely event that your work makes an enormous contribution to your society's productivity, the additional amount in your equal share of what is produced will be tiny—probably too small to notice, *certainly* too small to equal the added cost to you of working hard.

Most people will not work hard year in and year out unless doing so brings them greater benefits than costs. So, if they believed that goods would be divided equally and independently of how hard people work, then most would not work hard. Now, if there is less hard work than there could be, there will be less productivity than there could be. Thus, a system distributing material goods without regard to how productive individuals are will elicit less productivity than would some different system that rewards individual productivity.

If people produce less than they could, they will have fewer goods and services to share than they might have had. Fewer goods and services to share may result in less aggregate well-being than there could be. Therefore, because a distributive system that divides things equally will result over time in fewer goods and services, such a distributive system may fail to maximize aggregate well-being. The need for individual material incentives thus gives utilitarians a reason for accepting an unequal distribution of wealth. Let us refer to this argument as *the argument from the need for material incentives*.

I shall now answer five objections to this argument. The first is that *to reward productivity is not necessarily to reward hard work, and vice versa*. Some people are more productive than the rest of us without working harder than the rest of us (they might just be more talented). So, if the distributive system rewards these people's productivity, it will not thereby be rewarding hard work. There are also some other people who work harder than the rest of us and yet produce less of what others value (they might either be particularly *un*talented or decide to work hard at things that others do not value).

All this is true, but none of it counts against the argument from the need for material incentives. The point of the utilitarians' argument from the need for material incentives is not to justify a distributive system that rewards *hard work*. The point is instead that they have a reason for favoring a distributive system that rewards *productivity* in order to get people to be productive. Reference is made to hard work because productivity often (though not always) requires hard work. Because productivity often requires hard work, there is a need to provide some incentive to get people to be productive.

This brings us to the second objection. This objection is that *the argument ignores the internal, nonmaterial, rewards that hard work can bring*. Of course, I realize that working hard can make people feel good about themselves, give them a sense of accomplishment, or bring them some other internal reward. For some people in some jobs, the prospect of such rewards is sufficient to elicit hard work year in and year out. But, for many people and jobs, this is not the case. There must be significant material rewards if these people are to be willing, year in and year out, to do the hard work necessary for productivity.

A third objection is that *the idea that material incentives are needed takes people as they are now (selfish, lazy, materialistic), whereas we should be trying to improve humanity by making people less materialistic, less self-centered, and more concerned about the good of the whole*. Well, could most people's desire to promote aggregate well-being become so strong that it consistently drove them to work hard (even when there was no particular national emergency)?[5] To be sure, the culture in which people grow up can have profound influences on their motivations, habits of mind, and so forth. Could cultural changes, though, reshape human nature so that people cared so much about everyone else's well-being that productivity could be maintained without the provision of individual material incentives? Is human nature plastic in the sense that it takes the shape of whatever mold culture imposes on it? If evolution has left us with genes limiting the amount culture can change us, why not use genetic engineering to change the genes themselves? Perhaps we could then develop a more cooperative and selfless human being.[6]

For many people, however, the idea of attempting to refashion human nature via genetic engineering conjures up nightmare scenarios (with well-meaning scientists creating monsters by mistake or evil scientists doing so on purpose). I will therefore assume that we do not want to resort to genetic engineering. I will also assume that cultural changes could not make the majority of people care enough about aggregate well-being to ensure that they were consistently willing to work hard even though they garnered no significant additional material goods from doing so. I do not mean that people are entirely selfish. On the contrary, people are willing to make substantial sacrifices for the sake of their family or friends, or, less frequently, their wider community. But I will assume that their concern for people outside their circle of family and friends is not strong enough to eliminate the need for individual material incentives.

A fourth objection is this: *Our present, mainly capitalistic system does not actually reward the productive,* but instead rewards those who are underhanded or well-connected or rich already. This objection is completely misguided, for I am not defending our present distributive system. My point is only that the need for incentives calls for *some* material incentives. Let us refer to the distributive system that would result in the greatest sum of well-being over time as the *utility-maximizing distributive system.* Presumably, our present distributive system falls short of the utility-maximizing one in many ways. Maybe our present system is quite different from the one that would maximize utility. These points in no way, however, conflict with the conclusion that the utility-maximizing distributive system, whichever it is, would provide some material incentives for productivity.

The fifth objection to the argument from the need for material incentives is that *there is enough production already,* and so there is no need to reward productivity. True, there is a point at which the harm associated with further increases in productivity would be greater than the benefit.[7] Nevertheless, part of the reason there is so much production now is that there have been rewards for it. If there were no material incentives for productivity, there would be far less productivity than there is now. Indeed, productivity would be *too* low. Technological breakthroughs and sustained economic growth, both of which take hard work on the part of many people, can lead to large increases in aggregate well-being. So, while we should not pursue productivity beyond the point at which harms outweigh benefits, likewise we should not ignore the contributions to well-being that productivity can bring.

I have discussed two of the considerations that influence the opinions contemporary utilitarians have about the distribution of wealth: the declining marginal utility of material goods and the need for material incentives. I then replied to five objections to the idea that the need for material incentives provides utilitarians with a reason to favor unequal distributions of wealth. Now let us turn to the third consideration: *that great disparities in wealth can have corrupting influences.* For example, suppose legislators have before them a bill that would maximize utility overall but would be disadvantageous for the rich. Some of the rich may prevent the passage of the bill by bribing enough legislators (or by contributing to campaign war chests). One way to decrease the chances of this sort of thing happening is to equalize wealth. There might be less radical ways, however, of decreasing the chances that great disparities in wealth will corrupt politics (such as insisting on both public funding for political campaigns and careful public scrutiny of politicians' business relationships).

Thus, given the diminishing marginal utility of material goods, the need for material incentives, and the corrupting power of great disparities in wealth, what would the utility-maximizing distributive system be? This is a question for economists, who, as you probably know, disagree. If what I have argued is correct, however, we can be confident that the utility-maximizing distributive system would provide material incentives for productivity. And, because different people have different levels of talent and ambition, such a system would result in some material inequality.

This is not to say that the utility-maximizing distributive system would be a pure free-market system. First, there are overwhelming and relatively uncontroversial arguments for thinking that certain things from which everyone benefits—national defense, police, courts, public parks, protection of the environment, and so on—should not be left entirely to the free market, but should instead be arranged by the government and paid for by some mechanism intended to ensure that everyone who has more than some threshold of income or wealth helps pay for these things.[8] Second, some people are too young or too old or too infirm to earn enough in a competitive market to meet their basic needs. Nothing I have said about incentives militates against the social provision of a safety net to protect the well-being of these people. Almost certainly, the utility-maximizing distributive system would try to secure for these people what they need. Perhaps the most obvious way of providing a safety net would be through public-assistance programs funded by taxes on the better off. Third, what I have said about incentives does not preclude a form of distributive system in which, although there is a (relatively) free market for labor, there is virtually no private ownership of the means of production.[9]

Let me warn against some possible misunderstandings of a utilitarian conclusion about which distributive system would be just. Suppose the utility-maximizing distributive system would distribute goods much more equally than they are now. Does a utilitarian conclusion about which distributive system would be just require you to rush out and start giving all your time and money to the poor? Maybe not. First of all, your *unilaterally* redistributing wealth might not increase utility. Second, even if utilitarianism is a good approach to the social issue of which distributive system is just, it might not be a good approach to questions of *individual* morality (such as the question of what you ought to do with your money and time).[10] So, even if you conclude that utilitarianism is right about distributive justice, perhaps all this would require of you is that you support politicians whose policies would bring our system closer to the utility-maximizing one.

Another misunderstanding would be to think that if utilitarians conclude that a different distributive system would produce more utility than the distributive system we now have does, they must favor an overnight change to the different system. A gradual change might cause less economic disruption and social anxiety than an overnight change. So, the gradual change might have better consequences on the whole.

■ THE DESERT THEORY

Many people reject the utilitarian approach to distributive justice because they believe that what makes a distributive system just is not that it yields the greatest aggregate well-being, but that it leaves people with what they *deserve*. Let us refer to this view as *the desert theory*,[11] and let us call its proponents *desert theorists*.

We need to be careful about the locus of the disagreement between desert theorists and utilitarians. Desert theorists may agree *in practice* with utilitarians that the productive should get more than the unproductive. Indeed, desert theorists usually claim that what people deserve depends on what they do, in particular on how much they produce of what others value. Nevertheless, desert theorists disagree with utilitarians *about fundamental principle*. Desert theorists insist that whether a distributive system is just depends entirely on whether it leaves people with what they deserve; utilitarians insist that what people should get depends entirely on what distributive system would maximize utility.

This disagreement about fundamental principle can be illustrated as follows. Suppose for a moment that the utility-maximizing distributive system would *not* call for the productive to get more than the unproductive. Then, utilitarians would say that the productive should not get more. Desert theorists would say that the productive should get more because they deserve more, whether or not rewarding productivity is part of the distributive system that would maximize utility.

■ RAWLS'S THEORY

In the English-speaking world, John Rawls has been the most influential political philosopher of the twentieth century. This section contrasts his theory of distributive justice with that of the utilitarians. The following section discusses Rawls's answer to the desert theorists.

Rawls allows that justice may call for a different pattern of distribution in a poor country than it would in a reasonably affluent country. I shall focus on his view about what justice requires in a reasonably affluent country. He puts forward two principles of justice: *the liberty principle,* which is about the securing of basic liberties, and *the difference principle,* which is about how resources should be distributed given that the basic liberties have been secured.

The liberty principle states that "Each person is to have an equal right to the most extensive total system of equal basic liberties compatible with a similar system of liberty for all."[12] By "basic liberties," Rawls means the standard civil and political liberties, such as freedom of thought, freedom of speech, the right to vote and to run for office, freedom of assembly, the right to due process, and so on.[13] He gives these liberties special protection: At least in countries with developed economies, they are never to be restricted for the sake of promoting economic gains.

Rawls likewise contends that, in a reasonably affluent society, fair equality of opportunity should never be sacrificed for the sake of economic benefits, even for the sake of economic benefits to members of the worst-off class. This contention has been criticized, as has Rawls's contention that in a reasonably affluent society, sacrificing equal civil and political liberties for the sake of economic benefits can never be just.[14] Much more attention, however, has been devoted to Rawls's difference principle. Thus, let us also focus on this principle. To make doing so easier, suppose we are talking about societies in which basic liberties and fair equality of opportunity are securely established.

The difference principle states that social and economic inequalities are justified if and only if (a) the inequalities are "attached to offices and positions open to all under conditions of fair equality of opportunity,"[15] and (b) those who are worst off get more "social primary goods" than those who are worst off under any other distribution would get. "Social primary goods" are goods that (a) are under society's control and (b) "normally have a use whatever a person's rational plan of life."[16] Think of these as all-purpose means to the pursuit of the good life, whatever it is. Given that the greatest equal basic liberties have been secured and that there is fair equality of opportunity, the main social primary goods are income and wealth and the bases of self-respect.

There are two main differences between Rawls's difference principle and the utilitarian principle about how resources are to be distributed. First, whereas utilitarians assess distributive systems in terms of how much *well-being* results, Rawls is concerned with *social primary goods.* Second, whereas utilitarians give *equal weight to everyone's interests,* Rawls gives *special weight to the plight of the worst off.* His difference principle calls for the distributive system under which there would be the best worst-off position.

You might initially think that because Rawls favors the distributive system with the best worst-off position he would favor a distributive system that gives everyone an equal amount of goods. Rawls's principle, however, does not necessarily favor the most egalitarian distributive system. Here is an example illustrating the point (*units* in this example refers to amounts of social primary goods):

DISTRIBUTIVE SYSTEM 1	DISTRIBUTIVE SYSTEM 2	
gives to	*gives to each member of*	
Everyone 10 units each	Best-off class	25 units
	Middle class	20 units
	Worst-off class	15 units

Given these alternatives, strict egalitarianism would favor the first. Rawls's difference principle, in contrast, would favor the second.

Why might a system in which everyone gets an equal amount of material goods leave everyone worse off than he or she would be under a system leading to an unequal distribution? A system that distributes goods equally might result in so little productivity that another system, one that distributes goods *unequally* in order to supply material incentives, would produce more goods for everyone— *even for the worst off.*

Now, consider how Rawls's theory and utilitarianism can disagree about which distributive system is just. Consider two distributive systems. Under each system, there are only three socioeconomic classes, with 10^n people in each class. (Again, *units* refers to amounts of social primary goods.)

DISTRIBUTIVE SYSTEM 1	DISTRIBUTIVE SYSTEM 2	
gives to each member of	*gives to each member of*	
Best-off class 60 units	Best-off class	35 units
Middle class 30 units	Middle class	20 units
Worst-off class 10 units	Worst-off class[17]	15 units
Total 100×10^n units	Total 70×10^n units	

Because the units refer to amounts of social primary goods, not to amounts of well-being, utilitarians would say that they do not yet have the information they need in order to choose between these systems. But, for the sake of argument, assume that the first distributive system would indeed produce more total well-being than the second. So, utilitarians would favor the first system. In contrast, Rawls would say that the second is more just, because its worst-off class is better off than the worst-off class under the first distributive system would be. After all, why should anyone be left with as little as the members of the worst-off class under the first system, when there is an alternative system that would leave no one so badly off?

Which particular distributive system would Rawls's principle favor for your society? This again is a question for economists. The answer might be a system under which there is a large gap between rich and poor, or the answer might be a system under which there is little gap between rich and poor. Actually, Rawls himself explicitly leaves open the question of whether his theory supports market socialism or a system in which natural resources and the means of production are privately owned.[18] He suggests, however, as have others who have written about his theory, that his principle mandates more redistribution from the rich to the poor than occurs now.[19] If we accept Rawls's principle about the just distribution of wealth, and if we believe it calls for increased redistribution from the rich to the poor, then we should support politicians who will push for this increase.

Rawls put forward powerful arguments for his principle, arguments over which scores of books have been written. I shall not survey that literature. Instead, I shall focus on one of the most common objections to Rawls's principle—the objection made by those I am calling desert theorists.

■ THE DESERT THEORY REVISITED

Just as desert theorists reject utilitarianism because they think people should get what they deserve whether or not this accords with the utility-maximizing distributive system, they reject Rawls's principle because they think people should get what they deserve whether or not this accords with the system that produces the least bad worst-off position. Suppose for the sake of illustration that the least bad worst-off position would come from a distributive system giving only a tiny amount more to those who work very hard and produce much more than to those who are lazy and produce much less. Rawls would say that in this case the productive should get only that tiny amount more. Desert theorists would object that, where the difference in what people do is large, the difference in what they get should be more than tiny. They would object that to give only a tiny amount more to people who work much harder and produce much more is to give them less than they deserve.

Rawls's reply to the desert theorists starts from ideas he thinks we almost all accept.[20] Suppose you end up with a much more comfortable life than I do because you inherit more from your parents than I do from mine. It is difficult to believe that you therefore *deserve* these advantages more than I do. Desert, according to the common view, has to do with what you *do*, and to get that wealth you did not *do* anything that I failed to do. A system that allows people to pass on their wealth to their offspring is justified, if at all, by something other than the *desert* of the offspring.

Now suppose passing along wealth to offspring is made impossible. You may nevertheless end up with a much more rewarding job than I because of other things your parents did for you that my parents were unable to do for me. Perhaps your mother introduced you to important professional contacts, or your father taught you how to be exceptionally charming. You did not deserve these advantages any more than I did. Thus, how could you deserve the better job they helped you to get?

Desert theorists might say that *at least* if two people start out from the same position and one then outperforms the other, the one with the better performance deserves greater rewards. But what counts as the same starting position? Suppose that your parents were neither wealthier nor better connected than mine. It might nevertheless be the case that, because of the genes you inherited, you are much better looking than I am, and you therefore make more as a model than I can make. Or your reflexes may be quicker than mine because of your genetic inheritance, and this may enable you to make much more money as a professional athlete than I can make. Or you may have inherited a steady, easy-going temperament, which helps you become popular and professionally successful, while I suffer from a mercurial temperament, which alienates people and limits my career advancement. The beauty or quick reflexes or easy-going temperament would not have been advantages you deserved; you would have been merely lucky to inherit them. So, why would you *deserve* the advantages they help you obtain? This is Rawls's reply to the desert theorists (and utilitarians would agree with it). As Rawls writes, "Once we are troubled by the influence of either social contingencies or natural chance on the determination of distributive shares, we are bound, on reflection, to be bothered by the influence of the other. From a moral standpoint the two seem equally arbitrary."[21]

Many people would acknowledge that if you end up with more wealth than I do because you inherited more money, or because your parents provided you with better contacts, or because you inherited more brains, brawn, or beauty than I did, then you do not deserve to have more wealth than I. They would, however, go on to insist that if the cause of your ending up with more was that you were more *ambitious* than I was and thus worked harder, then you do deserve your additional wealth. The idea seems to be that things beyond your control (such as how much you inherit) cannot provide a basis for desert, but things within your control (such as your level of ambition) can.[22]

This line of thinking is questionable. Our ambitions were largely shaped by what environment we were born into, how we were raised, what alternatives we were encouraged to consider, what talents we found in ourselves. Thus, our ambitions were largely shaped by facts about us that were beyond our control. If facts about us beyond our control cannot provide a basis for desert, and if our ambitions were largely shaped by facts beyond our control, then so much the worse for ambition as a basis for desert.

If we are persuaded to reject the desert theory, there remains the question of whether Rawls or the utilitarians have the better theory of distributive justice. Moreover, the utilitarians and Rawls are far from the only ones to have put forward theories of distributive justice that contrast with the desert theory. In fact, there is a wide variety of competing theories to choose among, including some that mix Rawls with utilitarianism.

Which of the theories of justice is most plausible? I shall not try to answer this question. Instead, I shall put forward my own justification for redistributive taxation—a justification that does not require rejection of the desert theory. We should eschew, as much as possible, political justifications that appeal to controversial philosophical views.[23] Views about desert are certainly controversial. Indeed, most people believe—and probably will continue to believe—what we have called the desert theory. So, even if the desert theory is in fact wrong, any argument for redistribution that involves rejecting it is unlikely to gain general acceptance.

■ GOOD SAMARITANISM AND REDISTRIBUTION

I shall now argue for redistribution in a way that does not require rejection of the desert theory. Furthermore, I think that all of the premises on which I shall rely are more likely to gain wide acceptance, at least after due reflection, than is the rejection of the desert theory. My first premise is that the rest of us have a duty to help, if we can, those who cannot on their own obtain the food or shelter or medicine or basic education they need. My second premise is that the rest of us *can* help these people by making available to them the goods they need. The conjunction of these two premises entails the conclusion that the rest of us have a duty to help these people. Refer to this as *the Good Samaritan duty.*

What does this have to do with the state, you might be wondering. Consider this: If there is not an institution for *compelling* compliance with the Good Samaritan duty, many people will not comply. When some do not comply, others will no doubt make up *only some* of the difference. It follows that the badly off will not get some of the help that others have a duty to provide unless there is an institution that compels compliance with this duty. We might now add the premise that we should ensure that people get all the help that others have a duty to provide. This would generate the conclusion that we should have an institution that compels compliance (for example, redistributive taxation that funds public-assistance programs).

The premise that we should ensure that people get all the help others have a duty to provide is controversial, however. So, consider a different argument, one that starts from the premise that if some well-off people do not comply with the Good Samaritan duty, the Good Samaritan principle requires more of the conscientious compliers—that is, requires them to make up at least some of difference. This premise is easy to defend. Suppose you and I see ten innocent people drowning, and each of us is able to throw life vests to all of them. Suppose you throw life vests to five of them and then notice that I am doing nothing to help save the remaining five. Clearly, morality requires you to throw life vests to the other five.

Admittedly, there may be limits on the extent to which compliers are required to make up for the noncompliance of others. This acknowledgment, however, is perfectly compatible with the modest claim that compliers are required to make up at least *some* of the difference created by the noncompliance of others. This modest claim is enough for the purposes of my argument. Even making up only some of the difference created by others' noncompliance with the Good Samaritan duty is burdensome. So, if some people do not comply with the Good Samaritan duty, the burden on those who do comply will be greater.

As we earlier concluded, if there is not an institution that compels compliance with the Good Samaritan duty, many people will not comply. As we have now concluded, if some people do not comply with the Good Samaritan duty, the burden on those who do comply will be greater. The conjunction of these two conclusions entails that, if there is not an institution compelling compliance with the Good Samaritan duty, the burden on the well off who comply will be greater.

Now consider the following argument. We should do what will protect compliers from the extra burden placed on them by noncompliers, if we can do this in a way that is not morally objectionable. Having an institution compelling compliance with the Good Samaritan duty is not morally objectionable.[24] Thus, we should have an institution compelling compliance with the Good Samaritan duty.

Some would object to this argument by insisting that compelling people to do their duty *is* morally objectionable. Even if compelling people to comply with their duty is morally objectionable, I cannot see that it is so objectionable as to be more important than protecting the compliers from the extra burden put on them by the noncompliers. Some think that the moral value of people's complying with the duty to help others depends on its coming *from their own free will*, not from external coercion. But, again, I cannot see that the loss (if such it is) of the value of people's free compliance would be greater than the gain in preventing the increased burdens on them.[25]

Here is another argument against the premise that an institution compelling compliance with the Good Samaritan duty (such as redistributive taxation that funds public-assistance programs) is not morally objectionable. We have a duty to oppose injustice. Consider people who either are not actually needy or are needy because they refuse to help themselves: For any of these people to receive benefits paid for by the hard work of fellow citizens is unjust. Public-assistance programs funded by redistributive taxation distribute benefits to at least some such people. We thus have a duty to oppose such programs.

Here is how we should reply to this argument. Of course a distributive system should not encourage people to be lazy. With this in mind, many systems use forms of "means-testing" to try to channel aid to those who really cannot earn enough in a free market to meet their basic needs. But making sure that absolutely no one else gets these government benefits meant for these people would be ridiculously costly. (Imagine the costs of government agencies having to investigate *thoroughly* the neediness of every last person seeking government benefits.) Therefore, efficiency may be served by allowing for *some* "leakage" of benefits to those who could live a decent life without them. Is this leakage so morally terrible that it must be eliminated even if this means eliminating public-assistance programs? On the contrary, having public-assistance programs, even with some leakage, is morally better than having no public-assistance programs at all.

■ YOUR COUNTRY AND BEYOND

Governments normally have more control over what happens within their own country than over what happens in others, but governments can influence what happens to the poor in other countries.[26] Here are some examples of the many ways they can do this. Rich countries can push down interest rates. This leaves poor *debtor* countries with more money to spend on their poor. Rich countries can open their markets to agricultural products or textiles or other things that low-income countries can supply at low cost. This can increase the employment opportunities for the poor in those countries. Governments of rich countries can pressure the governments of poor countries to pursue policies that will reduce poverty.[27] One obvious way of doing this is to provide aid on the condition that those policies are pursued.

There are many millions of starving people in Africa and Asia. Why focus on distribution *within* a country and ignore distribution *across national boundaries?* Of course, questions about helping the poor in foreign countries can be more complex than questions about helping the poor in your own country. But for all their added complexity, they are no less urgent.[28]

■ NOTES

1. As Joseph Raz says, "[T]he state . . . is the political organization of a society, its government, the agent through which it acts, and the law, the vehicle through which much of its power is exercised," Joseph Raz, *The Morality of Freedom* (Oxford: Clarendon Press, 1986), 70.

2. Jeremy Bentham, *Introduction to the Principles of Morals and Legislation* (1789), many editions since; John Stuart Mill, *Utilitarianism* (1863), many editions since; Henry Sidgwick, *The Methods of Ethics* (London: Macmillan, 1874 and 1907).

3. See Derek Parfit, *Reasons and Persons* (Oxford: Clarendon Press, 1984), 493–502; and James Griffin, *Well-Being: Its Meaning, Measurement and Moral Importance* (Oxford: Clarendon Press, 1986), pt. 1.

4. I do not mean to suggest that these are the *only* considerations utilitarians can think relevant and important.

5. This is but one of many places where a question about human nature is relevant to political philosophy.

6. Jonathan Glover, *What Sort of People Should There Be?* (Harmondsworth, Eng.: Penguin, 1984) is a fascinating meditation on philosophical questions raised by the possibility of improving humanity through genetic engineering.

7. Why might increasing productivity beyond a certain point produce greater harms than benefits? There are any number of possible reasons. One is that beyond a certain point, increases in productivity might be obtainable only by means of cutting back on public-assistance programs for the needy, and the harm to the needy might be greater than the benefit to others of the increased productivity.

8. See any economics textbook for discussions of "externalities" and "public goods."

9. For a discussion of this sort of view, which is called *market socialism*, see Allen Buchanan, *Ethics, Efficiency, and the Market* (Totowa, NJ: Rowman and Littlefield, 1985), ch. 4.

10. Why? Perhaps utilitarianism requires a kind of impartiality that is appropriate when we are assessing social goals but not appropriate when we are making decisions as private individuals about what to do with our own resources. (Incidentally, it is also possible to think that utilitarianism is a good approach to private moral decisions but not to questions of justice. This thought might appeal to those of us who believe (1) that our conception of justice, though not our private morality, needs to be founded on beliefs others share, and (2) that others do not share some of the beliefs on which utilitarianism is founded.)

11. Arguably, it is the most common view of justice. "Popular morality continues obstinately in its belief that distribution ought always in justice to be according to desert," J. R. Lucas, *On Justice* (Oxford: Clarendon Press, 1980), 170.

12. John Rawls, *A Theory of Justice* (Cambridge, MA: Harvard Univ. Press, 1971), 302.

13. Rawls, *Theory of Justice*, 61.

14. Imagine a case in which giving up a small amount of liberty or equality of opportunity is necessary to bring about enormous economic gains. For an influential discussion of Rawls's giving liberty overriding importance, see H. L. A. Hart, "Rawls on Liberty and Its Priority," *Reading Rawls*, ed. N. Daniels (New York: Basic, 1975).

15. Rawls, *Theory of Justice*, 302–3.

16. Rawls, *Theory of Justice*, 62.

17. Do not assume that the particular people who would end up in the worst-off class under this system must also be the same people who would end up in the worst-off class under the other one.

18. Rawls, *Theory of Justice*, 265–74.

19. See, for example, Thomas Pogge, *Realizing Rawls* (Ithaca: Cornell Univ. Press, 1989).

20. Rawls, *Theory of Justice*, 65–75.

21. Rawls, *Theory of Justice*, 74–75.

22. Ronald Dworkin, "What Is Equality? Part II: Equality of Resources," *Philosophy and Public Affairs* 10 (1981): 283-345.

23. See John Rawls, "Justice as Fairness: Political not Metaphysical," *Philosophy and Public Affairs* 14 (Summer 1985): 223–51; and John Rawls, "The Idea of an Overlapping Consensus," *Oxford Journal of Legal Studies* 7 (Spring 1987): 1–25.

24. John Stuart Mill seems to concur—see *On Liberty* (Indianapolis: Library of Liberal Arts, 1956), 15, 95.

25. Contrast the last section of Baruch Brody, "The Role of Private Philanthropy in a Free and Democratic State," *Social Philosophy and Policy* 4 (1987).

26. See the World Bank, *World Development Report 1990* (New York: Oxford Univ. Press, 1990), ch. 8.

27. For discussion of what such policies are, see *World Development Report 1990*, chs. 4–7; and Jean Drèze and Amartya Sen, *Hunger and Public Action* (Oxford: Clarendon Press, 1989).

28. For very helpful comments on an earlier draft of this chapter, I am grateful to Frederick Adams, Roger Crisp, Will Kymlicka, Leemon McHenry, Guy Marsh, and Peter Vallentyne.

■ QUESTIONS

1. Which do you think matters more from the point of view of justice—the size of the gap between the richest and the poorest, or how badly off in absolute terms the poorest are?

2. Could an economic system depending on slave labor ever accord with utilitarianism?

3. Do you agree with the author that the best defense of redistributive taxation will be one that does not depend on rejecting the desert theory?

4. The author concluded that we should have an institution compelling compliance with the Good Samaritan principle. Which premise in his argument for that conclusion do you think is weakest?

5. We can calculate aggregate well-being only if we can compare amounts of benefit and harm to different people. Can we really do this in anything but an arbitrary way?

6. What importance should national boundaries have to the distribution of wealth?   ∎

∎ FOR FURTHER READING

Aristotle. *Nicomachean Ethics.* Available in many editions.

———. *Politics.* Available in many editions.

Arthur, John, and William Shaw. *Justice and Economic Distribution.* 2nd ed. Englewood Cliffs, NJ: Prentice-Hall, 1991.

Brown, Alan. *Modern Political Philosophy: Theories of the Just Society.* Harmondsworth, Eng.: Penguin, 1986.

Dworkin, Ronald. *A Matter of Principle.* Boston: Harvard Univ. Press, 1985.

von Hayek, F. A. *Law, Legislation and Liberty.* Vol. 2, *The Mirage of Social Justice.* London: Routledge and Kegan Paul, 1976.

Kymlicka, Will. *Contemporary Political Philosophy: An Introduction.* Oxford: Clarendon Press, 1990.

Marx, Karl. *Karl Marx: Selected Writings.* Ed. D. McLellan. Oxford: Oxford Univ. Press, 1977.

Nagel, Thomas. *Equality and Partiality.* New York: Oxford Univ. Press, 1991.

Pettit, Philip, ed. *Contemporary Political Philosophy.* New York: Macmillan, 1991.

Plato. *The Republic,* many editions, and *The Laws,* many editions.

Rakowski, Eric. *Equal Justice.* Oxford: Clarendon Press, 1991.

Wiggins, David. "Claims of Need." *Morality and Objectivity.* Ed. Ted Honderich. London: Routledge and Kegan Paul, 1985. Reprinted in David Wiggins. *Needs, Values, and Truth.* Oxford: Blackwell, 1987.

Social Philosophy and Policy 1 (1983).

CHAPTER SEVEN

Aesthetics

ROBERT STECKER

Art is always considered among the most important products of a culture. A book about almost any great civilization would discuss at considerable length its artistic achievements. Thus, a survey of the great achievements of ancient Greek civilization would include the invention of democratic forms of government, the discovery of philosophy and science, *and*, inevitably, its great artistic creations: its painted vases, its sculpture, its architecture, and its poetry. Artistic forms, like forms of government, religion, and philosophy, are commonly perceived (at least in retrospect) as central to the life of a civilization and are perhaps the only items that are *always* mentioned when we specify which of its products are to be most highly valued. It appears, then, that art is something very valuable. Why, then, can it seem that this value plays little or no role in the lives of most people? How many of us are art lovers? It may seem that the obvious answer is, not all that many of us.

The philosophy of art asks many questions, but among its central questions are several about the value of art: "What makes art seem so valuable to some people?" "Are other people, perhaps the majority, indifferent to these values?" "Is art really as valuable as it is sometimes said to be?" "Are different works of art, or different art forms—like painting and music—valuable in the same way?" "Most generally, what is valuable about art?" In this chapter, I shall try to answer these questions. I shall indicate what is valuable about art and argue that few of us are, and no one ought to be, indifferent to these values.

These questions, however, cannot be answered without answering several others. First, we need to have a clear conception of our subject matter; the most straightforward way to do this is to answer the question "What is art?" Second, we need to answer questions about what it is to understand and appreciate works of art.

■ WHAT IS ART?

Consider the following list:

Literature	Architecture
Painting	Pottery
Sculpture	Furniture
Music	Carpets
Opera	Jewelry
Musical Comedy	Wine
Cinema	Cigars

Which items on this list are arts? If only to avoid confusion, we should note that there is a sense of *art* according to which *all* of these items are arts. Art in this sense simply means (something like) a product of human skill. When people write books with titles like *The Art of Cooking, The Art of Renovating Old Houses,* they are using *art* in this sense. This is not the sense of *art* we are interested in defining. If art in the sense we are interested in could simply be defined as any product of human skill, there would be no explanation why items at the top of our list are so much more readily thought of as art than are items at the bottom.

In the relevant sense of *art*, few of us would classify a fine cigar or a fine wine as art. We may be less certain about furniture, carpets, jewelry, or musical comedies. The other items on the list, however, are definitely to be counted. Yet, it is not clear that they have more in common with each other than with the more questionable items. A fine wine or a fine cigar can be appreciated for the way it accents and harmonizes various sensuous qualities wines or cigars are capable of possessing—its bouquet of flavors, its odor, its visual appearance. It is sometimes claimed that this is the sort of thing we appreciate in painting; although with paintings, of course, our appreciation is confined to visual appearance.

If there is something peculiarly valuable about art, it is plausible to hope that we can define art precisely in terms of these valuable properties. Many definitions of art seem to be based on this hope. Let us examine three of the most important attempted definitions: (1) art as representation, (2) art as expression, and (3) art as aesthetic experience.

■ *Art as Representation*

For centuries, some of the most central art forms were devoted to the representation of reality. Ancient Greek sculpture, in its representation of gods and heroes, aimed to capture (and sometimes idealize) the human form. This aim dominated well into the nineteenth century (as can be seen in the sculpture of the French artist Rodin). Paintings commonly represented the human figure and human scenes: scenes from myths, from the Bible, from great historical events. Eventually, painters became interested in representing scenes from common life, things such as food, artifacts, and landscapes. Drama and poetry represent human beings acting in various ways. Until the seventeenth century, even music was seen as an exclusively representational art (one view was that it represented the human voice in the act of expressing various emotions). It seemed plausible, then, that art could be defined in terms of its representational function: art is the representation of reality (perhaps in certain specific media).[1]

We obviously value art for its representational capacities. For example, many people value certain novels for their ability to represent vividly the way of life of a time or place or of a particular class of people. Paintings are valued because they represent things in beautiful or surprising ways, or simply because they capture and preserve a bit of transient reality. For similar reasons, we value photographs, including the snapshots most of us take. We want to capture a certain moment. We are pleased when we find represented in the photograph an aspect that typifies what we valued in that moment. Sometimes, however, the photographs we most value reveal something surprising, something we did not expect to find.

Despite the fact that we value the representational aspects of art, the definition of art in terms of representation no longer appeals. Not only are we all familiar with nonrepresentational painting and sculpture, it seems so obvious now that there are many nonrepresentational art forms. Many now think of music, pottery, and architecture as such art forms. Furthermore, the mere fact that something is a representation gives it no claim to being art. Last year, I threw away an extremely ugly carpet that represented a hunting scene. It never occurred to me that I threw away a work of art. Furthermore, I just represented myself—by describing myself as throwing away a carpet last year. I didn't, however, just create a work of art.

■ Art as Expression

Many artworks that do not represent an outward reality, nevertheless, are *expressive*. And, of course, representational art can also be expressive. A piece of instrumental music that represents nothing can be expressive of sadness or joy, grief or anger (at least, many would claim this is so). A building can express power or stability or upward aspiration of one kind or another. Painting and poetry can express these things as well. Not only does art *possess* expressive qualities, art is valued *for* possessing these qualities. We enjoy sad music, tragic dramas, scary movies. The fact that the finest Gothic cathedrals are expressive of the arduousness and ardor of religious aspirations seems to make them better buildings—both more functional and more beautiful. A poem that represents someone's grief that was neither sad nor ironic would not be a good poem.

Because the expressive function of art is both highly valued and seemingly pervasive, it is not surprising that people have attempted to define art in terms of this function. What might such a definition look like?

There are several ways of thinking of artistic expression. Because it is standardly *people* who express things, it is plausible to think of artistic expression as a case of the *artist* expressing thoughts and feelings. During the nineteenth and early twentieth centuries, there were many attempts to define art in terms of *art-ist's expression*. Two of the most famous expression theorists, Benedetto Croce and Charles Collingwood, thought of expression as taking place wholly within the mind of the artist.[2] Collingwood liked to distinguish between betraying an emotion and expressing one. I might betray my anger with you by my face turning very red and my shouting at you. In order to express my anger, in Collingwood's sense, I must articulate the thoughts and perceptions and the likes and dislikes that under-lie it. Compare one's face turning red with these lines from William Blake's poem "London."

> I wander thro' each charter'd street,
> Near where the charter'd Thames does flow,
> And mark in every face I meet
> Marks of weakness, marks of woe.
>
> In every cry of every Man,
> In every infant's cry of fear,
> In every voice, in every ban,
> The mind-forg'd manacles I hear.

Here the speaker of Blake's poem is expressing the thoughts and informing us of the perceptions that cause (or constitute) his anger. One does not just hear the expression of *thoughts* in these lines, however. One hears a particular sort of *anger* with its indignant quality and its peculiar subject matter. Art, for Collingwood and Croce, is expression as articulation. Because such expression takes place within the artist's mind, that is where works of art primarily exist; it is at best in a deriva-tive way, for them, that works of art exist on pieces of canvas or in pieces of bronze.

Many people object to the idea that art is the expression of an artist. For an artist to express an emotion, he or she must actually have had that emotion. The Gothic cathedrals mentioned earlier, however, would express religious emotions whether or not their designers and builders experienced, much less personally expressed, those emotions. If we discovered that the designers and builders lacked the requisite emotions, we would not thereby discover that the buildings were not works of art. The same goes for poems expressing grief and for sad music. Look, for example, at these lines from an untitled poem by Alfred, Lord Tennyson:

> Break, break, break,
>   At the foot of thy crags, O Sea!
> But the tender grace of a day that is dead
>   Will never come back to me.

We don't have to know what Tennyson was feeling to know that what we are reading is an expression of grief. This is not to say that artists never express their thoughts and emotions in artworks or that we are never interested in an artist's expression when we are enjoying artworks. It is simply to say that the artist's ex-pression is neither what defines an object as art nor is it even a necessary condition for an art object being expressive.

Some people, by contrast, think the value of art consists in the evocation of emotion. So, for example, a proponent of this view might say that a work expresses anger if it evokes anger in us. The following consideration might seem to make this view plausible. As we have seen, the Gothic cathedrals could express religious aspiration even if their designers and builders neither had nor personally expressed such aspirations. What might seem to matter, however, is that the building gives us these feelings. Without them, why would we even think that religious aspirations were being expressed?

As an account of the expressiveness of art, the evocation view strikes me as implausible. When I express my depression, I might make you depressed. But my expressing depression is one thing; my evoking it in you is another. Likewise, when art evokes emotions in us (as I suppose it often does), that may be a symptom of its expressiveness (as spots are a symptom of measles), but it seems just wrong to say that it is what its expressiveness consists in (as it is wrong to say measles consists in having spots). It also seems wrong to say that I can only know that a work expresses something by feeling it myself. I can *hear* the sadness in music without feeling sad. I don't myself have to have religious aspirations to perceive them in the Gothic cathedral.

Even if we cannot define *expression* in terms of evocation, one might wonder if *art* can be defined in terms of an object's capacity to evoke such things as emotions in us. As I said above, artworks are often highly evocative. Unfortunately, so are many other things. Even if we confine ourselves to standard artistic media such as paint, photography, the written word, and so on, there are many highly evocative items produced in these media that are not works of art. Advertisements are just one type of such evocative items.

I said earlier that it is standardly people who *express* things. It is not standardly people who are *expressive of* things, however. A person expresses sadness, but a person's face or behavior is expressive of sadness. Furthermore, some faces are expressive of sadness even when the person whose face it is is not sad. It is just a sad face. The property of being expressive of a feeling is not confined to human faces. It is obvious how the weeping willow tree got its name; it has that sad *look* that makes it expressive of sadness. Until now, I have not carefully distinguished *expressing* and *being expressive*. Many contemporary philosophers think that this distinction is crucial for understanding expression in art. Art is essentially expressive of such things as emotions and moods. As with the sadness of the weeping willow tree, such expressiveness is a perceptual property, something we see or hear. It is not necessarily indicative of anyone's state of mind, either the artist's or the spectator's.

This conception of expression brings us no closer to defining art. Our discussion should make it obvious that many things other than artworks are expressive in the sense just specified. Nevertheless, some people would claim that expression is at least a necessary condition of art. This is a hard claim to refute partly because there are, as we have seen, many senses in which works of art are expressive, and partly because whether a work is expressive and what, in particular, it is expressive of, is so much a matter of disputable interpretation. Still, it is not clear that art-works *must* possess expressive properties. There are artists who just don't seem interested in expression in any of its varieties. Some painters want to capture the appearance of a landscape without making it expressive of anything (such as impressionists like Monet). Expression is one, but only one, of the many things an artist can try to achieve, and some artists may wholly exclude it in favor of other things.

■ Art as Aesthetic Experience

Sometimes we enjoy works of art because we perceive in them expressive qualities; for example, we might enjoy a piece of music because of the sadness we hear in it. Sometimes we enjoy works of art because they represent things in fascinating ways. Although in one case we are enjoying works of art for their expressive properties and in another we are enjoying them for their representational properties, in both cases our perceiving these properties gives us enjoyable *experiences*. These experiences have a lot in common: They typically result from closely attending to the sensuous qualities of the work. Having such experiences also requires, commonly, the exercise of the imagination. The people and scenes we see in pictures, after all, are not literally there. Similarly, music isn't literally sad. Hearing sadness in music might require perceiving analogies between patterns of sound and patterns of sad human behavior. Finally, the experiences this attentive, imaginative perception gives us are enjoyed for their own sake, whatever further benefits they might bring.

Furthermore, there are other enjoyable experiences we have in perceiving artworks that seem to follow the same formula. We sometimes enjoy patterns we perceive in the organization of a piece of music or a painting. Thus, we enjoy following the development of a theme in a musical work, and we can take pleasure in the way different parts of a painting form a balanced whole or stand in tension with each other. Though such properties are neither representational nor expressive, their perception requires close attention and imagination. The experience of these properties is enjoyed for its own sake.

Such reflections have encouraged many philosophers to suppose that what is peculiarly valuable about artworks is a certain experience they are capable of giving in terms of which they might be defined. This experience has been dubbed *aesthetic experience*.

Unlike the terms *art*, *expression*, and *representation*, the term *aesthetic* is a technical one—a term coined by philosophers for a special purpose—so, one would expect it to have a precise meaning. Unfortunately, such expectations are unfulfilled. When the word *aesthetic* was first used, in the eighteenth century, to characterize a new discipline that would study the human experience of art *and* beauty (as well as the sublime, the gorgeous, the awe inspiring, and so on), the seeds were sown that grew into a concept covering a diversity of experiences. Beauty can be found almost anywhere—certainly in nature, in art, and in mathematics and science.

There are many different attempts to define the aesthetic and, hence, little agreement about the boundaries of aesthetic experience. From the remarks above, one might think that an aesthetic experience is any experience that is enjoyed for its own sake resulting from close and imaginative attention to the sensuous features of an object. Well, that *is* a possible definition, but it excludes things that many, including myself, would regard as aesthetic experiences. *Imaginative* attention is not always required to enjoy natural beauty. Our enjoyment of a pretty flower, a gorgeous sunset, or an awe-inspiring snowstorm is aesthetic pleasure, but the element of imagination often does not seem required. The fact that imagination is much more commonly required in the enjoyment of works of art might suggest that we are dealing with two quite different types of experience and that we should give the enjoyment of natural beauty a different name. Unfortunately, this will not work. For we often enough experience pleasure from the sights and sounds of artworks, the appreciation of which also requires little imagination: the shape and color of a ceramic bowl, the beautiful colors of a painting. If we deny that *these* enjoyable experiences are aesthetic, we risk making aesthetic experience a rather specialized experience we have in connection with art (and perhaps other things), rather than the pervasive and dominant feature of our intercourse with art that it is often said to be.

So far I have spoken of aesthetic experience as a kind of perceptual experience, in particular, a kind of visual or aural experience. This raises the question whether, on the one hand, it extends to other senses, and on the other, whether it extends beyond perception. A connoisseur of cigars is able to discriminate among and enjoy the tastes and smells (as well as the color and shape) of fine cigars. Is the sort of experience the connoisseur enjoys an aesthetic experience? Although aestheticians are by no means unanimous, the majority answer has been "no" for reasons I shall let readers try to determine for themselves. On the other hand, there is considerable pressure to extend aesthetic experience beyond perceptual experience, primarily because there is at least one extensive and important art form the enjoyment of which is primarily not perceptual, namely, literature. When we read a novel or a poem, the sound of the words, and even their visual appearance on the page, can be important, but what is more important is the meaning these words convey. What is typically conveyed is a world we contemplate in our imagination rather than with our senses. But because, as we have already seen, even perceptual aesthetic experience often requires a good deal of imagination, it seems natural to extend the concept of aesthetic experience to those pleasurable experiences we have when attending to the imaginary worlds found in literature. Once we allow this extension, the problem of the cutoff point once again arises. Are the pleasurable experiences we get when attending to an elegant mathematical demonstration or an ingenious scientific experiment also aesthetic experiences? The word *aesthetic* often enough crops up in characterizing these experiences.

For the purposes of defining art, this would not matter if there was a special variety of aesthetic experience *peculiar* to the enjoyment of artworks or at least particularly intended by artists. This however, does not seem to be the case. Furthermore, in the twentieth century whole artistic movements as well as individual works have attempted to separate art and the aesthetic. Probably the most famous example of these are Marcel Duchamp's readymades: mass-produced objects that Duchamp simply chose, sometimes scribbled on, mounted, and exhibited.[3] One of Duchamp's criteria in choosing these objects was a complete lack of aesthetic interest. It could be argued that insofar as Duchamp succeeded in "making" artworks with his readymades, he necessarily failed in his intention to present unaesthetic objects. The fact is that some of the readymades are rather beautiful—the bicycle wheel being one of these. The consensus, however, is that many of the readymades are aesthetically boring and that they are art for other reasons. For example, they suggest certain compelling questions: "What does an artist have to do to make an artwork?" "Can unaesthetic artworks exist?" "What does it mean for an artwork to be original?" "How do artworks differ from functional artifacts?" To not only raise but make compelling such questions by embodying them in a striking object also seems to be a function of art. So, artworks cannot be defined as those objects that give, or are primarily intended to give, aesthetic experience.

■ Some Recent Attempts to Define Art

The failure of definitions of *art* in terms of representation, expression, and aesthetic experience has led many philosophers to suspect that there is something fundamentally mistaken in these attempts. For one thing, there seems to be no fixed set of valuable properties or functions that characterize all works of art. What counts as a valuable artistic property or function is subject to continuous evolution.

This realization has suggested at least three quite different views about the definition of art: (1) the open-concept theory, (2) the institutional theory, and (3) the four-factor theory.

The first view is simply that art cannot be defined. Proponents of this view claim that art is an open-ended concept, meaning by this that it has no necessary or sufficient conditions. The concept of a game is often given as an example of an open-ended concept. It is claimed that there is nothing that all games have in common. Many games are competitive but some (solitaire) are not. Most games involve winning and losing, but some do not. Something is a game if it resembles one of the standard examples of a game. This results in different things being games for different reasons. Similarly, we classify particular items as art in terms of a "family resemblance" they share with one or another of the works that are, at a given time and place, considered standard examples of art.[4]

One point that early proponents of the open-concept theory failed to make clear is how classification by family resemblance works. The problem is that, if we think of the resemblance of two objects as their sharing some properties, then everything resembles everything, and we have no reason for picking one object over another as a work of art. Thus, consider the office chair on which I am now sitting. Why isn't it a work of art? (Believe me, it's not.) It resembles works of art in many ways. It resembles some Henry Moore sculptures in, among other things, being a material object, being partly composed of objects with rounded shapes, having legs, having lots of green in it. Take any work of art at all. There will be some property or other it shares with my chair. What family-resemblance theorists failed to give us was a rationale for taking certain properties as relevant and others as irrelevant for classification.

The second view is that art can be defined but that traditional attempts look for a definition in the wrong place. It should not be sought in the properties that traditional definitions focused on, such as representation, expression, or the capacity to give aesthetic experience. The best known version of this view is the *institutional theory* of art. According to this view, arthood is a matter of sociological fact, in particular, an object standing in the appropriate relation to something called "the artworld" or "the institution of art." Thus, George Dickie, a contemporary philosopher, has proposed that an artwork is an artifact of a kind created to be presented to an artworld public.[5]

I believe that a third view is more promising than either of the preceding views. It incorporates the insights of these views, but it also finds insight in the traditional definitions. The basic idea of this view, called the *four-factor theory*, is that, at any given time, there are a finite number of functions works of art fulfill and a finite number of media in which artworks fulfill these functions. Whether some object is a work of art depends on (1) the intention with which it is made, (2) whether it fulfills one or more of these functions, (3) the medium in which it is made, and (4) when it is made.

According to the four-factor theory, the criteria for determining whether something is art are more complex than is recognized by any of the theories so far discussed. In order to state these criteria, two distinctions have to be made. First, we have to distinguish between the art of the present and the art of the past. Second, we have to distinguish between central and peripheral art forms.

It is important to distinguish between the art of the present and the art of the past precisely *because* more complex criteria come into play when classifying objects from the past. Basically, *an object belongs to the art of the present* if it fulfills at least one of the functions now given to art, *or* is intended to fulfill such a function and is made in a recognizable art medium. *An object from the past is a work of art* if it satisfies these criteria, but it is also a work of art if it fulfilled functions given to art at the time it was made and is in a medium then recognized as an art medium.

It is also important to distinguish central and peripheral art forms. At any given time, certain forms or media are the standard ones in which art is produced. Thus, a writer with literary aspirations will most likely write poetry, novels, short stories, or drama. These standard ways of producing art are what I am calling the central art forms. (A form can lose its centrality, while new central forms are constantly coming into existence. In the eighteenth century, the essay was a central literary form—which it no longer is—while the novel was just emerging as such a form.) For an object made in such a form to be art, all that is needed is that it is intended to fulfill one of the functions given to art. There are, however, other objects not belonging to one of these central forms that are also art. Thus, a work of philosophy, such as a dialogue by Plato, may be correctly considered a work of art. What is needed for such objects to be art is not merely the intention to fulfill a function but excellence in the fulfillment of an artistic function.

The four-factor theory accepts the idea that motivated traditional definitions, namely, that art is to be understood in terms of the valuable functions it fulfills. It also, however, accepts the insight of the more recent theories discussed in this section that the whole of art—the art of the past, present, and future—cannot be characterized in terms of a single function or even in terms of several functions. It accepts from the open-concept view the idea that these functions evolve in an open-ended fashion so that there will be resemblance rather than identity between the valuable functions of art at one period and those at another. From the institutional theory, it accepts the idea that, for an object to be art, it does not necessarily have to fulfill one of these functions. Roughly, for works produced in the central art forms—such as poetry, painting, and music (but not philosophy or furniture)—the intention to fulfill is enough.[6]

Despite its advantages, I can see how someone might feel that this is the most unsatisfactory view of all those discussed. Not mentioning a single function art actually has or has had, it may seem peculiarly empty. However, what the demise of earlier theories shows is that the substance missing here cannot be provided *a priori* or by an examination of a handful of examples. Those earlier theories suggest certain preeminent functions, but they do not replace a painstaking, historical, artform by artform investigation into the functions of art.

■ UNDERSTANDING ART

Works of art differ from many artifacts we value in the way they are commonly supposed to be *known*, and in the relationship between knowing them and valuing them. We would never talk about understanding a chair the way we talk about understanding a work of art. Certainly, if a friend does not like a new chair you have just installed in your living room, you could not try to change her mind by getting her to understand it better. If she does not like the new painting you have hung above the chair, however, trying to get her to understand it better may be just the thing.

Works of art are not the only synthetic objects that can be understood. Machines, such as computers and automobiles, can be understood too. There are, however, important differences between understanding a computer and understanding a painting. Understanding the inner workings of a computer is not necessary to appreciate it, but understanding how a painting works may be just what is needed to appreciate it. Furthermore, there are experts on computers who *know* just how computers work, and different experts will tell pretty much the same story. There are something like experts on paintings too—critics. Like computer experts, they receive special training. Critics, however, do not tell the same story about paintings. It is very common for them to have different understandings of the same painting, which is sometimes expressed by saying that paintings need to be interpreted.

What is involved in understanding a painting? Is the same thing involved in understanding all works of art? First, it is not clear that it is even appropriate to talk of understanding all works of art. It is about as appropriate to talk about understanding a ceramic bowl as it is to talk about understanding a chair. Second, understanding at least seems to involve rather different things for different arts. If I don't understand a poem or a painting, it would be natural to express this by saying "I don't understand what it *means*." If I don't understand a piece of music, however, it seems less right to put this by saying "I don't understand what the music means." Music, especially instrumental music, needn't mean anything. (This may be true of certain types of paintings as well.)

There is at least one uniform way of trying to understand works of art, however, that can be applied not only to poems and paintings, but equally to music and even ceramic bowls. This is to try to understand what the artist was up to, or intended, in making the work.

The idea that understanding a work of art consists in understanding the artist's intention in making the work has been subjected to severe criticism.[7] One problem concerns the accessibility of intentions. How can we know what the artist intended? How can we know what is going on in the artist's mind while he or she is creating a work? Put this way, the question does seem rather daunting. No one can *observe* the inner workings of the artist's mind, and, while artists sometimes leave evidence of their thoughts in the form of letters, diaries, and recorded conversations, this evidence is often unreliable and invariably fragmentary.

To illustrate the problem about the availability of intention, consider Henry James's famous novella *Turn of the Screw*. It is not just that there are many different interpretations of this story; there is basic disagreement about its point. Some critics read it as a ghost story about two children under the spell of evil ghosts and about their governess who struggles to disenchant them. Other critics claim that it is a psychological tale about the mind of a neurotic governess: The ghosts are merely figments of her psyche. Henry James's text seems to offer plenty of support for *both* interpretations. Not only that, an abundance of further evidence leaves the issue unsettled. James wrote about his story in a preface, in letters, and in diaries. Furthermore, we know a great deal about James's life and mind. But the interpretive dispute only seems to escalate, rather than get settled.

Despite cases like that of *Turn of the Screw*, however, the problem of recovering the artist's intention is easily blown out of proportion. We are actually quite adept at figuring out the intentions with which people do and make things. This is no accident. This is our standard procedure for understanding the behavior of our fellow human beings. To understand any conversation, we must understand what our interlocutor means by his or her words. To recognize any artifact, we must understand what *it is for*. We not only succeed in doing this with familiar people and objects; archaeologists use the same procedure with the artifacts of long dead, newly discovered civilizations—not, of course, by peering into the minds of either the living or the dead. Archaeologists do it by consciously formulating hypotheses about the point of a certain artifact. We do the same thing, but usually unconsciously and automatically, in understanding conversations. We can equally well formulate such hypotheses about the point of poems, paintings, and piano concertos. Some of these will be obviously true (Shakespeare intended *Hamlet* to be a tragedy); others may always be debatable (Shakespeare intended to represent Hamlet as irresolute). This variation, however, simply reflects the fact that we never have a perfect understanding of the behavior of our fellow human beings.

A second objection to the idea that understanding a work of art consists in understanding the intention with which it was made is that, although intentions no doubt exist and may in principle be accessible, they are not, it is claimed, what determines a work's meaning. Proponents of this objection like to point out that there is no guarantee that an artist (say a writer) will succeed in realizing his or her intention. Whether he or she succeeds or not, however, we will be able to assign a meaning to the lines he or she wrote. Hence, we must assign meaning in some other way than by discovering intentions. A common proposal is that we assign meaning (in the case of a piece of writing) by our knowledge of linguistic and literary conventions that exist independently of any specific individual, such as the writer.

Just as the problem of accessibility of intentions was exaggerated by anti-intentionalists, however, so here the power of conventions to determine the sorts of meaning we are looking for when we interpret works of art is being exaggerated. To understand why this is so, it is convenient to distinguish sentence meaning from utterance meaning. Perhaps it is true that conventions wholly determine sentence meaning. Thus, the meaning of the sentence "This suitcase is heavy" does not depend on the intentions of any individual (though some think it depends on the shared intentions of a community of individuals). Utterance meaning is the message a speaker gets across by using a given sentence on a given occasion. The utterance meaning of "This suitcase is heavy" may vary wildly from situation to situation. On one occasion, a speaker may indicate that he needs help carrying the suitcase; on another, he may be bragging about how strong he is; on a third, complaining about how much is packed in it; on this or another occasion, worrying about the overweight fee he will have to pay at the airport. In general, we determine utterance meaning by determining a speaker's intention. In doing this, we are helped by context and convention, but, if for some reason we believe that the speaker did not intend the meaning we initially assign to the utterance, we will look for a different interpretation. Only in the rare case when it is impossible to find a suitable fit between his words and a hypothesized intention will we say he uttered something *other than* what he intended.

A final objection to the idea that we should try to understand works of art in terms of artists' intentions concerns the aim of interpretation. The intentionalist supposes that the aim of interpretation is to figure out something like the artist's utterance meaning. The objection is that this is not the aim of interpretation. Unfortunately, proponents of this objection do not agree among themselves about the aim of interpretation. Some propose that it is to discover the way of reading or perceiving the work that is aesthetically best (or, at least a way that is aesthetically superior). Others claim that the aim is to make the work of art relevant to the contemporary audience. Still others claim that it is to discover *any* of the indefinitely many ways of reading or perceiving the work that the interpreter finds interesting for *whatever* reason. The only constraint on the interpreter is that the interpretation be compatible with commonly agreed on features of the work. These are only a sampling of the many alternatives proposed to intentionalist interpretation.

When we combine this objection with a survey of critical practice, it has to be admitted that it shows something, namely, that the attempt to understand works by recovering their creator's intentions is not the only aim with which critics interpret art. Critics also interpret artworks with, among others, the aims mentioned in the preceding paragraph. If, however, the original point of this objection was to show that the recovery of intentions is not even among the legitimate aims of interpretation, then merely proposing alternatives does nothing to establish this.

In the beginning of this section, I emphasized that the understanding of art is different from the understanding of other things. Now, at the end of the section, in defending intentionalist interpretation I am suggesting that art *can* be understood in a way that is just like the way we understand other kinds of human behavior and human artifacts. Let me try to reconcile these two points of view.

Even when we approach a work of art by seeking out its creator's intention, we still need, usually, to *interpret* the work. We call what we are doing interpretation because many of the intentions we are seeking are not, and may never be, obvious. By contrast, we don't interpret cars and computers even when we seek to understand the intentions with which they are made. Artistic intentions seem to have, frequently, a depth and complexity usually lacking in the creation of more obviously functional artifacts. In fact, intentionally interpreting a work of art can be quite like trying to understand the people around us or, for that matter, ourselves. We can become intimate with works of art, and this is another reason for which we value them. So, even when we approach a work intentionalistically, we approach it somewhat differently than we do other artifacts.

It is no longer the case, however, that we exclusively seek to understand works by understanding their creator's intentions. We seek *an understanding* of a work of art with many other aims—our own aims rather than its creator's. In doing this, we do seem to treat works of art differently than most other products of human agency. We also value art for allowing us this flexibility.

■ THE VALUE OF ART

In the previous two sections, in discussing what art is and how we understand it, I mentioned many features of works of art that people value. Let us now, by way of concluding this chapter, bring together some of these thoughts by focusing on the questions about value raised at the beginning of this essay.

■ *What Makes Art Valuable?*

While there is no completely satisfying simple answer to this question, a good *partial* answer can be given by mentioning three functions that art fulfills especially well, though they can be fulfilled by other things too.

Earlier in this chapter, I introduced the notion of an *aesthetic experience*—a pleasurable (sometimes intensely pleasurable) experience we have when we closely and imaginatively attend to the sights and sounds of things or when we vividly imagine certain represented states of affairs. Such experiences are by no means confined to art, but many works of art are the richest sources of these experiences. This is *one* reason why art is found in all cultures. To be a human being with eyes and ears and an imagination is to be a seeker of aesthetic experience. Aesthetic experience is not simply a pleasure human beings are capable of having; it is a human need, although we can be conditioned or can condition ourselves to ignore this need, unlike certain physical needs.

Second, in addition to fulfilling the function of giving aesthetic experience, many works of art are especially good at helping us understand ourselves, the world around us, and the possibilities open to us. (Let us call this art's cognitive value.) The key word is *possibility*. Works of art present to us possible ways of experiencing things, of conceiving things, and of valuing things. They exhibit surprising ways of seeing the world around us. They suggest ways of thinking about ourselves and our actions. They explore what may be of value or disvalue in experiences, relationships, and ways of living. It would be wrong to say that art gives us *knowledge* of any of these things for, as I have been saying, a work of art can only present us with a possibility. Knowledge requires something more—that the possibility be realized in the world we live in, not just in the imaginary world of the artwork. But to find out anything, we have to have possible ways of seeing, thinking, and valuing. Many works of art are better than anything else at enabling us to make these explorations.

In our own century, a third function has been assigned to works of art that is as highly valued as the first two (and is not entirely independent of the first two). This is the function of being an object *for* interpretation—an object to be construed in accordance with aims we bring to it, rather than in accordance with the intentions with which it was made.[8] In the last section, I argued that it is perfectly legitimate to interpret in the latter way. I also pointed out, however, that the intentionalistic approach no longer monopolizes interpretive practice. The sort of interpretation that has fascinated many contemporary critics is a kind of revisionary, creative interpretation that attempts to blur the distinction between artist and critic. While this sort of criticism has shocked more conservative practitioners, it seems to me that it is simply an extended pursuit of the artistic values already mentioned. A creative critic does not aim to discover something but to "collaborate" with the work to create something new—a new work with its own aesthetic and cognitive properties. Such criticism is simply the attempt to *create more* aesthetic and cognitive value. The only question such critics need to ask themselves is whether they create enough new aesthetic and cognitive value for their efforts to be worthwhile.

■ Are All Art Forms Valuable for the Same Reason?

I have been speaking of the value of *art*, but this requires qualification. Not all the broad categories of value apply equally well to all art forms. Aesthetic value does apply, but this is not surprising because we can try to appreciate almost anything aesthetically. The cognitive value just discussed is a different story. It applies preeminently to representational arts such as literature, painting, and dance, and much more dubiously elsewhere in the artworld. So, largely for reasons of space, the above account of artistic value is somewhat biased in favor of the representational arts. To make up for this, let us very briefly examine what sort of value (other than aesthetic value) might be attributed to two largely nonrepresentational artforms: instrumental music and architecture.

Music possesses something that is at least analogous to the cognitive value discussed above. Many writers about music have observed that we perceive music as movement. We hear it moving slowly or quickly, as moving up or down, as moving with a certain rhythm. We hear parts performed by different instruments moving together or in different directions. In addition to hearing movement, we hear many other dynamic qualities. Music can sound languid or bouncy, aggressive or peaceful. It would be wrong to say music *represents* these qualities, for if it did, we could say that a piece of music is about languor or bounciness, and that is hardly necessary for the music to be languid or bouncy. Furthermore, very often it would be wrong to say that a work of music represents anything as having these qualities. The *music* is simply perceived as having them. Nevertheless, many things besides music literally or metaphorically have these qualities too. Bodies move through space. We walk, run, work, play with a certain pace and rhythm. Our breathing and heartbeat are movements within our body. Our thoughts and feelings have dynamic qualities as well and impart dynamic qualities to our bodies. (Think of your body when you are sad and when you are filled with joy.) I believe that music helps us conceptualize the qualities of movement and other dynamic qualities that permeate our lives. When we talk about sad music, we are thinking of sadness as a certain kind of dynamic quality. Because such conceptualization is not easily accomplished with words (at least in English and many other languages), this is one reason we value music.

Architecture intervenes in our environment much more aggressively than most other arts. Once a building is put up, we may have little choice whether to look at it, move through, and move around it. When an architect or planner is considering what building to build, he or she is choosing among possibilities, but once the building exists, *we* are not being presented with a possible way of thinking or experiencing things beyond the artwork. Rather, we are being presented with a new set of actual experiences. It is in these terms that we have to evaluate a work of architecture. If we like, we can confine this evaluation to the aesthetic experience such works give us, which, in the case of architecture, means evaluating our visual experiences of buildings and their surroundings. Because this is only one aspect of the way we experience buildings, however, there is no reason why we must confine our evaluation to this aspect. Our evaluation can include all the ways buildings shape the environment and affect our lives.

The best approach to understanding the value of art would begin by considering the value of individual artforms and work from there to sets of generalizations. Limitations of space make that approach impossible here. I hope that the alternative I have adopted is not wholly unenlightening or off base.

■ Who Cares about Artistic Value?

Everyone cares about the values I have been describing. Everyone seeks aesthetic experience; everyone seeks new, fruitful ways of thinking about themselves and the world. Everyone would like an enhanced rather than an impoverished environment. Of course, great works of art are not the only place to find these valuable things, and not everyone seeks them there. There are many reasons for this, but one is that many, though not all, great works of art can be daunting either because they are difficult and demanding or because they come from a distant era. Such works cannot be appreciated effortlessly and without preparation. But if you become prepared and make the effort, the rewards will be surprising.

■ NOTES

1. The classical sources of the representational definition of art are Plato's *Republic*, Book 10, and Aristotle's *Poetics*. Though *sources* of the definition, it is probably a mistake to think of Plato and Aristotle as defining art in these works.

2. R. C. Collingwood, *The Principles of Art* (Oxford: Oxford Univ. Press, 1938); B. Croce, *Aesthetic*, trans. D. Ainslie (London: Macmillan, 1929).

3. Duchamp was a member of the movement known as Dada, which sometimes claimed to create "anti-art" rather than art. However, anti-art seems to have been used ambiguously to denote either something other than art or art stripped of its usual presuppositions. I think Duchamp's readymades are best understood as anti-art in the latter sense. The most famous readymade is a urinal known as *Fountain*.

4. The best known statement of this view is found in Morris Weitz, "The Role of Theory in Aesthetics," *Journal of Aesthetics and Art Criticism* 15, no. 1 (1956). The notion of family resemblance is borrowed from Ludwig Wittgenstein, *Philosophical Investigations*, trans. G. E. M. Anscombe (New York: Macmillan, 1953), 67.

5. George Dickie, *The Art Circle* (New York: Haven, 1984). Though very influential, this view has received a barrage of criticism. See Richard Wollheim, *Art and Its Objects*, 2nd ed. (Cambridge: Cambridge Univ. Press, 1980) and Robert Stecker, "The End of an

Institutional Definition of Art," *British Journal of Aesthetics* 26, no. 2 (1986). Dickie replies to me in "Reply to Stecker," G. Dickie, et al., *Aesthetics: A Critical Anthology*, 2nd ed. (New York: St. Martin's, 1989), 214–17.

6. For a more detailed presentation of this view see Robert Stecker, "Boundaries of Art," *British Journal of Aesthetics* 30, no. 3 (1990).

7. See M. C. Beardsley, *The Possibility of Criticism* (Detroit: Wayne State Univ. Press, 1970) for many of the criticisms stated below.

8. The expression "object for interpretation" was coined by R. A. Sharpe, "Interpreting Art," *Proceedings of the Aristotelian Society*, supp. vol. 55 (1981). This function of art has been incorporated into many schools of contemporary literary theory, for example, reader-response theory, pragmatism, deconstruction. Comparable ideas are to be found in the criticism of other arts.

■ QUESTIONS

1. Which items from the list at the beginning of the chapter are arts or works of art? Can you explain why you chose those items and rejected the others?

2. How would you answer the question "What is art?" Among the definitions discussed in this chapter, to which one does your view most closely correspond?

3. The Dutch artist Van Megeran took the artworld by storm by claiming to discover several unknown works by his great predecessor Vermeer. These works attracted intense interest until it was discovered that Van Megeran himself painted them. Are Van Megeran's "Vermeers" works of art? Are these works less valuable, or of no value, because Van Megeran rather than Vermeer painted them?

4. Can enjoying a good meal be an aesthetic experience? Can a good meal be a work of art? Why, or why not?

5. How would you explain what it is to understand the following things: a song, a piece of instrumental music, a poem or short story, the chapters in this book?

6. According to the author, what are we doing when we interpret a work of art? Do you agree with the author's acount of the interpretation of art?

7. Is it true that not many people today are art lovers? If so, do you think those people who are not art lovers are missing something important? ■

■ FOR FURTHER READING

Beardsley, M. C. *Aesthetics: Problems in the Philosophy of Criticism*. New York: Harcourt, Brace, 1958.

Dickie, G., R. Sclafani, and R. Roblin. *Aesthetics: A Critical Anthology*. 2nd ed. New York: St. Martin's, 1989.

Hirsch, E. D. *Validity in Interpretation*. New Haven: Yale Univ. Press, 1967.

Kivy, Peter. *The Corded Shell: Reflections on Musical Expression*. Princeton: Princeton Univ. Press, 1980.

Sheppard, Anne. *Aesthetics*. Oxford: Oxford Univ. Press, 1987.

Tolstoy, Leo. *What Is Art?* Indianapolis: Bobbs-Merrill, 1960.

■ CHAPTER EIGHT

Philosophy of Religion

GALEN K. PLETCHER

■ INTRODUCTION

That human beings are religious is one of their most interesting and distinctive features. No matter where they are found on the globe, human beings form such religious patterns of response to the world as (1) the veneration as sacred of both objects and traditions; (2) belief in the reality and power of unseen forces; and (3) identification of some class or classes of people who have special knowledge and authority concerning the relationship to unseen powers; as well as (4) the elaboration of a code of behavior, informed and inspired by these beliefs and traditions; and (5) extensive patterns of social organization formed in relation to these beliefs and traditions. (Surprisingly, belief in a supernatural being who created the world and is in some ways responsible for it is not a universal component of religions, although it is very common.)[1]

When philosophy considers the phenomenon of religion, it is concerned with the analysis and assessment of claims made by religion, with regard both to the meaning and consistency of these claims and to the relationship of religious claims to nonreligious beliefs. Philosophers find the religious practices and beliefs of human beings to be of interest because religions make, explicitly and implicitly, claims about the ultimate nature of reality (metaphysics), the basis of belief (epistemology), and the proper conduct of human beings (ethics)—all of which are traditional subject areas of philosophy.

Philosophy and religion are by no means identical, even though the impression that they are is very common. Whereas philosophy is concerned with critical analysis, religion is an intellectual and emotional response to the universe that may be practiced without any attempt to scrutinize it in a philosophical way. But neither, to cite another common misconception, is philosophy in principle concerned with criticizing and refuting religion. Critical analysis results in the clarification and strengthening of religion as frequently as in attempted refutations of religion. In fact, philosophy of religion is practiced by a large number of people whose express intent is to use the central philosophical tools of reason and analysis to defend religious belief.[2]

Over the course of the past half century or so, there have been two related shifts in emphasis in the conduct of philosophy of religion in the Western English-speaking world. The first is an emphasis on the need to understand and analyze religious concepts with careful attention to the way they are actually *used* by people who practice religion. The second is a conception of philosophy of religion as ranging over many or even most of the religious traditions of human beings, instead of being confined to an examination of one particular religion. Discussions of philosophy of religion earlier in the century often left religions other than Christianity completely out of account. This is now increasingly rare. Many philosophers have come to believe that the examination of the concepts of religion can be enhanced by considering the same or similar concepts in different traditions.[3]

When we look at religion, it is natural to consider philosophical questions and problems as they arise in each of the three categories mentioned earlier. *Epistemology* is the theory of knowledge, the study of the ways in which we may be said to know things. *Metaphysics* is the study of the ultimate nature of reality. *Ethics* is the study of the nature and defense of moral judgments.

■ EPISTEMOLOGY

Try to imagine that you have grown up in an environment in which the idea of religious belief has never been suggested to you. Under these circumstances, would religious ideas and/or beliefs occur to you? It is possible to take rather different views in answering that question. One view holds that the most important features of religious belief come to us through revelation—the direct communication of religious truths from God[4] to humans. Another view holds that religious truths can be discovered and supported by normal operations of human reason. A third view—a common view in Christianity and the orthodox view of Roman Catholicism—is that of St. Thomas Aquinas, to the effect that some religious truths are revealed and others discoverable by reason.[5] The view that religion is communicated to humans in a special way and that without this communication human beings would not be religious, or would not know about religious truths, emphasizes *religion as revealed*. The view that the normal operations of human reason could discover religious truths emphasizes *natural religion*.

Those who emphasize revealed religion must confront a number of philosophical problems regarding religion, foremost among which is how we are able to identify revelations as such. We cannot comfortably base our religion on revelation unless we can be confident that we can tell a revelation from an hallucination. We shall consider this problem in the section on religious experience.

A similar problem arises when we are asked to accept a book or other record as containing a revelation of God. Some versions of Christianity hold the doctrine of the inerrancy of the Bible, believing that it contains the actual words of their God. Similarly, most Muslims accept that the Qu'rān contains the words of Allah, revealed to the prophet Muhammad. Works such as the Bible and the Qu'rān, however, seem to many readers to contain contradictions, duplications, and other problems that raise serious questions as to their reliability as records of a divine revelation. One of the tasks for epistemology of religion is to evaluate answers that have been offered to such questions.

Views of religion that construe its beliefs as naturally discoverable by human beings face unique philosophical problems of their own. Perhaps the foremost of these problems is this: "If reason is sufficient to establish religious truths, and if human beings are everywhere pretty much the same, why is the religious experience of human beings so widely divergent across the face of the Earth?"

One's views of the proper relationship between philosophy and religion, and of the proper substance of the philosophy of religion, will depend to some extent on which of these views of the source of knowledge about religion one finds more credible. If one views religion as a revealed phenomenon, then philosophy's role will be to assess the coherence of the revelations with the rest of what is known about the world and to remove possible inconsistencies that may creep into one's expansions on and explanations of the revelations one accepts. For believers in revealed religion, however, philosophy will not be the *source* of religious truths. If, on the other hand, one views religion as a natural phenomenon, then one will see philosophy as intimately involved in the *discovery*, as well as in the assessment, of religious truths.

The attempt to decide which of these views is correct takes us into epistemology and raises questions of the following sort: "What is the nature of religious belief?" "It is sometimes claimed that religion calls for faith rather than knowledge, but what does this mean?" "Is faith a different kind of knowing?" "Is it more or less reliable than knowing?" "Is it like opinion?—or perhaps like opinion held with strong emotion?"

■ Arguments for the Existence of God

The question of the basis of religious beliefs is sometimes addressed by considering so-called arguments for the existence of God. It must be stressed at the beginning, however, that ordinary believers, going through their lives relying on religious belief, may not *base* their views about religion on these arguments. Two considerations must be kept in mind. First, these arguments, in some *implicit* form, may underlie much of what makes religious beliefs seem reasonable to many people. If so, these arguments may account to some extent for the tenacity with which religious beliefs are held, even if it would be incorrect to say that the beliefs are *based on* these arguments. Second, even if the arguments for the existence of God are not related to the motivations for holding the belief, they may well offer *justifications* for such beliefs. That is, they can be used to give reasons for beliefs that are challenged by those who believe otherwise. As such, they would be of interest to someone who was concerned to show that his or her religious belief was reasonable.

As noted earlier, not all religions have a central concept of God or deity;

moreover, the nature of deity can be very differently conceived among the religions that do make reference to God. But in the Judeo-Christian tradition, the concept of God is central. We shall consider in this section some of the many arguments that people have given for believing that such a God exists.

The evidential basis in arguments for the existence of God can be of two broad kinds. One type, often called *a posteriori*, relies on facts drawn from experience of the nature of the world. By far, the largest number of arguments for the existence of God have fallen into this category. I shall presently examine two of them. The other category relies on modes of reasoning based on an analysis of the concepts of religion, independent of experience. These are often called *a priori* arguments. They have always held a deep attraction for philosophers because if one of them were valid, it would demonstrate God's existence without any reliance on experience, and, hence, without the possibility of invalidation by later experience. I shall examine one *a priori* argument for the existence of God, the ontological argument.

■ THE ONTOLOGICAL ARGUMENT

The *ontological argument* for the existence of God does not depend on facts about the nature of the world but concentrates, instead, on purely conceptual considerations. With many concepts, we can make deductions about the nature of the things to which the concept applies from the concept itself. From the concept "equilateral," we can deduce the concept "equiangular." This means that from the fact that a triangle has all its sides equal, we may deduce the fact—without even looking at the triangle at all—that all its angles must also be equal. Similarly, if I tell you that I have a sibling who is a bachelor, then you may deduce not only that the sibling is unmarried, but also that the sibling is male.

The ontological argument does a surprising and dramatic thing. It attempts to deduce the *existence* of God from the concept of God. The version by St. Anselm is the most famous. Anselm thought everyone would agree to this concept of God: God is that than which nothing greater can be conceived. Therefore, he reasoned, it must be the case that God exists. For suppose (S) that the being than which nothing greater can be conceived exists in the understanding alone (that is, not in reality). Then a being greater than it *can* be conceived after all, namely, one that exists not only in the understanding but also in reality. So the supposition (S) must be contradictory, because it leads to its own denial. Anselm assumed that to exist in the understanding and in reality is greater than to exist in the understanding alone. Hence, Anselm concluded, if God is truly the greatest being that can be conceived, then God must exist.[6]

This is a singular argument. In no other case, Anselm himself insisted, can one deduce the *existence* of anything merely from its concept. You may deduce the maleness of my bachelor sibling from his bachelorhood, but you may not deduce the fact that he exists from this or any other characteristic that is true of him. Of course, it would be very peculiar if I were to talk about this person if he did not exist. But that he exists does not *follow from* any characteristic that is true of him; belief that he exists is based on assumptions we all reasonably make when someone introduces a topic into discussion. By contrast, Anselm thought that the existence of God followed simply from the concept of God. He thought that once we achieved a clear grasp of the nature of God, we would see that God must exist.

As appealing as this argument is in its simplicity, it sometimes seems to have something of the air of illegitimacy about it. It may appear to derive a major conclusion with far too little effort. I think it is important to resist this psychological distrust of the argument. Like any argument, it stands in need of evaluation, and it may well be unsound, but some good arguments are simple arguments, and it would not do to reject the ontological argument solely on the basis of its simplicity.

One objection to the argument holds that a being existing only in the understanding does not seem to acquire greatness by coming into existence. It would certainly acquire the capacity to affect, and to be affected by, other existent objects, but would that capacity enhance its greatness? Immanuel Kant, an eighteenth-century German philosopher, argued that we add nothing to a concept by thinking of its object as actually existing. "Otherwise stated, the real contains no more than the merely possible. A hundred real [dollars] do not contain the least coin more than a hundred possible [dollars]." If they did, he continued, their concept would not be an adequate representation of the object. "My financial position," he admits, "is . . . affected very differently by a hundred real [dollars] than it is by the mere concept of them . . . ; and yet the conceived hundred [dollars] are not themselves in the least increased through thus acquiring existence outside my concept."[7]

A second objection is this: "Are we sure that we understand what it means to ask whether something is greater or more perfect when it exists than when it does not exist?" If I ask about a cake I am decorating for my son whether it would be better if I added a baseball glove and a soccer ball down in the lower corners, I know perfectly well what I mean. A cake exists in one form, and I am asking whether changing it into another form would improve it. If I ask of something that does not exist at all whether it would be better if it did exist, however, it is not clear exactly what I am asking, because the item referred to seems to be different in each case. "It" refers at first to a concept in my understanding, whereas in the second case "it" refers to an actually existing thing. An adequate defense of the ontological argument would have to clarify and defend the argument in the face of these questions.

■ THE COSMOLOGICAL ARGUMENT

The *cosmological argument* infers the existence of God from the generally accepted principle that all events and objects in the world are caused. The reasoning can go something like this:[8] Whenever we see an object or event, we naturally assume that it was caused; some set of circumstances is assumed to be responsible for its having come into existence and for its having the nature that it does. My own most recent brush with this principle involves my automatic coffee maker, which can be set so that when I get up in the morning, the coffee is already brewed. One morning I came downstairs to find coffee all over the kitchen cabinet. The water had entered the basket with the coffee grounds but, after a little while, had stopped flowing into the coffee pot and started running over the rim of the basket. This condition persists, and I have not been able to discover its cause. The morning on which it first occurred was just like any other morning. I was using filters out of the same box I had been using for weeks; I was using the same kind of coffee and the same amount of water. I had done everything exactly the same as I had always done it, and yet, on that particular morning and ever since, the coffee will not run through the basket after the cycle is about halfway complete.

Because coffee is an important part of my morning ritual, I have spent considerable time trying to solve this mystery. But it has never, in the course of the investigation, occurred to me to think that maybe there is no cause for this, that things sometimes just happen like this, and you have to be prepared for them. I am convinced that someone who knew more about coffee makers would eventually be able to unearth an explanation for its malfunctioning.

In the cosmological argument, this pervasive principle is extended to the universe. The argument maintains that if we believe that every event or object has a cause, and if, in fact, we hold to that principle even when we have no idea of what the cause might be, then it would be irrational to deny that the universe also must have a cause. If everything has a cause, then the universe must have a cause, and that cause is God.

Appealing as this method of argumentation may be, it has long been thought to contain a number of defects that considerably weaken the evidence it gives for its conclusion. First, it seems to necessitate an endless causal chain in which every link must itself have a cause. The reasoning of the cosmological argument makes it appear that God is in need of explanation and causal antecedents every bit as much as the universe is. God's causing the universe cannot, then, provide an ultimate explanation of the existence of the universe. Moreover, in some theological traditions, notably Judaism, Christianity, and Islam, the idea that something could have caused God, and that God would consequently depend on something else in order to exist, is unorthodox and inadmissible.

There is a second difficulty. It seems possible that the universe may have existed forever. God in some religious traditions is conceived as eternal. If God can be eternal, why can't the universe be eternal? But if the universe is eternal, then there would be no initial state of the universe, any more than there would be a largest or smallest number in an infinite series of integers. Although each individual event in the world would have a causal history, under this supposition the universe as a whole would have no causal history, and there would, therefore, be no antecedent situation that brought it into being. The cosmological argument does nothing to eliminate this possibility, and its introduction considerably weakens the support that the argument provides for its conclusion.

■ THE TELEOLOGICAL ARGUMENT

The cosmological argument would be valid no matter what the world is like, because according to the principle that the cosmological argument employs, a very bad world would require a cause just as would a very good world. The *teleological argument*, in contrast, begins from the fact that although the world seems to be well designed for the production of a large number of ends, no designer in the world can be found who could be responsible for these instances of design. William Paley, an eighteenth-century English theologian and moral philosopher, took special note of the efficiency of the eye as an organ for perceiving the world and argued that, if we found anything so well designed and functional in a natural setting (he imagines someone who has never seen a pocket watch finding one lying in a meadow), we would not hesitate to infer that it had been designed and manufactured by someone. Therefore, when we observe the eye, we can similarly infer that something must have designed it and brought it into existence.[9]

Another version of the argument calls attention to the extraordinary balances in nature and to the specialized features of natural organisms that are precisely the ones necessary for them to exist. Predators have precisely the kinds of claws, teeth, physical strength, and speed necessary for obtaining their prey, and they have digestive systems particularly well designed for the digestion of meats and other foods high in protein. Browsers and vegetarians have similarly well designed features for their needs. Something, so the argument continues, must have designed the world to make it as harmoniously intertwined as we find it to be.

Perhaps the strongest objection to this argument is based on the apparent fact of the evolution of life on this planet. The theory of evolution by natural selection is almost universally embraced by scientists as an explanation of the existence and features of life-forms in the world. According to it, the world's life-forms are precisely those that were best equipped to survive the pressures of competition for food and safety. Over the long course of development of life-forms on the Earth, changes have occurred in them by chance mutation. Those chance mutations that were beneficial to the species have been preserved by virtue of the fact that the animals in which they occurred were better able to compete with other members of the species than were animals without the changed characteristics. Hence, when we admire the ability of the salmon to return to the very stream in which it was hatched and to swim long distances in an exhausted condition up the stream to lay its eggs or to fertilize eggs laid by other fish, we need not infer the existence of a designer who designed the fish to carry out these tasks. According to the theory of evolution, those salmon in which this urge to reproduce was not successfully acted out did not live to reproduce their own genes, while those that did successfully act on this urge were successful in perpetuating the very genetic strain responsible for it. Similar comments can be made about the features of all other living things, including human beings.

One possible objection to this line of reasoning is that the theory of evolution does not fully explain all the features that we find in currently existing life-forms. For example, why do salmon return to the very *same* stream in which they were hatched when a similar stream would do (from the reproductive point of view)? In response to this, however, we can suggest that even if there is no obvious answer to this question, the general fact of salmon reproducing the way they do is probably much more simply and effectively explained on the basis of evolution than it is on the basis of a creator whose operations are, at best, mysterious.

A further consideration disinclines many people from accepting the teleological argument: the problem of evil, which we shall discuss below. David Hume, an eighteenth-century Scottish philosopher, suggested that we are a long way from demonstrating the existence of the Christian God, who is alleged to be perfect in every respect, from a mere consideration of the nature of the world, because the world is so far from perfect.[10] He claimed that even if the teleological argument were valid, it would not show what Christian theists need it to show, because we cannot infer about a designer any more excellence than is found in the object alleged to have been designed by it.

If we ask what type of God the design of the universe might suggest, we have to consider the fact that the universe does not seem to be designed as well as it could be. For example, why is it necessary that life-forms survive only at the expense of other life-forms? Not only must organisms give their lives so that other organisms may live, but they often must do so in painful and terrifying circumstances. Again, why are there naturally developing difficulties in the universe, such as cancer? The world presents a mixture of extraordinarily well-designed features together with features that seem to have absolutely no intrinsic or beneficial relationship to other parts of the universe. This does not show that the teleological argument is invalid, because its proponent might well maintain that at least those things that *are* well designed still stand in need of explanation, even if those that are not well designed cannot be explained. But in general, considerations of the evils of the universe have made this argument far less appealing to many people than it at one time was.

■ Religious Experience

Philosophers frequently value cognitive thought above all other forms of human relationship to the world. A concern for arguments for the existence of God certainly reflects a preoccupation with the examination of the cognitive dimensions of beliefs. It is, therefore, worthwhile reminding ourselves that the major religions of the world, whose cognitive claims we examine in the philosophy of religion, had their birth, not in cognitive thought, but in *experience*. Religion has rarely sprung from people sitting down and reasoning out the truths of the universe by stepwise argumentation. Religions have frequently begun by their founders' being seized by tremendous experiences that carried them away and made them speak and act in ways that they themselves at first may have found objectionable or at least peculiar. One thinks of Muhammad, alone in the caves of the Arabian peninsula, seeking enlightenment and hearing the voice of Allah say "speak, recite," and being terrified that he was going crazy until his wife was able to encourage him to listen to the voice.[11] One thinks of Moses, tending his father-in-law's flock, turning aside to watch a bush that burns but is not consumed, and then hearing the voice of Yahweh commanding him to take off his shoes, for the ground on which he stands is holy.[12]

Religious experiences need not be dramatic. They can vary from mild feelings of mood elevation to the utter overcoming of the subject-object distinction and the loss of a sense of self that occur in mystical experiences. In philosophy of religion, our first concern regarding religious experience is that our understanding of its varieties be as full and accurate as possible. A taxonomy of religious experience must take account of the continuum from ordinary to exotic experiences and must look for some of the characteristics that may be common to a large number of religious experiences. One of the most useful books for this purpose is *The Varieties of Religious Experience* by William James.

A characteristic of many religious experiences (not, we have just seen, of that of Muhammad) is a sense of certainty, or what William James called a *noetic quality*: The conviction that the experience has conveyed important truths to the experient.[13] The experient may not be able to describe these truths even to himself or herself, but this so-called ineffability of religious experiences does not prevent their being felt as of tremendous importance; nor does it prevent their resulting in dramatic changes in the lives of the people who have them.

The philosopher's major interest in religious experience is to determine its epistemological value. The fact that the people to whom religious experiences occur do not generally doubt their authenticity, as Muhammad did, does not mean that they should not doubt their authenticity. The mere fact that something seems to me to be true is not an unmistakable and infallible mark that it *is* true. Two questions must be raised. The first is, "If such an experience should happen to me, would I be justified in drawing from it the conclusions that seem to follow?" If I seem to see an airplane in the sky, most of us believe that I am justified in concluding that there is an airplane in the sky. If I seem to see the Virgin Mary in the sky, am I justified in concluding that the Virgin Mary is in the sky?

The other question is "To what extent am I justified in drawing conclusions from someone else's religious experience?" Consider an example. A close friend and professional associate of mine told me of spending a vacation on the grounds of a now defunct religious community that had thrived for 150 years. Just as he drifted off to sleep one night, his chest became almost unbearably constricted, and he began to fear for his life. Gradually, it began to seem to him that there was something or someone on his chest and that the constriction was not due to a heart attack or other physical malady. Eventually overcoming his fear, he said, "Who are you?" into the darkness. A voice identified itself as that of a devout resident of that place whose death a hundred or so years before had left his spirit very troubled; he had not been able to get free of the place to go to a higher world. My friend has said that the question of distrust of this experience never occurred to him, but instead he immediately asked the disembodied voice if it would like him to pray for its spiritual welfare. Receiving an affirmative response, my friend began to pray that this being should be freed of its ties to that place and be allowed to go to a higher world. Gradually the constriction on his chest lifted, and it became clear that the spirit had taken its leave of him.

I have complete trust in my friend, who is a person of sound mind and body and who does not drink in excess nor abuse drugs in any way. I find it unlikely that this story is something he has made up for his own amusement. Should I believe my friend's description of what happened, or should I suspect that he was dreaming or hallucinating? Suppose that my friend said that just as he was drifting off to sleep, he felt a heavy weight on his chest that startled him, and he awoke to discover that it was a cat kept in the inn as a mouser who had decided that his chest would be a good place to catch some shut-eye. I do not believe I would have any trouble accepting this story and believing on its basis both that there was a cat kept as a mouser in that retreat house and that it had climbed on my friend's chest one night when he was there. The mere fact that I didn't see it for myself is no bar to my belief, nor is the mere fact that it was a very unusual circumstance. If it would be reasonable to accept his testimony in the case of the cat, why not in the case of the disembodied spirit?

Here we are on a continuum of sorts. If my friend said that as he was falling asleep, an elephant came into the room and jumped on his chest and caused him discomfort for some time until he succeeded in shooing it away, we would not believe him, no matter what evidence he provided. This is primarily because we believe that if an elephant had jumped on his chest, he would not be here to tell us about it. Although the cat story is unusual, there is nothing about it that violates our beliefs about the ordinary course of events. By contrast, the story of the disembodied spirit is a little more like the elephant story, in that it does conflict with some, at least, of what many of us believe. If we are materialists, we may not believe in disembodied spirits at all. Even if we do believe in disembodied spirits, we may not think it makes any sense to conceive of them as having weight, or to suppose that they would have trouble moving from one place to another.

But are we as confident of our beliefs about disembodied spirits as we are of our judgment that a man could not withstand an elephant's weight on his chest? A religious person might think that we are not justified in such confidence, arguing that it is just through such novel experiences that we can learn how wrong our general views of the world are and how much they need to be supplemented in the direction indicated by the experience my friend had. You can begin to appreciate the strength of this argument if you imagine the "strange" occurrence happening several times or to different people. If such incidents happened regularly to my friend, or if several reliable people independently reported similar experiences, we might conclude that this concurrence of testimony is too striking to dismiss out of hand. It would seem unlikely that they were all having hallucinations of the same kind.

This reasoning explains why people who have written about religious experience have often been interested in trying to assess how much commonality there is among the "varieties of religious experience." For if there were some one or two or six common elements to the experiences, no matter how diverse they were in other ways, then it might well be that they would form a kind of collective testimony in favor of those one or two or six features similar to what we have when people agree in mundane matters.[14] By the same token, an effective way for an opponent to attempt to discredit the possible evidential value of religious experience is to try to show that there are no common unifying themes to be found in them, so that the best explanation for them is that they are aberrations, each of a different personality.

In *The Varieties of Religious Experience*, James tries to establish that there *are* common features to these experiences and argues that their occurrence in many ages and climates has to be explained. Perhaps they crop up time and again all over the globe because there is some element of reality that is somehow breaking through in these instances and making itself known or at least felt. James speaks of a "more" to the universe that may be revealed through these experiences. Now, of course, even if we felt justified in drawing such a conclusion, we would still be a long way from reliable conclusions about the nature of the "more" that we may be experiencing. (Remember our discussion of a similar point, raised by David Hume.) There is no unanimity in the whole range of such experiences that would entitle us to conclude that there exists an anthropomorphic God—that is, a God having many humanlike qualities and characteristics. James, however, concludes that these experiences point to a dimension of the world that can bring about real transformation in the lives of those who experience it.[15]

■ Naturalistic Analyses of Religion

Another concern in the epistemology of religion stems from the wide disagreement about the claims of religion, both within the social group that is involved in a particular tradition and between the various religious traditions of the world. Moreover, religion makes claims that are sometimes at variance with what would seem to be straightforward observations of the world. These differences with other beliefs and with other people have prompted some people to suggest that religion is not based in fact and observation, but is rather an unthinking reaction to the circumstances of life. For example, Karl Marx held, in a famous phrase, that religion is the opium of the people.[16] By this, he meant that religion and its claims of compensation for hardship, survival of death, and the like, were necessary analgesics to help people cope with the everyday difficulties of their lives, particularly economic difficulties. Sigmund Freud, the Viennese psychiatrist and founder of psychoanalysis, held that religious beliefs were primarily motivated by wish fulfillment, showing very little relationship to reality but revealing a great deal about what people *wanted* reality to be like.[17]

Both Marx and Freud held that a full analysis of religious belief would show that religious beliefs spring entirely from certain naturalistic conditions. These beliefs do not report accurately about the world, because they are nothing more than symptoms of serious problems and maladjustments on the part of human beings. (With Marx, the unease is basically economic, whereas with Freud it is basically psychological.) Human beings are completely unaware of the true origins of these beliefs, and so they take them to be accurate representations of the nature of the world. If the problematic circumstances responsible for the formation of religious beliefs were to be ameliorated, however, the beliefs would simply evaporate, just as the symptoms of a disease disappear when the disease is cured.

Even though both Marx and Freud are interpreted (by themselves and others) as posing deep challenges to the rationality of religious belief, it may be possible to reconcile some of their insights with religious belief. One might point out, for example, that the fact that religious beliefs offer compensation for economic hardship does not by itself establish that they are not true. Similarly, one might hold that God has instilled in people certain wishes that naturally influence their beliefs, and that, because the wishes were instilled by God, the resultant beliefs are, in fact, accurate reflections of reality. Such a compromise position would admit that religious beliefs certainly do offer compensations for economic hardship and certainly do provide psychological security, yet without admitting that their only value lies in the fulfillment of those functions.

We can also argue that although Freud and Marx are correct in thinking that religious faith does not have the epistemological character it is normally thought to have, religion is crucially important to human beings nonetheless. In a well-known essay in 1955, R. B. Braithwaite, a professor of philosophy at Cambridge University, argued that "the primary use of religious assertions is to announce allegiance to a set of moral principles."[18] Moreover, religion is superior to morality in getting people to behave morally because religion also emphasizes the internalization of the moral code—changing what the person wants as well as how he or she acts. In addition, by reference to certain stories accepted as portraying exemplary action (for example, the parable of the Good Samaritan), religion makes the allegiance to moral principles vividly and deeply felt.[19] In Braithwaite's view, although religion seems to offer statements about the world of a metaphysical sort, it is best seen as a successful system for assuring moral behavior. We consider a similar view in our discussion of the relation between morality and religion later in this chapter.

■ METAPHYSICS

■ God

Metaphysics is the study of the ultimate nature of reality. Religions offer a range of theories about the nature of reality, and philosophers are interested in examining the coherence and consistency of these theories, as well as the arguments that can be put forth in their defense. For example, the religions familiar to most readers of this book have held that there is a supreme spiritual being in the universe who created the universe and who is in some way still responsible for it, who has from time to time manifested itself in human circles but is invisible, and whose effects are felt in the world around us.

This is a remarkable claim, and we must not let its familiarity blind us to that fact. It raises epistemological questions with which we have already been concerned, but it also raises a metaphysical question: "What kind of being is God?" Although we systematically discourage belief in fairies and ghosts in our children, we readily believe in the existence of invisible magnetic fields, because their effects can be felt or observed under regular conditions. Believers have rarely claimed any such predictable regularity for the activities of God. In fact, many have insisted that humans cannot hope to understand God's ways. An invisible being who acts in ways that are difficult to anticipate beforehand is quite different from most of what we encounter in human experience.

The irregularities (if such they should be called) in the appearances of God may be explained by the attribution of personality to God. We know from human experience that beings possessing personality are not completely predictable. A difficulty with this attempt to understand God's actions is that most believers want to think of God as *good*, perhaps as supremely good, and this conception may be hard to reconcile with an unpredictable personality. We touch on this issue again in the section on the problem of evil.

■ Human Beings

Metaphysical claims about the universe are also made regarding human beings. In many religious traditions, human beings are thought of as *dualistic* in nature. There is a physical part, which obeys the law of gravity, bumps into things, and makes noises, and there is another, invisible part, which is the soul or spirit, or perhaps, the mind, and which manifests itself primarily through changes that it induces in the physical part.[20] It is not uncommon for religions to claim that the spiritual side of human beings is completely independent of the physical side, or that it can be made to be so through disciplines of various kinds. Indeed, the claim is sometimes made that the spiritual side of human beings does not suffer the well-known and mournful fate of the physical side, but continues to exist even after the body dies. Not surprisingly, teachings about the ultimate fate of human beings are among those most treasured by the adherents of religion. Some people find considerable consolation in the assurance that the death we see in our loved ones and anticipate for ourselves is not annihilation but is only a change from one form of existence to another.

By contrast, I think it can fairly be said that the current scientific view of human beings is materialistic. This means that scientists do not consider it necessary to take account of anything other than the physical dimensions of human beings in explaining their behavior and experiences. This is an alternative metaphysical view, a *monistic* one as opposed to the dualistic one just outlined. According to this materialistic version of monism, human beings are basically bodies. Hence, the death of the body marks the end of the person.

Although it is held by almost all Christians, dualism is not clearly the orthodox Christian view. A contrary view is suggested by Paul in 1 Corinthians 15, which is, in fact, one of the few places in the Bible where the issue of the fate of the human being after death is clearly addressed. Paul explicitly avoids dualism when he describes his understanding of human death. He says that we are sown a physical body and we are raised a spiritual body. The phrase *spiritual body* is striking because it seems self-contradictory; spirit and body are ordinarily thought to be exclusive of one another. Paul's view is that each human being exists as a physical body for a number of years and then "falls asleep" in Christ until Christ's expected Second Coming. At the time of the Second Coming, humans will be raised in this new form of being, which thereafter does not itself suffer death of any kind.

Another striking feature of this view is that it is profoundly monistic, even materialistic, in its metaphysical analysis of human beings prior to death. (We are *sown* as *physical bodies.*) Moreover, it makes the survival of human beings a miraculous occurrence. According to the usual dualistic view, the mind or soul or spirit is itself something that cannot die. Consequently, the fact that it lives after death is nothing remarkable. It simply *cannot* be killed. In Paul's view, it requires divine intervention to transform the completely disintegrated bodies of dead people into a new form of existence. Survival is assured, in his view, only by an act of divine re-creation, a "raising up" or "resurrection."

■ Nonhuman Beings

In company with metaphysical views of the universe as a whole (for example, that there is a great spirit underlying it or somehow responsible for it) and about human beings (for example, that they are composed of spirit and body), religions typically offer analyses of the nature of the other items in the universe, such as animals. Are animals on a par with human beings, beneath them, or perhaps above them? In the Judeo-Christian tradition, there are pretty clear indications that animals are thought of as inferior forms of being. Alternatively, animals might be thought to be gods, having powers that transcend human beings. After all, many of them can run much faster than we can and many are much stronger than we are. Moreover, many of them can sense features of the world that we cannot sense (for example, smells, sounds). In Hinduism, animals may very well be the current manifestations of formerly existing human beings who have been reborn in animal form in accordance with their behavior in earlier lifetimes. In southern Africa among the Bushmen, it is not uncommon to address an animal respectfully and even lovingly before killing it for food and skin for the family. There is among such people a vivid awareness of the dependence of human beings on the life-forms around them.

And what about rocks? Are rocks really dead? In religious traditions of aboriginal human beings in northwest Australia, a large rock may be regarded as the current embodiment of a previously active God. A rock face of a sheer cliff may be thought of as a place where the gods assemble and may be imbued with special significance because of the attachment the gods have for the place. Muslims venerate a black stone embedded in one corner of the Ka'ba, a shrine in Mecca in the shape of a cube that is ceremoniously circumambulated seven times during one of the rituals of the annual pilgrimage, or Hajj. It appears to be a meteorite that fell to the earth well before the time of Jesus. Although Muslims would be deeply offended if it were suggested that this stone is regarded by them as divine, it is nevertheless clear that it has become for them a powerful and vital symbol.

Similar questions can be raised about the vegetable kingdom. A tree is alive, unlike a rock, but does it have a personality? Can it interact with human beings? When I was a child, my house was surrounded by four enormous American elm trees. I used to interact with these trees in various ways, and I believed as a young child that they had a good knowledge of what I was doing. Was this view mistaken? To give up such a belief as one grows older, as I did, is to change one's metaphysics and to adopt a different view of the ultimate nature of the things in the world.

■ ETHICS

Some philosophers have maintained that ethics depends on religion, suggesting that religion is important because it makes people behave morally or that religion is important because it teaches people the difference between right and wrong. This view can be combined with the view that there would *be* no right and wrong if there were no religion. Religions do teach moral codes to their adherents. Confucianism, for example, consists primarily of rather elaborate moral and social codes. Nothing is more well-known to people living in the Judeo-Christian tradition than the story of Moses descending from the mountain holding two tablets on which are inscribed Ten Commandments from God, some of which deal directly with human ethical behavior.

So strong is the association between ethical behavior and religion that there is an argument for the existence of God based on the moral sense that human beings have. C. S. Lewis, in his book *Mere Christianity*, argues that everyone has an inborn conscience, the "Law of Decent Behavior," that tells us what we should and should not do. He argues that this moral faculty is evidence of the existence of a God who instilled it in us.[21] Its presence in us and its influence on us, he thinks, cannot be explained in any other way.

■ *Religion and Moral Behavior*

To clarify the relation between religion and morality, we must first distinguish between behavior that is *motivated* by morality and behavior that is merely *in accordance* with morality. An example may help clarify this distinction. If I take morality seriously, in the sense that I want very much to be an ethical human being, then my reason for not cheating on my income taxes may be that to do so would be inconsistent with my view of what an ethical human being should do. It violates my code of ethics. Consider now the person who would dearly love to cheat on his income taxes but is prevented from doing so by a vivid fear that, if he does so, he will be audited, fined, and perhaps imprisoned. In this example, both my behavior and the behavior of the man who fears the audit are *in accordance with* morality, but it can be argued that the behavior that is done for nonmoral reasons, from fear of punishment, is not moral behavior at all. It is behavior that happens to come out in accordance with morality for entirely nonmoral reasons.

The view that religion is a principal source of morality seems to be based on a belief that without the fear of God, and perhaps of God's punishment, to spur us on, we would not behave in a moral fashion. Indeed, one of my students once told the class that the only reason that he was at all interested in behaving morally was his own fear of hell. To the extent that this is the connection between religion and morality, then religion is not a source of morality any more than your father is a source of morality when he assures you that if you do not share the cookies with your sister, he will spank you. This may eventually teach you morality, but at the point that you obey your father's admonition, you are not behaving morally; you are behaving *in accordance with morality* for nonmoral reasons. Indeed, a religion with a prominent belief in hell may in fact make *moral* behavior impossible on the part of its adherents: These people may behave in accordance with morality only out of fear, rather than on the basis of moral considerations. Because of this, one of the ethical issues that arises in the philosophy of religion concerns the very *possibility* of a religious morality when fear is the primary motivation for behavior.

■ Religion as the Source of Moral Knowledge

It is possible, however, to assert a connection between religion and ethics that has nothing to do with the motivation to behave one way or another. Someone may claim that nothing would be good or bad if God did not command certain things to be good and other things to be bad. Someone may, that is, assert not that one would not be *motivated* to be moral without belief in God, but the rather different claim that there would *be* no good and bad without God's existence. One may also maintain, as a related but distinct claim, that one would not *know* what was good and bad, right and wrong, without God's having instructed us in that regard. Because it is rather difficult to discuss issues of right and wrong, and we often have rather vivid disagreements with our friends about these issues, the possibility that there might be some such divine answer to questions of right and wrong is very attractive. Tempting as this position may seem to be, there are strong arguments to the effect that the commands of God could not be the basis for an ethical system.

Let us imagine that we define good in the following way: *good = commanded by God*. Under that definition, to say that it is good to practice marital fidelity and to be honest is to say that God commands those actions. Let us similarly define bad in the following way: *bad = forbidden by God*. According to this approach, to say that it is bad to murder, to beat one's child, and to cheat on one's income taxes is to say that God forbids such behavior. Would this understanding of the concepts of good and bad be adequate?

A problem arises if we ask whether God has any reason for commanding what God commands and forbidding what God forbids.[22] Let us suppose that God commands us to practice marital fidelity. Does God do this for reasons? If so, then it would seem that the reasons God has for commanding marital fidelity are independently good enough to warrant marital fidelity whether or not God commands it. After all, we do not need a command from God to eat foods containing vitamin C. If God did command us to do that, it would be on the basis of reasoning that is open to all of us to understand, namely, the prevention of scurvy and considerations of nutrition in general. Similarly, if there are reasons for God's commanding marital fidelity, then we ought, as moral agents, to be primarily concerned with the reasons God has for the command, not with the fact that God commands it.

Recall now our earlier distinction between *behaving morally* and *behaving in accordance with morality*. It is, of course, possible to skip the moral reasoning once you have concluded that God commands something, and to do it simply because if you don't, God will make you very sorry you did not. By our earlier distinction, however, that is not behaving morally; it is behaving in a way that saves you from dire punishment. Our question, then, is whether God's commands could make any *moral* difference in how we ought to behave. It would seem that if God's commands are based on reasoning, then they do not make any moral difference. We ought rather to get right to the business of examining the reasons themselves and use those as the basis for our decisions about what is right and wrong.

On the other hand, suppose that we say that God has *no* reason for commanding what God commands and forbidding what God forbids. It would seem to follow that it is important to know what God commands and forbids, because if it were not for God's commanding and forbidding, we would not be able independently to discover what is right and what is wrong, what is good and what is bad. This alternative is equally unacceptable, for it implies that murder might be good, if only God had decided to command it instead of the opposite, and it implies that marital fidelity might be bad, if only God had decided to forbid it instead of commanding it. Good *reasons*, however, can be given for these evaluations that are entirely independent of a knowledge of God's commands. It is difficult to understand how this ethical reasoning (for example, in favor of the view that murder is bad) could be invalidated simply by the command of a supreme being, no matter how powerful that being might be. For when we reason about right and wrong, good and bad, we are always right in the thick of the details of the world. We call attention to the fact that pain is universally avoided, that pleasure is universally sought, and on and on, through a whole host of natural consequences of actions and events. It is on the basis of these considerations that we make our decisions about moral right and moral wrong, about good and bad. In order for a command of God to change good into bad, the very nature of the world in which we live would also have to change.

The upshot of our discussion of a theological basis for ethics is this: It would appear that God's commands are either irrelevant to ethics (if the commands are based on ethical reasoning we can understand), or arbitrary and without basis in our lives (if the commands are not based on ethical reasoning such as we employ). It thus appears that God's commands cannot be an appropriate basis for morality and a moral code.[23]

■ The Problem of Evil

The problem of evil arises because some conceptions of God strongly imply that God could and would eliminate all evil from human existence. Because there is obviously evil in the world, God must either not exist or be wrongly conceived. Specifically, the problem of evil arises because it appears that not all of the following propositions can be true:

1. God exists.
2. God is benevolent.
3. God is omnipotent (all-powerful).
4. Evil exists.

As David Hume says in a famous passage: "Epicurus's old questions are yet unanswered. Is [God] willing to prevent evil, but not able? then is he impotent. Is he able, but not willing? then is he malevolent. Is he both able and willing? whence then is evil?"[24]

The problem of evil as conceived above can be solved simply by denying any of the numbered propositions. If the problem is structured in this way, we can see that an argument taking some of the numbered propositions as premises need not be directed against the existence of God (proposition 1). The argument could just as well be directed against any of the other three claims, for the problem disappears if any of the four is given up.

For example, we could deny that evil exists (proposition 4). The religion of Christian Science holds that evil is an illusion of the mind. Buddhism and many forms of Hinduism can also be understood as claiming that much of what we judge to be evil is not in fact evil. This denial of the existence of evil should not be taken as a silly claim. Theorists who hold this view do not necessarily deny that people die, that they cut their fingers, and that they sometimes are tortured, but they deny that these things, if properly understood, are really evil. One version of this position suggests that just as darkness is nothing but the absence of light, so what seems to be evil is simply the absence of good. Because this interpretation requires us to understand evil in ways that make it difficult to continue our ordinary ways of thinking and speaking about good and evil, this solution has been thought by many to carry an intolerably high price.

As we saw, Hume conceived the problem of evil as the basis for an argument to the effect that God cannot exist *as traditionally conceived*. Following this out, we could deny that God is omnipotent (proposition 3). Perhaps evil exists because

God is not powerful enough to eliminate it. William James was partial to this view,[25] and a view very similar to it has been developed by the various forms of process theology inspired by Alfred North Whitehead's *Process and Reality*.[26] Views of this kind basically see God as actively working, often with the cooperation of human beings, toward the creation of a more valuable world. Evil exists because of limitations in the abilities of humans and of God.[27]

In a variation of this position, Zoroastrianism sees the whole history of the universe as a cosmic drama between a powerful evil force (*Angra Mainyu*) and a powerful good force (*Ahura Mazda*). *Ahura Mazda* is the source of light and life and is, as far as it goes, perfectly good. The resulting world is not as good as it could be because *Ahura Mazda* is effectively opposed, at least from time to time, by the evil *Angra Mainyu*.

The other logical possibility for solving the problem posed by the above four propositions has not seemed very attractive. To deny that God is benevolent (proposition 2) would change most theistic religions to such a drastic extent as to produce completely different religions. It is also difficult to imagine how one could *worship* a God who is not good. Perhaps Satanism may best be understood as a form of this response to the problem of evil.

A further possibility for solving the problem of evil is to hold that there *is* in fact no contradiction among the above four propositions, even though there seems to be. To defend this, we might try to show that evil is essential to goodness in some way. We might call attention to the value of suffering, or we might claim that it is necessary to be tempted by evil in order for our good will to win out, and so forth. Such an attempt would try, in other words, to preserve God's goodness and omnipotence in the face of the existence of evil.[28]

Some Christians also explain evil by reference to the existence of the devil, but they may fail to realize that the existence of the devil may compromise God's omnipotence in a considerable way. A truly omnipotent God must be able to eliminate evil in spite of the activities of any being, devil or otherwise. It becomes difficult to understand, then, why God does not do so. What reason could God have for permitting the devil's evil efforts to succeed? This puzzle is at least as challenging as the original problem of evil.[29]

Like many questions in philosophy, the problem of evil is worth a lifetime of reflection. My view is that the problem of evil is a logical problem, as I have presented it above, in only one of its aspects. In another aspect, the problem concerns how we are to come to terms with the fact that the things we love most deeply contain within them, or closely associated with them, other things that we reject most strenuously and that we deplore. This is true of people, of occupations, of the world as a whole. This is an enormous puzzle. It is not clear that there can be a final answer in anyone's thinking as to why there is such an admixture of good and evil. What there can be is a resolution of the dissatisfactions that this situation occasions in the hearts and minds of sensitive human beings. What we can hope for is to become more comfortable with the world as we find it, so that we do not feel it necessary to reject or devalue its good parts simply because we are so painfully aware of the bad.

■ CONCLUDING REFLECTION

We should remind ourselves, in closing, that ordinary men and women embrace religions not by the strength of the argumentation offered in their behalf, but because those religions help them make sense of their situation. Religions help their adherents believe that the mysteries of the universe are, at least to some extent, accessible. It may be that Freud was right that religious beliefs are ways of accommodating ourselves to a largely hostile universe, partly through the manifestations in human thought of unconscious wishes. If so, then whether or not we agree with him that this forms a definitive criticism of religion, we must, in the study of religion, always remember the depth with which religious beliefs are held. We misunderstand religion if we think of its beliefs as superficial—easily revised or rejected. If we revise our religious beliefs, we revise our orientation to the world, and if we reject them, as many reflective people have thought they must, we usher in a revolution in our thinking that will result in deep and pervasive changes in our lives. It is because of this that the examination of religion must always proceed with concern, with care, and with a certain kind of love.[30]

■ NOTES

1. Jainism and Buddhism are religions of India that reject belief in a personal God. In China, Taoism and Confucianism place little emphasis on the gods.

2. See, for example, Alvin Plantinga and Nicholas Wolterstorff, eds., *Faith and Rationality: Reason and Belief in God* (Notre Dame, IN: Univ. of Notre Dame Press, 1983).

3. An example of an approach to philosophy of religion that attempts to do justice to many different traditions is John Hick, *An Interpretation of Religion* (New Haven: Yale Univ. Press, 1989). The work of Ninian Smart has also consistently made use of insights from all the world religions. See, for example, *The Philosophy of Religion* (New York: Random House, 1970), and *Reasons and Faiths: An Investigation of Religious Discourse, Christian and Non-Christian* (London: Routledge and Kegan Paul, 1958).

4. The word *God* may be used as a proper name, for example, when it is used to name or address the divine being of some religious tradition. Or it can be a common noun, referring to some being or thing regarded as divine by some person or tradition (as in "Money is his god"). In the first use, the word has an initial capital, as do most proper names; in the second use, the initial letter is usually not a capital. Although I am comfortable with this distinction, which often helps to remove ambiguities, I have in this chapter followed the more usual practice of capitalizing the initial letter whenever the word is used.

5. St. Thomas Aquinas, *Summa Contra Gentiles*, 1, 3–8, trans. Anton C. Pegis as *On the Truth of the Catholic Faith*, vol. 1 (Garden City, NY: Doubleday, 1958), 63–76. For Aquinas, all truths that are discoverable by reason could also be revealed to us, if God chose to do so. But some truths known by revelation could not be discovered by reason. (This does not exhaust the possibilities for the relation between faith and reason. Some philosophers, notably Søren Kierkegaard, have held that religious truths are *contrary* to reason.)

6. See Alvin Plantinga, ed., *The Ontological Argument* (Garden City, NY: Double-day, 1965), 3–6.

7. The passage is from Immanuel Kant, *Critique of Pure Reason*, trans. Norman Kemp Smith; qtd. in Plantinga, *The Ontological Argument*, 61–62.

8. The most widely cited versions of the cosmological argument are probably the first three of St. Thomas Aquinas's "five ways." See *Summa Theologica*, 2.3, "Whether God Exists," *Introduction to Saint Thomas Aquinas* by Anton C. Pegis (New York: Modern Library, 1945), 24–27. The argument I present most closely resembles the second way, but differs from it somewhat.

9. See William Paley, *Natural Theology, or Evidences of the Existence and Attributes of the Deity Collected from the Appearances of Nature* (1802). It is reprinted in many places; for example, John Hick, ed., *The Existence of God* (New York: Macmillan, 1964), 99–103.

10. David Hume, *Dialogues concerning Natural Religion* (1779), pt. 5. This work, published after Hume's death, is available in many editions.

11. See David S. Noss and John B. Noss, *A History of the World's Religions*, 8th ed. (New York: Macmillan, 1990), chapter on Islam.

12. Exodus 3.

13. William James, *The Varieties of Religious Experience* (New York: Modern Library, 1902), chs. 16–17.

14. I have discussed the argument based on agreement in one type of religious experience (mysticism) in "Agreement Among Mystics," *Sophia*, 11, no. 2 (July 1972), 5–15.

15. James, *Varieties of Religious Experience*, 498–99: The individual, through religious experience, "*becomes conscious that this higher part* [of himself] *is conterminous and continuous with a MORE of the same quality, which is operative in the universe outside of him, and which he can keep in working touch with, and in a fashion get on board of and save himself when all his lower being has gone to pieces in the wreck.*" (The entire passage is italicized in the original.) In a later passage (again italicized), he says: "*the conscious person is continuous with a wider self through which saving experiences come*" (505).

16. The passage occurs in the introduction to his *Contribution to the Critique of Hegel's Philosophy of Right*. See Karl Marx and Friedrich Engels, *On Religion*, introduction by Reinhold Niebuhr (New York: Schocken, 1964), 42.

17. Sigmund Freud, *The Future of an Illusion* (1927), *The Standard Edition of the Complete Psychological Works of Sigmund Freud*, ed., James Strachey, vol. 21 (London: Hogarth, 1961), 3–56.

18. R. B. Braithwaite, "An Empiricist's View of the Nature of Religious Belief," *The Eddington Lecture* (Cambridge: Cambridge Univ. Press, 1955), 19.

19. Braithwaite, "Empiricist's View," esp. 21–24.

20. I am for the moment ignoring the possibility of paranormal phenomena such as telepathy, in which a mind is alleged to contact another mind without the intermediate influence of a body. This topic deserves a fuller discussion than I could here devote to it.

21. C. S. Lewis, *Mere Christianity* (London: Macmillan, 1952).

22. I would like to avoid even the implicit ascription of gender to the deity. Hence, rather than use a personal pronoun for subsequent references, I repeat the proper name.

23. There is much more to be said on this issue. For a collection of relevant readings, see Gene Outka and John P. Reeder, eds., *Religion and Morality* (Garden City, NY: Doubleday, 1973). A recent comprehensive treatment is found in Philip L. Quinn, *Divine Commands and Moral Requirements* (Oxford: Clarendon Press, 1978).

24. David Hume, *Dialogues*, pt. 10. (Hume obviously felt comfortable ascribing gender to the deity!)

25. See especially Lecture 18 ("Philosophy") and the "Postscript" to William James, *Varieties of Religious Experience*.

26. Alfred North Whitehead, *Process and Reality: An Essay in Cosmology* (New York: Macmillan, 1929), particularly pt. 5, ch. 2. A current delineation of a similar view is Charles Hartshorne, *Creative Synthesis and Philosophic Method* (London: SCM, 1970).

27. *Omniscience* (the quality of knowing everything that can be known) is often considered part of omnipotence, and I have followed this practice, but the practice can be questioned. For example, in human affairs, our power (that is, what we *could* do) often exceeds our wisdom (that is, our knowledge about what we are *well advised* to do). Moreover, our knowledge about a state of affairs often exceeds our power to bring it about. So, it in fact appears to make logical sense to separate power (agency) from knowledge, but this is a larger topic than we can pursue here.

28. One of the best known attempts to treat the problem this way is John Hick, *Evil and the God of Love*, rev. ed. (San Francisco: Harper and Row, 1978).

29. For a view in which (contrary to the position of this paragraph) reference to Satan plays a fundamental role in an answer to the problem of evil, see Alvin Plantinga, *God and Other Minds: A Study of the Rational Justification of Belief in God* (Ithaca: Cornell Univ. Press, 1967), 149–151.

30. I thank Leemon McHenry and Frederick Adams for the invitation to write this chapter, for careful readings of successive versions of it, and for many suggestions regarding its improvement. John Barker, John Danley, Ronald Glossop, Edwin Lawrence, and Clyde Nabe offered extensive and very helpful suggestions, for which I am deeply grateful. The chapter also owes much, as does the majority of my work, to the expert stenographic and editorial assistance of Donna Ireland.

■ QUESTIONS

1. Discuss the differences between faith, opinion, belief, and knowledge. Are there some areas of life in which it is appropriate to apply different standards of evidence and justification for our beliefs than we apply in most areas?

2. Compare these two descriptions of faith: "Faith is the assurance of things hoped for, the conviction of things not seen" (Hebrews 11:1, Revised Standard Version); and "Faith is when you believe something that you know ain't true" (William James, "The Will to Believe," *The Will to Believe and Other Essays in Popular Philosophy* [N. p.: Dover, 1956], 29).

3. Could there be a conclusive disproof of the existence of God? That is, can you imagine something that, if it were ever to happen, would convince you that God does not exist? If so, what would such an event be and why would it disprove God's existence? If not, what difference does the existence of God make in the world?

4. Suppose that you came to the conclusion that none of the arguments for the existence of God is valid. What influence should that conclusion have on your evaluation of the rationality of belief in God?

5. Under what circumstances would you be inclined to believe a friend's report of a religious experience? Under what circumstances would you use someone else's report of a religious experience as a basis for your own belief?

6. Try to defend, perhaps with the help of examples, St. Anselm's belief that it is a greater thing to exist in reality than to exist only in the imagination.

7. Could the universe have come about just as it is completely by accident? Why, or why not?

8. Do you think that someone could be justified in believing that an entire book, such as the Qu'rān, contains the inerrant word of the divine being? What would be a *rational* basis for this belief?

9. In what way(s) can someone be said to believe in another human being? Would a person's *belief in* his or her best friend be anything like his or her *belief in* God?

10. Do you think it is possible that any species of animal besides human beings believes in God? If so, what animal behaviors might be the manifestations of this belief? If not, what is necessary for belief in God that animals do not have?

11. Try to state in brief form what you think is the fate of the human being at death. Then examine the *bases* that you have for these beliefs. (One way of doing this is to ask yourself how you would try to make those beliefs credible to another human being.)

12. What solution to the problem of evil seems to you most convincing? Why? ∎

■ FOR FURTHER READING

Alston, William P. *Religious Belief and Philosophical Thought*. New York: Harcourt, Brace and World, 1963.

Collins, James. *The Emergence of Philosophy of Religion*. New Haven: Yale Univ. Press, 1967.

Edwards, Paul, ed. *The Encyclopedia of Philosophy*. 8 vols. New York: Macmillan, 1967.

Flew, Antony, and Alasdair MacIntyre, eds. *New Essays in Philosophical Theology*. New York: Macmillan, 1955.

Hick, John. *An Interpretation of Religion*. New Haven: Yale Univ. Press, 1989.

———, ed. *The Existence of God*. New York: Macmillan, 1964.

———. *Philosophy of Religion*. 3rd ed. Englewood Cliffs, NJ: Prentice-Hall, 1983.

James, William. *The Varieties of Religious Experience*. New York: Modern Library, 1902.

Noss, David S., and John B. Noss. *A History of the World's Religions*. 8th ed. New York: Macmillan, 1990.

Plantinga, Alvin, and Nicholas Wolterstorff, eds. *Faith and Rationality: Reason and Belief in God*. Notre Dame, IN: Univ. of Notre Dame Press, 1983.

Russell, Bertrand. *Why I Am Not a Christian and Other Essays on Religion and Related Subjects*. Ed. Paul Edwards. New York: Simon and Schuster, 1957.

Smart, Ninian. *The Philosophy of Religion*. New York: Random House, 1970.

———. *Reasons and Faiths: An Investigation of Religious Discourse, Christian and Non-Christian*. London: Routledge and Kegan Paul, 1958.

CHAPTER NINE

Personal Identity

GARY FULLER

■ INTRODUCTION

You and I are persons. We persist, or survive, over time. The problem of personal identity is mainly the problem of saying what it is for a person to persist, or survive. This is a problem of *identity* because it is natural to think that one and the same person is crucially involved in persistence, or survival. The boy who (supposedly) cut down the cherry tree was one and the same person as (was identical to) the first American president. The boy George Washington did not die young: He survived and became President Washington. For a person to survive is for there to be a person at a later time with whom he or she is identical. I used to fear flying. During turbulent flights, I would fear that the plane would crash and that I would not survive. My fear can be expressed in terms of personal identity: It was the fear that the next day there would be no person who was identical to me. Some of you may have hopes about life after death. Your hopes involve the notion of personal identity: You hope that after your death there will be a person, perhaps in a pleasant, heavenlike setting, who will be identical to you.

The problem of personal identity is to explain what personal identity involves. An adequate account, or theory, of personal identity will tell us, among other things, what is required, or necessary, for personal identity. It will tell us what is necessary for a person to survive over time. In order for me to survive, must my body survive? An account of personal identity will also tell us what is enough, or sufficient, for identity. Suppose that President Washington remembered cutting down the cherry tree as well as many other experiences connected to the cherry-tree incident. A good theory should be able to tell us whether Washington's having such memories is enough to guarantee that he was identical to the boy who chopped down the tree.

Before we try to come up with an adequate account of personal identity, we need to make a few preliminary clarifications. We need to distinguish between identity and similarity, to say something about the important role personal identity plays in our lives, and, finally, to make a few remarks about constructing and testing theories of personal identity.

First, it is important to stress that there is a difference between personal identity and personal similarity. To say that a person X is identical to a person Y is quite different from saying that X and Y are qualitatively similar, even to a very high degree. Washington the boy was identical to Washington the president— they were one and the same person—although they were dissimilar in many respects. The boy was shorter than, and much less worldly than, the man. Conversely, two *identical* twins can be qualitatively very similar, although they are not identical in our sense. If X is identical to Y, then there is just one person: If they are not identical, then there are two. The identity that we are interested in is, then, *numerical* identity and not similarity, or even exact similarity.

Consider the remark that you might make on running into an acquaintance after a number of years and being shocked by the changes in her physical appearance and personality: "Greta is not the same person that she was." Here, of course, you do not mean, paradoxically, that Greta is not identical to Greta, or, perhaps less paradoxically, that the person whom you knew, namely Greta, has died and no longer exists. Rather, what you mean is that Greta has survived but is now very dissimilar in many respects to what she was when you knew her. The person whom you knew is one and the same person as the person you just ran into, but she has undergone great changes in personality.

Second, the problem of personal identity is not merely an academic problem. Personal identity plays an important role in our lives. There is, to begin with, an obvious connection between personal identity and that special concern that we have about *our* future. You have good reason to believe that a terrorist group is going to kidnap and torture an innocent person in the near future. You feel sympathy and some pity for the victim. Suddenly, you discover that the victim is going to be you! Your whole attitude changes drastically.[1] True, you may be an altruistic person, so your initial concern, sympathy, and even identification with the supposed victim may have been deep and genuine. Still, there seems to be a big difference between even the most altruistic concern for others and your own special concern for yourself.

Personal identity is connected to our special concern about our future and, hence, to our hopes and fears about an afterlife. It is also deeply connected to our moral attitudes regarding punishment, commitment, fairness, and so on. Think of our attitudes about punishing a person for a crime. Suppose that yesterday a person stole Bob's valued 1971 Buick. Should Leemon be punished today for the crime? Only if Leemon is identical to the real thief. Or again, think of our attitudes about fairness. It may be morally permissible to make a certain person suffer now for that very person's own future benefit (for the benefit of a future person identical to him), but it is unfair and wrong to make a person suffer solely for *another* person's future benefit.[2]

Third, we need to say something about constructing and testing a theory of personal identity. A theory of personal identity can be more or less ambitious. It can try to provide only necessary conditions, or only sufficient conditions, or, ideally, conditions that are both necessary as well as sufficient. A theory of personal identity that attempts to provide necessary conditions, for example, will have the following form:

X = (is identical to) Y only if X _____ Y.

X is a person picked out at an earlier time, Y a person picked out at a later time, and the blank space is to be filled in with an appropriate relational term, for example, *has the same body as*. A theory that attempts to provide sufficient conditions will have the form:

X = Y if X _____ Y.

Finally, a theory that attempts to provide both necessary and sufficient conditions will have the form:

X = Y if and only if X _____ Y.

When we talk about conditions for personal identity, we mean conditions that hold not simply in all actual cases but in all possible cases. Suppose that you hold that having the same body is a necessary condition for personal identity. Now, it may well be that there never has been a case of body switching, for example, your waking up one morning and finding that you have a completely different body. Your theory, however, makes a much stronger claim than that. It claims that there never *could* be such a case. If I can show that there could be such a case, then, I will have shown that your theory is false.

How do we think up a good theory, or even a tentative theory, of personal identity? In other words, how do we discover what to put in the blank in "X _____ Y"? Here a certain amount of creativity is needed, but a good way to start is by looking at typical cases. Among other things, in typical cases of personal identity there is bodily identity as well as brain identity, and even though there are many physical and psychological changes, these changes take place gradually.

In thinking up a theory, two dangers need to be avoided: obscurity and circularity. The terms in our theory must be clear and must be defined without appealing back (around in a circle) to the idea of personal identity. Later in this chapter, we shall explore the *soul theory* of personal identity. If such a theory is even to get off the ground, however, it must avoid our two dangers: the term *soul* must be made clear and must not just be a synonym for *person*.

Of course, it is not enough for a theory of personal identity to be well formulated, clear, and noncircular: We want it to be true. How do we find out whether it is true, or at least reasonable to believe? We do so by submitting it to various tests. An especially important kind of test is that of hunting for counterexamples. If we find no counterexamples, this provides some reason for thinking that the theory is true; if we do find a counterexample, then this shows that the theory is false and needs either to be revised in such a way that it can accommodate the counterexample, or, in extreme cases, be abandoned altogether.

We are now in a position to examine and think through various theories of personal identity. In the following section, we shall look at three theories: the *body theory*, the *psychological continuity theory*, and the *brain theory*. In the third section, we shall consider the *soul theory*. Finally, in the last section, we shall relate the issue of personal identity to other issues about persons.

■ BODY, PSYCHOLOGICAL CONTINUITY, AND BRAIN THEORIES

■ *The Body Theory*

An initially plausible theory of personal identity is the *body theory*. According to this theory, personal identity is explained in terms of the identity of the person's body as follows:

$X = Y$ if and only if X's body $= Y$'s body.

What makes Ronald Reagan identical to the Hollywood actor who starred in *Bedtime for Bonzo* is that the actor's body is identical to Reagan's.

Let us try to make the body theory somewhat clearer. Two points need to be made. First, the body theory does not restrict itself to human bodies. Of course, according to the body theory the identity of you, me, and Reagan will be explained in terms of persisting human bodies; but E.T.'s identity will be explained in terms of his extraterrestrial body, and, if there could be robots that are persons, their identity would be explained in terms of the persistence of their inorganic bodies. Second, bodily identity can tolerate many changes, including loss or replacement of at least some parts. If I lose an arm or leg, or have a heart transplant, my body does not go out of existence; similarly, if my brain is replaced by the brain of someone else, my body also remains in existence—it has simply acquired a new brain.

Does the body theory give us a true account of personal identity? It certainly seems initially plausible, for in just about every actual case body identity and personal identity go together. Remember, however, that the theory is supposed to apply to all possible, as well as actual, cases. Can we think up any possible cases that are counterexamples to the body theory? Unfortunately, at least for the body theory, we can. One example will show that bodily identity is neither necessary nor sufficient for personal identity. Here is the example. I go to bed tonight and wake up tomorrow morning, not with my body, but with the body of Ronald Reagan. I am amazed. I get up and look in the mirror: What is reflected is not my old familiar face, but Reagan's face. I weigh myself: The scale registers not my old weight, but Reagan's weight.

Surely, this example is possible. I can easily imagine such a thing occurring. And if it is possible, then the body theory fails. Bodily identity is not necessary for personal identity because in the example I survive, although my body is replaced by Reagan's. Nor is bodily identity sufficient, because Reagan's body was formerly associated with Reagan, but now it is associated with me.

Someone might question whether the imagined example really *is* possible. Sometimes what initially seems possible turns out to be impossible when we try to fill in details. Can we fill in the details in a consistent way in the example? Is the body that I end up with really the body of former president Reagan? If so, how did I end up with it? For that matter, what happened to my original body and what happened to Reagan himself? Luckily, there is a consistent story that we can tell that answers these questions. What has happened is that during the night my brain and Reagan's brain have been switched, Reagan's brain ending up in my body, my brain in Reagan's body.[3] (We can imagine that the doctors who performed the operation used incredibly advanced surgical and postsurgical procedures.) Because it is the brain of a person that supports the person's mental life—his or her beliefs, memories, personality, and so on—it seems plausible to think that persons go where their brains go, and that I end up in Reagan's original body and he in my old body. What has happened, then, is best described as two persons switching bodies rather than brains. The original example of my waking up with Reagan's body is thus quite possible, and, consequently, the body theory really does fail.

The body theory of personal identity has failed. The brain switching example used to refute the body theory, however, suggests an alternative theory—the brain theory. According to this theory, a person survives if and only if his or her brain survives.

The brain theory looks promising, but we need to ask why it seems promising. Surely, this is because there is (or at least it is widely assumed that there is) an especially close association between a person's mental, or psychological, life and what goes on in his or her brain. Before turning to the brain theory, then, it will be worthwhile to consider a theory that brings in a person's psychological life in a more explicit way: the psychological continuity theory.

■ The Psychological Continuity Theory

According to the *psychological continuity theory*, personal identity is explained in terms of psychological continuity as follows:

X = Y if and only if X and Y are psychologically continuous.

The idea of psychological continuity requires some elucidation. We can proceed in two stages. First, we introduce the idea of psychological *connectedness*, and then, we explain psychological *continuity* between X and Y in terms of a chain of appropriate psychological connections between them.

Consider what was going on in my life yesterday. I was in a number of psychological states and had many psychological characteristics: I had various beliefs, desires, emotions, memories,[4] mental skills, and capacities. States and characteristics of these types tend to persist or evolve over time in familiar ways. Yesterday, I was listening to Mozart's D-Minor Piano Concerto; today, I remember listening to the concerto. Yesterday, I believed that no human has lived past the age of 150; today I will continue to believe it unless I am presented with strong evidence to the contrary. Yesterday, I could do arithmetic, understand and speak English, and play the piano; today, I am also able to do these things. Notice that there is a causal connection between my states and abilities of yesterday and those of today. If yesterday I had not been listening to the concerto, I would not have remembered doing so today. If I had not had the ability to play the piano yesterday, then I would not have that ability today.

The person I was yesterday and the person of today are psychologically connected. More generally, X and Y are psychologically connected if and only if one or more of Y's psychological states (abilities, and so on) have evolved out of X's psychological states in the familiar way illustrated above. Further, we can talk about degrees of psychological connectedness. The degree of psychological connectedness will be determined by the number of psychological connections and perhaps by their type as well—experiential memory may count as more important than the retention of certain skills. I am psychologically connected to the person I was yesterday to a very high degree: I have retained most of the beliefs, memories, and skills that I had yesterday. I am also psychologically connected to the six-year-old me, but to a much lesser degree: Among other things, I remember very few of my experiences back then, and my emotional patterns have changed greatly. There might have been no psychological connectedness at all between the nine-hundred-year-old Methuselah and his six-year-old self!

We are now in a position to explain psychological continuity: X and Y are psychologically continuous if and only if there is a chain of psychological connections of a suitably high degree between them (included here as a chain will be the simplest chain, namely, that of one link). Here there are two new ideas. First, there is the idea of a suitably high degree of psychological connectedness—of enough connectedness. The degree of psychological connectedness of me today with the person I was yesterday is easily high enough; indeed, it is far over the threshold. That of me today with my six-year-old self is probably too low. To be sure, the idea of a suitably high degree of psychological connectedness is somewhat vague—there will be cases where it is unclear whether or not there is enough connectedness. Second, there is the idea of a chain of suitable psychological connections. The old Methuselah may have had no psychological connection with his younger self, but there probably was a chain of suitable psychological connections linking them: The 900 year old was suitably linked to the 899 year old, the 899 year old to the 898 year old, and so on.

The psychological continuity theory of personal identity, to repeat, is that:

X = Y if and only if X and Y are psychologically continuous.

We are now in a position to evaluate the theory. Is the theory a good one? What are its strengths and weaknesses?

One of its strengths is that it gives the right answer about what happens in the brain-switching—or, much better, body-switching—example. That example was the downfall of the body theory. The psychological continuity theory implies that the person who ends up in Reagan's body is identical to me, because he is psychologically continuous—because he is psychologically connected to a high degree—with me. This implication squares well with our intuitive judgments.

Are there weaknesses with the psychological continuity theory? Amnesia seems to present a problem. It seems to provide a counterexample to the theory's claim that psychological continuity is necessary for personal identity.

The American philosopher William James describes the case of the Reverend Ansel Bourne, a preacher living in Rhode Island, who in 1887 suddenly moved all the way to Pennsylvania where he set up a shop under the name of Brown.[5] For two months, he could not remember anything about his earlier life as a preacher. Then, again suddenly, he recovered his "identity" as Bourne the clergyman, only to become amnesiac with respect to Brown's life. This example seems to present a counterexample to the claim that psychological continuity is necessary for personal identity, for although there was a sharp break in psychological continuity, most of us would agree that Bourne did not cease to exist: We would agree that he became Brown, that Brown was numerically identical to him.

Further reflection shows that this example is not a genuine counterexample. Psychological continuity requires that Bourne just before the attack of amnesia and Brown just afterwards should be psychologically connected to a suitably high degree. It is true that the two were connected to a lesser degree than normal: Brown, for example, did not have experiential memories of Bourne—of living in Rhode Island, of preaching on such and such a day, and so on. Nevertheless, we can assume that he retained a great number of other psychological features of Bourne, for example: psychological abilities, such as the abilities to speak English, do arithmetic, read a map, and start a business; and general knowledge of various sorts, for example, knowledge about politics or geography.[6] The psychological connectedness between the two was lower than normal, but still high enough to be counted as psychological continuity.

The Bourne case, as well as many other examples of actual amnesia, then, presents little threat to the psychological continuity theory. What about cases that do not occur, but are at least possible? Can we find counterexamples among them? Philosophers have concocted cases of total amnesia in which, perhaps as a result of extreme shock treatment, what are obliterated are not only all of a person's memories in the ordinary sense, but also all psychological features that are the result of learning and experience over the years. We can assume that what remains is an individual with the mentality of something like that of an infant—although, of course, the brain will be more developed.[7]

Is total amnesia a genuine counterexample to the psychological continuity theory? There are three possible reactions to such cases. First, one could hold that the original person does not survive and that this is precisely because all, or at least most, psychological continuity is indeed broken. Second, one could hold that the original person does survive, but, again, that this is because there really is much more psychological continuity than meets the eye. Such a person might be impressed that the individual after the shock treatment does have, just as an infant has, many innate psychological capacities—capacities for consciousness, for learning language, for primitive reasoning of various sorts—and that these capacities are continuous with the innate capacities of the original person. Finally, one might hold that there is no psychological continuity, but that the original person still does survive. Total amnesia would be a counterexample to the psychological continuity theory only if this third reaction were plausible. It does not seem plausible. If there really is no psychological continuity at all, how can there be survival? The other two reactions, or perhaps a hesitation between the two, seem much more plausible.

Total amnesia, then, does not undermine the psychological continuity theory. It does show, however, that our idea of personal identity is somewhat vague—total amnesia seems to be a borderline case—and, hence, that the idea of psychological continuity needed to explain it may also be somewhat vague.

Psychological continuity seems plausible as a necessary condition of personal identity. Is it also plausible as a sufficient condition? In other words, does the existence of psychological continuity guarantee personal identity? Here the theory has to confront examples of teleportation.

Mr. Spock is beamed down from the spaceship *Enterprise* to the nearby planet. What happens, we can suppose, is this. Spock enters the teleportation machine, which takes a detailed blueprint of the precise states and configurations of all of his molecules and at the same time completely vaporizes his brain and body. The blueprint is then beamed by radio to a replicator machine down on the planet. The replicator makes use of the blueprint to construct out of new molecules (similar but nonidentical molecules) a body and brain just like Spock's.[8] The new Spock is of course psychologically similar to the old. Moreover, the new Spock is psychologically continuous with the old Spock: The old Spock's psychological features cause the new Spock to have similar features. (Notice that psychological continuity does not require temporal continuity. There may well be a temporal gap between the old Spock and the new Spock—a time during which no person exists—but psychological continuity can pass over such a gap, as it does here.)

Is the new Spock numerically identical to the old, or just an exactly similar, but nonidentical, replica of the old? If you were confident that the teleporter always functioned perfectly, would you be willing to be beamed down? Or, do you think that teleportation is tantamount to death? If it was clear to everyone, at least on reflection, that Spock does not survive—that identity is not preserved—then this example would be a counterexample to the psychological continuity theory as giving a sufficient condition for personal identity. Unfortunately, most people probably do not feel confident about what to say about Spock here. (The assumption common to the creators of and characters in *Star Trek* that Spock does survive may complicate our reactions here and make it difficult to come up with a confident verdict.)

Altering a number of nonessential features of the Spock example, however, does enable us to come up with a more decisive counterexample. This time it is you who is going to be "transported" from the spaceship to the planet below. As before, a complete blueprint is taken just before you are "destroyed," but this time destruction involves not the vaporization of brain and body but simply your being shot through the head ("death" will be instantaneous, so you will not feel a thing). Another difference is that this time the transportation process is somewhat slower. The blueprint is not beamed down to the planet; rather it is stored on disc, which in turn is filed away in the *Enterprise*. After a few weeks, the *Enterprise* lands on the planet, the disc is carried over to and inserted in the replicator, and the new you is created. Here, surely, our reactions are much more confident: You do not survive. This second example, then, shows that the psychological continuity theory, as it stands, fails as a sufficient condition of personal identity. Further, because it is relevantly similar to the Spock example, it provides support for a verdict of no survival there as well.

We need not, however, abandon the psychological continuity theory. We can try to modify it in such a way that it will rule out teleportation cases (and variations of such cases). Psychological continuity requires causation, or chains of causation, between earlier and later psychological states. The trouble is that it requires nothing more specific than that. There is causation between my listening to the concerto yesterday and my remembering listening to it today. There is also a causal connection between old Spock's experiences on the *Enterprise* and new Spock's "memories" of these experiences (these "memories" are of course not genuine memories, for that would require that new Spock is identical to old Spock—which we have decided he is not). Our modified psychological continuity theory needs to restrict causation in such a way as to rule out teleportation.

How should we restrict it? In normal cases, psychological continuity occurs when causation stays within the body, indeed the brain, of the person. My experience of listening to the concerto yesterday caused my remembering the experience today by way of a causal process that probably involved a memory trace, a persisting neural structure, within the brain. On the other hand, the psychological continuity in teleportation proceeds outside of the body and brain via the blueprint.

A modified psychological continuity theory is going to have to involve within-brain causation, and not merely causation within the body. Psychological continuity with causation within the body is not sufficient for personal identity. An extreme variation on the *Star Trek* process shows that. This time there is a device inserted in my body, say in my arm, which performs three tasks: It takes a detailed blueprint of my brain; at the same time, it vaporizes my brain, without harming the rest of my body; and finally, after a certain time, it uses the blueprint to construct out of spare cells in my head and neck a new brain relevantly similar to the original one. The whole process occurs within my body. Surely, however, if I do not survive the original *Star Trek* process, then I do not survive this inside-the-body process. Our modified account, then, will bring in the brain and will look like this:

X = Y if and only if X and Y are psychologically continuous via within-brain causation.

This looks like a pretty good theory. It gives the right answer to the examples we have discussed so far. Another good consequence of the theory involves examples of memory, or better, "memory transfer." Philosophers and science-fiction writers have imagined cases in which your and my memories are somehow peeled off our respective brains and switched: Your memories are stuck on my brain in the appropriate places, and vice versa. The details of the transfer are usually obscure, but what is clear is that the process involves a causal story that goes outside of the brain, indeed outside of either brain. Our modified theory, then, will rule out saying that I end with your brain and body and vice versa. This consequence seems intuitively satisfying.

There is one last hurdle that our theory must surmount. This is the problem of splitting.[9] Suppose that person A divides into persons B and C. We can actually imagine such a case without being too unrealistic. Apparently, a person can survive quite well with only one of the hemispheres of his or her brain, and so the following seems possible: A's brain is removed from her body, divided into two, and each hemisphere is rehoused in a new (brainless) body. We start with A, then, and end up with B and C, each functioning perfectly well with just one hemisphere. To make things easier, let us suppose that the two hemispheres are very similar to each other, so that B and C each end up with all the "memories," psychological abilities, character traits, and so on, of A.

In this example, B will be psychologically continuous via brain causation with A and so will C. Indeed, B will be confident that she is A and so will C. The modified psychological continuity theory will imply that this is so: that $A = B$ and that $A = C$. But that *cannot* be so! If Fred is identical to Colleen's father and also identical to that red-haired man in front of me, then Colleen's father is identical to the red-haired man. Similarly, if $A = B$ and $A = C$ then it must be that $B = C$. It is clear, however, that it is false that $B = C$: B and C are two different persons—if a bee stings B, C will not feel any pain, and if someone kills B, C will still survive. Our theory, then, implies something false and will have to be modified one more time.

The way to modify the theory is simply to insert a clause that prohibits the branching of paths of psychological continuity. Our final psychological continuity theory, then, looks like this:

> $X = Y$ if and only if X and Y are psychologically continuous via within-brain causation, and there is no branching—(roughly) there is no person Z who is psychologically continuous with X but not with Y.[10]

■ The Brain Theory

Let us at long last go back to the brain theory. The *brain theory* asserts that

> $X = Y$ if and only if X's brain $=$ Y's brain.

Here, as in the body theory, what counts as a brain will include not only human brains but human-brain analogues, like E.T.'s brain and robot "brains."

The brain theory appears much simpler than the psychological continuity theory (in its final version), and so we need to know why we should not prefer it to the psychological continuity theory.

The brain theory and the psychological continuity theory are really very close to each other. Indeed, both theories require brain persistence as a necessary condition of personal identity. It would be nice if we could just accept the brain theory outright. Unfortunately, it has one drawback that the psychological continuity theory does not have: It seems to permit survival in the case of brain scrambling.

Suppose that as a result of a powerful electric field, the insides of your brain are completely scrambled—all the connections between neurons are broken, and all persistence of neural structures disrupted. As a result, all psychological capacities are lost, including even the capacity for some kind of minimal consciousness. Suppose also that later, this time perhaps as the result of another completely coincidental electrical field, the neurons are reconnected completely differently, but still in such a way as to support psychological life.[11] Notice that this case is much more extreme than even the case of total amnesia: Here, all psychological continuity is broken.

It seems clear on reflection that you would not survive such a brain scrambling. Even if the reconnected individual turned out to have many psychological similarities to you, he or she still would not be you—even less so than in teleportation cases—for here there is no causation at all between your psychological states before the scramble and those of the reconnected individual.

Your brain, however, does survive the scrambling: It stays alive throughout the whole process. According to the brain theory, then, you do survive. The brain theory gives the wrong verdict here, and so comes off worse than the psychological continuity theory.

■ THE SOUL THEORY

We have ignored one of the most widely believed theories of personal identity— the *soul theory*. According to this theory, persons have, indeed they must have, souls, and personal identity is explained in terms of soul identity as follows:

$X = Y$ if and only if X's soul $= Y$'s soul.

If we are going to continue to hold the psychological continuity theory, then we need to show that the soul theory is not a serious competitor.

Persons, unlike unicorns, really do exist and persist over time. This is an assumption that we have been making, and will not question, in this chapter. It follows that if the soul theory is correct, there really are such things as souls that exist and persist over time. Rather than ask directly whether the theory is true or whether there are counterexamples to it, we shall ask the easier question of whether there are such things as souls. If it turns out that souls do not exist, or at least that there is no good reason for thinking that they do, that will of course mean that we should reject the soul theory.

To find out whether or not there are souls, we need to understand what souls are supposed to be. We need to clarify the idea of a soul, which admittedly is pretty unclear. Not surprisingly, the soul is generally associated with the soul theory of personal identity. Think of the role that the soul plays in many religions. According to some versions of Christianity, it is the soul that survives death and, after a period of disembodiment, goes to heaven where it acquires a glorified, or transformed, body. In some Eastern religions, the soul is reincarnated in a series of different human (and perhaps nonhuman) bodies. In all of these cases, survival of the soul means survival of the person.[12]

In addition, most people would agree on the following two general features of souls. First, souls must have psychological features—they must have beliefs, desires, intentions, and so on. Second, they must be nonphysical: They can exist separately from body and brain, and, hence, are not identical to either. A third feature, more closely associated with philosophical than with popular conceptions, is that of simplicity. Souls are simple: They cannot be divided into parts, and so cannot be split into two souls in the way that an amoeba can divide into two amoebas.

Let us look at the last two features in more detail. Souls are supposed to be nonphysical, but what exactly does this mean? An extreme view, often associated with the French philosopher René Descartes,[13] is that this means that souls have no spatial features at all. Not only do they lack solidity, like ghosts, and size and shape, like the North Pole or the Equator, but they also fail to have spatial *position*; strictly speaking, it makes no sense to ask where a particular soul is located. The trouble with this conception of the soul as something nonphysical is that we can hardly understand what is meant by it. Suppose you are told that there is a heaven populated by souls, but that this heaven and its inhabitants are completely nonspatial. Can you really understand what you are being told? Do you not have to think of this heaven as a spatially extended area and of its souls as occupying positions within the area?

A more intelligible conception of the soul as nonphysical is that souls do have spatial features—position as well as size and shape—but they are made up of stuff that physicists have not as yet discovered. The picture here is that of the soul as a kind of second brain in our heads, made out of mysterious, but still very spatial, "soul" stuff.[14]

Souls are also supposed to be simple: They cannot be divided into further parts. This means that one soul cannot divide, or be divided, into two souls like an amoeba or, say, a long garden hose. This has consequences for the splitting example introduced earlier. Remember that we started off with A and ended up with B and C, each with half of A's brain. According to the psychological continuity theory, identity cannot be preserved here. There is a branching of psychological continuity that had to be ruled out by the final version of that theory. On the soul theory, however, identity can be preserved. It can turn out that A is identical to just one of the offshoots, say to B: for A to be identical to B, rather than C, is for A's unsplittable soul to be transferred to B.

The simplicity of souls can also mean that souls and soul identity have no borderline cases. Either there is a soul here or there is not; either this soul is identical to that soul or it is not. Contrast souls with tables. Someone has decided to use your favorite antique table for firewood. What is left is a badly burned chunk of it. Is what is left a table or not? There may be no definite answer. Later, using the chunk plus a lot of new lumber, you build a "new" table that looks quite similar to the old. Is the new table identical to the old? Again, there may be no definite answer. In the case of souls, there is always a definite answer.

The picture of the soul that is emerging is that of a kind of second brain that has or supports psychological states, is made of spatial soul stuff, and is somehow unsplittable into parts. Notice that an important consequence of this picture is that the scientific view of the brain (the actual brain) as the sole supporter of psychological states and psychological continuity must be wrong. According to the soul theory, much of my mental life, indeed the essential features of my mental life, are explained by appeal to my soul; my brain, on this account, plays a secondary role.

Are there good reasons for believing that there are souls? There could be.[15] Suppose that we found that many persons seemed to remember in detail experiences of persons who existed centuries ago, and that later on historians came across completely new evidence that confirmed that there were such persons and that they had such experiences. Further, suppose that we could find no physical explanation of all these "memories." Then we would have some reason for postulating something nonphysical, like a soul, to explain them. Again, suppose that we found that psychological changes in people occurred in such a way that there were never any borderline cases of personal identity. For example, suppose that no amnesia cases were ever like Bourne's—where there was a medium amount of psychological continuity—but all involved either just a very small psychological change, a small memory loss for example, or a radical psychological change involving all psychological states and characteristics. If that were so, then it would give us some reason for postulating something simple, again like a soul. Finally, discovering that large areas of a person's brain could be damaged with little effect on his or her mental life would certainly provide further reason in favor of the existence of the soul.

Unfortunately, at least for those who would like to believe in souls, we have no such evidence.

Surely, however, there must be reasons in favor of souls, for otherwise why would anyone believe in them? Indeed, there are reasons, but they are not good reasons. Some people believe in souls because this provides them with hope for an afterlife. Unlike most of the theories we have mentioned or discussed, the soul theory does make an afterlife possible; many people would like there to be an afterlife, and so they would like the soul theory to be true. Merely wanting something to be true, however, does not provide a good reason for its being true.

Philosophers have suggested, and often been seduced by, nonempirical reasons for souls and the soul theory. These arguments rely on such things as the special features of the word *I*, imaginings of situations from the first-person point of view, and our supposedly special knowledge about ourselves and our identity. These arguments are often intriguing, but it is questionable whether any of them are sound.

Here is one example of such an argument. I can know certain facts about myself and my identity—for example, that I now exist and that I was experiencing anxiety a few moments ago (and, hence, that I am identical to the anxious person)—without knowing anything about my body, brain, or any other physical thing. This premise seems true. If I had been knocked out in a bad car accident and was just recovering consciousness, I might well wonder whether I still had a body or brain but *know* that I existed and that I was feeling anxious a short moment before. The conclusion of the argument is that my existence and my identity do not depend on any facts about my brain or my body (or any other physical object), and so that I must be a soul.

The argument is seductive but invalid. It depends on the general claim that if one can know that p without knowing that q then the fact that p is not dependent on the fact that q. It is easy to think of a clear counterexample to this general claim. A child can know that there is water in front of her without knowing that there is H_2O in front of her (she will not know about H_2O until she studies some science), but the two facts are clearly dependent.

■ **FURTHER QUESTIONS**

We have been concentrating on personal identity, on what it is for a person to persist over time. There are, however, other questions about persons that are related to a greater or lesser extent to that of personal identity. Becoming aware of these questions, and of possible answers to them, should help deepen our understanding of personal identity. In this concluding section, then, we shall list and briefly discuss some of these questions.

Here is a list of questions which philosophers ask about persons.

1. What is it to be a person?
2. What is it for a person to persist over time?
3. What is it for there to be one, rather than two (or more) persons at a certain place at a certain time?
4. Where are persons located?
5. Are there different concepts, or ideas, of personhood?

What follows are brief discussions of each of these questions.

1. "What is it to be a person?" You and I are persons, but can the same be said about the insane or the mentally impaired, or even about normal infants? Could computers ever be persons? What about families, business corporations, or nations? We want to know what are the features, or conditions, that are central to being a person (to personhood).

Compare persons with nonhuman animals. Many people think that dogs, cats, and even apes are not persons. What is the difference between them and us? Animals, like us, have desires, beliefs, and intentions, and so have, or are, *minds*; but something more is needed. One plausible suggestion is that persons must have, or be capable of having, higher-order psychological states—states *about* psychological states.[16] My cat, K.K., can want to eat her food, but she cannot want to want, or to want to stop wanting, to eat her food. I can. I want to lose weight and therefore want to stop having my present strong desire to eat the sundae in front of me. Higher-order states are connected to the ability to choose and act *morally*, to being a moral agent. To make a moral decision, I must be able to think about and evaluate the desires of others as well as my own.

2. "What is it for a person to persist over time?" This, of course, is just our main question about personal identity, and we answered it by appealing to psychological continuity.

What is important to notice here is that there is a connection between questions 1 and 2. Question 1 is about the essential conditions for personhood. Question 2 is about persistence conditions for persons. What counts as persistence for persons, however, may depend on what one takes to be the essential features of personhood. Suppose that you reject the suggestion above that persons must have higher-order states; for you, persons are just *minds*. Then you will certainly hold that continuity of higher-order states or capacities is *not* necessary for personal identity. On the other hand, if you sympathize with the suggestion, you will probably hold that such continuity *is* necessary. Suppose that Al is in a horrible accident as a result of which he loses all higher-order capacities: He now has the condition of an impaired individual. Then, if you think that higher-order capacities are necessary for being a person, you may claim that the *person* Al ceased to exist as a result of the accident. On the other hand, if you think that persons are just *minds*, then you will hold that Al survives.

3. "What is it for there to be one, rather than two (or more) persons at a certain place at a certain time?" This usually becomes the question of how many persons inhabit a single body at a certain time. This time we do not have to turn to fiction, or science fiction, for an illustration; science gives us the example of brain bisection.

The two hemispheres of the brain divide their labor with respect to many functions. For the most part, the functions of each hemisphere are associated with the opposite side of the body. For example, the left hemisphere receives visual input from the right side of the visual field and controls the right arm. One of the most important "communicative" channels between the hemispheres is the band of fibers known as the *corpus callosum*. In brain-bisected subjects, these fibers are severed. In normal everyday circumstances, these subjects show little behavioral change; under special experimental conditions, however, they exhibit somewhat odd behavior.[17]

Here is an example of such behavior. The subject is placed in front of a screen. The words *key ring* are flashed on the screen quickly enough so that the subject's left hemisphere receives *ring* alone and the right hemisphere receives *key*. The subject is then asked to search through a group of objects which are hidden from view, and to pick out with both hands what he or she saw. The left hand will select a key, the right hand a ring![18]

It seems plausible to say that someone saw *key* and that someone saw *ring*, but that no one saw *key ring*.[19] Does this mean that we should say that there are really two persons existing in the subject's body, or would it be more reasonable to say that there is just one person there, but with a divided consciousness?

4. "Where are persons located?" This looks easy: Persons are located where their brains and bodies are located. My brain and body are here in this room, so I am in this room. Suppose, however, that we pry apart my brain from my body. We put my brainless body in the Swiss Alps and hook it up to my brain (in a vat) here in Michigan via radio transmission. If you ask me where I am, and to do so you will have to travel to Switzerland (where my ears and mouth are), I, of course, will say that I am in Switzerland. On the other hand, if you try to kill me and successfully push me off a mountain precipice, I will almost instantaneously travel back to Michigan where I will survive indefinitely in my vat.[20]

5. "Are there different concepts, or ideas, of personhood and of personal identity (or persistence)?" This question opens up fascinating territory about which we can make only a few brief comments and raise yet further questions.

There are concepts more or less similar to our concepts of a person and of personal identity. We have already suggested that there might be a distinction between *person* and *mind*. Others have argued that we can pry apart and distinguish *personal identity* from *personal survival*.[21] According to this view, there is a sense of survival that does not require identity. Consider again the example in which person A divides into B and C. If we describe this example in terms of identity, then we must say that A ceases to exist. A can be identical to neither B nor C, because identity does not tolerate branching. If, however, we describe the example in terms of *survival* (in the new sense), then A survives as both B and C. Personal survival here is simply psychological continuity (via within-brain causation, of course) minus the stricture against branching. Personal survival is important, it is also argued, because it is reasonable to extend our special concern about the future to our *survivors* (again in the new sense). According to this view, if A knows that either B or C, or both of them, is going to be tortured after the division, then A should indeed worry about being tortured rather than treat the splitting operation as tantamount to death.

Social scientists have employed the somewhat vague notions of self-concept, of social role, and indeed of "*identity*."[22] These concepts, however, are different from our concepts of personhood and of personal identity. When a psychologist, for example, tries to characterize a person's "identity," he or she will most likely mention significant beliefs of the person about what he or she is and what he or she ought to do and be. An opera singer's identity in this sense might be closely connected to his or her beliefs that he or she has great musical and vocal talent, and that music, and especially opera, is a very valuable human activity that ought to be seriously pursued. It is clearly possible, however, for the opera singer to cease to hold these beliefs, and thereby to lose or change his or her "identity," without ceasing to be a person or to exist.

Our concepts of a person and of personal identity are different from the social scientist's concepts of social role, "identity," and so on. Perhaps things could be different. Perhaps they are different in some cultures. It has been suggested, for example, that the people of the Indonesian island of Bali have a concept of personhood that is much more closely connected to *social role* than is ours.[23] This suggestion is intriguing, but there is a problem. The problem is that it is not very clear what the suggestion means. If it means that the Balinese think of change in social role as the death of one person and the birth of a new one, then (at least at first glance) that would seem extraordinary!

Finally, our concepts of a person and of personal identity are closely tied to our commonsensical notions of desire, belief, intention, and so on. Perhaps psychologists and other cognitive scientists will refine these folk-psychological notions into more scientific ones. This may lead to the development of a more *scientific concept of personhood* and of personal identity.[24]

As we saw early on, our concepts of personhood and of personal identity—and this means our *ordinary* concepts—play an important role in our lives. They are bound up with our attitudes and concerns about our own future, about punishment, and about fair treatment. If there really are many different concepts of personhood and of personal identity, then this raises the question of whether one of them, or some of them, are *better* in some sense, or for some purposes, than others. It raises the question of whether, and if so on what grounds, we should revise or change our ordinary concepts of a person and of personal identity.[25]

■ NOTES

1. See John Perry, "The Importance of Being Identical," *The Identities of Persons*, ed. Amélie Rorty (Berkeley: Univ. of California Press, 1976), 67.

2. See Derek Parfit, *Reasons and Persons* (Oxford: Clarendon Press, 1984), 333.

3. Sydney Shoemaker introduced this type of example to contemporary philosophers in *Self-Knowledge and Self-Identity* (Ithaca: Cornell Univ. Press, 1963), 22–25.

4. Historically, the psychological continuity theory is an ancestor of John Locke's memory theory. See John Locke, *An Essay concerning Human Understanding*, vol. 1 (New York: Dover, 1959), 439–70. In recent times, psychological continuity theories have been articulated by a number of philosophers, including: Paul Grice, "Personal Identity," *Personal Identity*, ed. John Perry (Berkeley: California Univ. Press, 1975); John Perry "The Problem of Personal Identity," *Personal Identity*; David Lewis, "Survival and Identity," *The Identities of Persons*, ed. Amélie Rorty (Berkeley: Univ. of California Press, 1976); and Sydney Shoemaker, "Personal Identity: A Materialist's Account," *Personal Identity*, eds. Sydney Shoemaker and Richard Swinburne (Oxford: Basil Blackwell, 1984).

5. See William James, *Principles of Psychology*, vol. 1 (London: Macmillan, 1891). 391–93. I owe this citation, as well as much of my discussion of the Bourne example, to Kathleen Wilkes, who deals with the example in some detail in *Real People* (Oxford: Clarendon Press, 1988), 103–106.

6. See Wilkes, *Real People*, 104–105.

7. The case of total amnesia is taken from Sydney Shoemaker, "Personal Identity," 86–88.

8. This description of teleportation is essentially from Parfit, *Reasons and Persons*, 199. See also pp. 199–306 and 474–77 for detailed discusssion of teleportation and related cases. Parfit should not be held responsible for any views about how the beaming-down process is supposed to work in *Star Trek* (he does not mention the well-known science-fiction series); indeed, *Star Trek* fans will probably claim that Spock's atoms, and not simply his blueprint, are beamed down. I shall stick to the "mere blueprint" version, however, because it provides a better example for philosophical purposes.

9. David Wiggins was one of the first of recent philosophers to discuss splitting cases. See David Wiggins, *Identity and Spatio-Temporal Continuity* (Oxford: Basil Blackwell, 1967), 50.

10. Some philosophers think that the prohibition on splitting here is too *ad hoc*. See, for example, John Perry, A *Dialogue on Personal Identity and Immortality* (Indianapolis: Hackett, 1979).

11. This example is due to Michael Lockwood. See his discussion remarks in Arthur Peacocke and Grant Gillett, eds. *Persons and Personalities* (Oxford: Basil Blackwell, 1987), 94–96.

12. See Martin Gardner, "Immortality: Why I Do Not Think It Impossible," *The* WHYS *of a Philosophical Scrivener* (New York: Quill, 1983), 307–8.

13. See René Descartes, *Meditations on First Philosophy*, esp. 2 and 6 (London: Cambridge Univ. Press, 1931).

14. See Paul Churchland's discussion of this account of the soul in his *Matter and Consciousnes* (Cambridge, MA: MIT Press, 1984), 9–10.

15. The paragraph that follows is heavily indebted to Derek Parfit, *Reasons and Persons*, 227–28.

16. See Harry Frankfurt, "Freedom of the Will and the Concept of a Person," *Journal of Philosophy* 68 (1971); and Daniel Dennett, "Conditions of Personhood," *Brainstorms* (Cambridge, MA: MIT Press, 1981), 267–85.

17. Kathleen Wilkes has an excellent discussion of brain bisection in *Real People*, 132–67.

18. This account of the *key ring* example is taken from Charles Marks, *Commissuratomy, Consciousness, and Unity of Mind* (Cambridge, MA: MIT Press, 1981), 4–6.

19. See Marks, *Commissuratomy*, 5.

20. For an amusing discussion of this question see Daniel Dennett, "Where Am I," in Dennett, *Brainstorms*, 310–23.

21. See Derek Parfit, "Personal Identity," *Philosophical Review* 80 (1971) 3–27. The summary below of Parfit's views is greatly oversimplified.

22. Eric Erikson is a well-known example of such a social scientist. See *Identity, Youth and Crisis* (New York: Norton, 1968), 15–44.

23. See Clifford Geertz, "Person, Time, and Conduct in Bali," *The Interpretation of Cultures* (New York: Basic, 1973), 360–411, esp. 386.

24. Some philosophers hold that scientific advances will force us to *eliminate* altogether from science the notions of desire, belief, and so on, and with them those of personhood and of personal identity. See, for example, Paul Churchland, *Matter and Consciousness*, 43–49.

25. Thanks to Frederick Adams, Ann Bardens, Chuck Hastings, and Leemon McHenry.

■ QUESTIONS

1. Dora is going through an *identity* crisis and is consulting a psychotherapist. Would it be helpful for her to read this chapter on personal identity?

2. How is the topic of personal identity related to real-life concerns?

3. What is the difference between giving a *necessary* condition and giving a *sufficient* condition of personal identity?

4. Consider the stuff theory of personal identity:

X = Y if and only if X is made of the same stuff as Y. (We can define the stuff of X as the collection of physical atoms that make up X, and same stuff to mean *numerically* the same.)

Is the stuff theory a good theory?

5. Suppose that you are caught in an arctic blizzard and literally frozen solid. A hundred years from now, your frozen brain-body is discovered, unthawed, and brought to life. Does the original you survive here, or is what is brought to life a mere replica? Compare this case to the teleportation case in which Spock is beamed down to the nearby planet.

6. The psychological continuity theory (in its final version) prohibits splitting. According to this theory, if A splits into B and C, then A does not survive; on the other hand, the theory gives a verdict of survival in the case where during the splitting operation half of A's brain (say the half that would have become C) is destroyed and the only resultant person is B. According to the theory, then, whether or not A continues to exist depends on something other than A's relations to B: It depends on the fate of C. But this seems counterintuitive. Division just does not seem as bad as death. What do you think? If you were split, would that be as bad as death? If it is not, what does this mean for the psychological continuity theory?

7. The soul theory allows for the possibility of an afterlife. Do any of the other theories that we have considered allow for that possibility?

8. What is it to be a person? How is that question relevant to the question of what is it for a person to persist over time?   ■

■ FOR FURTHER READING

Gardner, Martin. Essays 17, 18, and 19. *The whys of a Philosophical Scrivener.* New York: Quill, 1983.

Kolak, Daniel, and Raymond Martin, eds. *Self and Identity.* New York: Macmillan, 1991.

Marks, Charles. *Commissuratomy, Consciousness, and Unity of Mind.* Cambridge, MA: MIT Press, 1981.

Parfit, Derek. "Personal Identity." *Philosophical Review* 80 (1971): 3–27.

Perry, John. *A Dialogue on Personal Identity and Immortality.* Indianapolis: Hackett, 1978.

————, ed. *Personal Identity.* Berkeley: Univ. of California Press, 1975.

Shoemaker, Sydney, and Richard Swinburne. *Personal Identity.* Oxford: Basil Blackwell, 1984.

Wilkes, Kathleen. *Real People.* Oxford: Oxford Univ. Press, 1988.

CHAPTER TEN

Philosophy of Mind

JOHN HEIL

■ INTRODUCTION

If you are capable of reading and understanding these words, then you possess a mind. That is not to say that *only* creatures capable of reading and understanding words have minds. Nevertheless, an investigation of the character of mind is bound to begin with one's own case. Were we clear about that, we might come to appreciate what it is in general to possess a mind, and thus to gauge the breadth of the concept. People evidently have minds. What about nonhuman creatures? Does Koko the Stanford-educated gorilla have a mind? Koko certainly *behaves* intelligently; and it seems natural to describe Koko as having thoughts and feelings. If evidence of thoughts and feelings is evidence enough for the possession of mind, however, then Spot, the neighbor's dog, would seem to qualify. What of the squirrel that Spot chases? Or the flea on Spot's ear?

Perhaps, by the end of this chapter, we shall be in a position to evaluate these and related questions sensibly. Before pushing ahead, however, a word is due concerning the relation of the philosophy of mind and the discipline of psychology. After all, someone might think, if we want to discover whether squirrels or fleas have minds, we should consult those who profess competence in the science of mind. The suggestion is off base. Philosophy of mind, though certainly related to empirical psychology, differs both in approach and in subject matter. Psychologists engage in experimental research. This research presupposes some *conception* of what is under investigation. Philosophers, in contrast, focus on those conceptions of mind. We might wonder whether minds are thinking and feeling *things*, for instance, or whether possessing a mind is merely a way of being organized (or "programmed"). This way of characterizing the distinction is somewhat artificial. In practice, there is no sharp division of labor. Conceptual investigations reflect empirical discoveries at the same time they serve to direct those studies. The aim of this chapter is, among other things, to illuminate such matters and to provide a basis for more serious consideration of the mind and its place in the universe. Let us begin by looking at some traditional conceptions of mind.

■ MIND-BODY DUALISM

It is in many ways natural to regard the mind and body as distinct *entities*. Minds and bodies are no doubt intimately related, but, in death the body persists, at least for a time, without any sort of obvious mental accompaniment. Perhaps minds are forms of energy—analogous to heat energy. On death, bodies cease to produce heat. Perhaps they cease also to generate minds. This thought may be dispelled, however, by another: It is at least imaginable that minds exist *independently* of bodies. Many religions envision the soul departing the body and traveling elsewhere. It does not follow, of course, that minds and bodies *are* distinct entities, but the apparent ease with which we can imagine minds persisting apart from bodies suggests that our everyday conception of mind is consistent with *dualism*: Minds and bodies are separate, though intimately related, entities.

■ *Interactionism*

An interactionist version of dualism was first worked out in detail by René Descartes in the seventeenth century and has enjoyed considerable popularity since. Descartes was struck by three things. First, mental items and physical items seem, on the face of it, utterly different. Physical bodies, for instance, are inevitably *spatial*: They have a definite location in space relative to other physical objects, they exclude other bodies, and they possess measurable dimensions. Mental objects, however, seem different. It is at least odd to imagine that thoughts or ideas have a precise location, and it is even odder to suppose that they could have some definite size or shape. True, we do locate thoughts in the head, emotions in the breast, and pains in teeth and toes, but this may be largely metaphorical. An idea may be in my head, but not in the way that a neuron is. Neurons are in particular locations. Neurons, like physical objects generally, exclude one another from the space they occupy. It makes little or no sense to speak of thoughts excluding one another in this way—or being next to or on top of one another. Moreover, while pains are straightforwardly locatable, the sense in which they have a location seems special. If I have a pain in my right index finger and clutch that finger in my left hand, I do not then have a pain in my left palm. The phenomenon of *referred pain* suggests that pains may be *felt* to be at locations other than their sources. An extreme case of referred pain occurs when pain is felt to be in an amputated limb.

The second thing that Descartes noticed was that, despite their apparent differences, minds and bodies continuously *interact*. Goings-on in the mind affect the body (as when my decision to eat a Whopper, a mental act, leads me to place an order), and bodily occurrences are reflected in the mind (I delight in the Whopper's heft and aroma). Interaction of this sort seems obviously *causal*. Mental events cause bodily events, perhaps by affecting processes in the brain that lead to the stimulation of output—*efferent*—nerves, and bodily events induce mental counterparts via input—*afferent*—nervous stimulation.

Third, Descartes noted that we employ different patterns of explanation for mental and physical events. Whereas ordinary physical occurrences are explained *mechanically*—that is, by reference to material causes—the behavior of people, insofar as it was influenced by thought, requires explanation in terms of *reasons*. This suggested to Descartes that mental systems and physical systems are governed by very different principles: physical systems by mechanical, *natural laws*, mental systems by the laws of reason, *logic*. This, in turn, suggests that mental and physical things belong to very different *realms*.

The implications of such a view are momentous. If minds and bodies are distinct entities (Descartes called them *substances*) governed by distinct sorts of law, and yet minds and bodies causally interact, then the physical universe is not, as we should like to think, *causally closed*. That is, the occurrence of some physical events—certain events in the brain, for instance—would be *physically* inexplicable: Their causes would include a nonphysical, mental event. If physical events are influenced by nonphysical happenings, however, then the principle of the conservation of energy does not hold. Energy would be introduced into the physical universe every time a mental cause had a physical effect, and perhaps physical energy would be lost whenever a physical cause induced a mental event.

Anyone with strong scientific leanings will be repelled by this prospect. Interactionism, if it requires us to abandon such fundamental principles as the conservation of energy, perhaps requires too much. Even if it did not, however, interactionism gives rise to other, related worries identified by Descartes's contemporaries. If we regard bodies and minds as distinct substances, the former spatial, the latter not, how can we make sense of the notion that mental and physical things interact causally in the first place? Indeed, how are we to understand mental *causation* at all? Causal interactions occur when one thing bumps into, or pushes, or pulls another thing. Our concept of causality, at least as it concerns the physical realm, incorporates a strong spatial component. If minds are nonspatial, however, it is not easy to see how they might affect or be affected by spatial objects.

■ Parallelism

Although such objections to interactionism are scarcely decisive, they have encouraged philosophers to look elsewhere for an understanding of mind. Some, attracted to Descartes's dualism but not to his picture of causal interaction, have advanced a view according to which minds and bodies operate independently, yet *in parallel*. Minds function in accord with their own principles. Bodies function in accord with principles governing physical systems. The world is organized, however, in such a way that the two systems are perfectly coordinated—just as two clocks may keep the same time, not because they are causally connected, but because their own internal workings are synchronized. (The metaphor was advanced by the philosopher Gottfried Leibniz, a prominent advocate of this sort of parallelism.) To an observer, of course, it will appear that the mental and the physical interact causally. Every time I stub my toe, I feel a throbbing pain; but the stubbing is not the cause of the pain. The stubbing and the subsequent pain belong to isolated systems operating in perfect harmony.

Many philosophers have contended that this way of solving the problem of causal interaction makes the relation of mental and physical things more, rather than less, mysterious. If it is difficult to grasp causal relations between mental and physical events, it is not much easier to grasp the notion that the mental and physical realms, though entirely self-contained, are miraculously coordinated. What could account for such coordination? Leibniz's solution depended on the postulation of a benevolent and all-powerful God. Even if one grants that such a being might exist and might so arrange the world, however, it is far from clear that we have any very good reason to suspect that the world *is* so arranged. Parallelism, while fitting our evidence, is an extravagant hypothesis, one it would be unwise to endorse so long as simpler explanations are available. (The hypothesis that my watch keeps time because it houses tiny, punctual leprechauns is *consistent* with the facts, but there is a simpler explanation available, one framed in terms of springs and gear wheels.) The question is whether there *are* simpler accounts of minds available.

■ *Epiphenomenalism*

Concerns over the plausibility of parallelism and interactionism have led theorists to *epiphenomenalism*, the view that mental occurrences are dependent on physical happenings, but that physical occurrences themselves constitute a self-contained system. Consider conscious human beings: We have evolved as finely tuned biological mechanisms. Our bodies are monitored and controlled by a complex and highly organized nervous system. One by-product of this nervous system is, according to epiphenomenalists, our capacity for conscious thought. Mental states and processes *arise from* physical—biological—states and processes. But mental goings-on themselves have no causal role: They have neither physical nor mental effects. In this regard, they resemble smoke given off by a steam locomotive, or the shadows cast by someone pumping water. Puffs of smoke and shadows result from ongoing physical processes. Neither contributes to the production of those processes, however. Nor do puffs of smoke and the motions of shadows contribute to the production of further puffs of smoke and movements of shadows. One puff of smoke follows another, but the puffs are not causally connected. A shadow moves now this way, now that way, but its so moving is due exclusively to motions of the physical system casting the shadow.

As in the case of parallelism, it may *seem* to us that our conscious states have bodily effects. This, say epiphenomenalists, is an illusion arising from the fact that physical events responsible for those bodily effects are *also* responsible for certain mental accompaniments. When I decide to eat a Whopper, my body moves appropriately. This is not a result of my *decision*, however, but the product of a particular neurological occurrence. As in the case of a steam locomotive, one occurrence gives rise *both* to a certain conscious state (or a puff of smoke) *and* to my subsequent bodily motions (the locomotive's moving forward). Because conscious states of the one sort inevitably precede bodily motions of the other sort, I mistakenly infer the presence of a causal connection—just in the way a child might imagine that the puffs of smoke emitted by the locomotive push it along the tracks.

Interactionism and parallelism divide the world into mental and physical *substances*. Epiphenomenalism, in contrast, envisages only a single sort of substance, material substance. According to the epiphenomenalist, complex material systems give rise to *im*material, mental events and states. The epiphenomenalist conception of our world, then, though dualistic, is in this respect *simpler* than those advanced by substance dualists. There is a single world—the material world—though that world contains events and states of two fundamentally different kinds, mental and physical. Mental events (like my feeling a sudden pain) are effects of physical causes, but do not themselves cause anything. The world is a self-contained system of physical causes that, when the conditions are right, can have mental side effects.

There are many bad arguments against epiphenomenalism. According to one, epiphenomenalism implies that the world might have been exactly as it now is in every nonmental detail, even though no one was ever conscious, no one ever had a thought about anything. All of Shakespeare's sonnets could have been written, astronauts sent to the Moon, and groups persecuted for their religious practices, despite no one's having a single thought or conscious experience. This is said to follow from the epiphenomenalist's insistence that mental occurrences themselves have no physical effects. Were that so, the argument continues, mental occurrences *could* be eliminated without altering the physical domain in any way. It is unlikely that epiphenomenalism entails such possibilities, however. Certainly, epiphenomenalists need not allow that the physical world might have been exactly as it now is in every detail without producing the mental world as a by-product. Thus, the laws of nature might be such that, given a physical world with the complexity of ours, a mental world is guaranteed. If that were so, it would be wrong to suppose that mental occurrences could be absent while leaving physical processes intact—just as it would be impossible to build a steam locomotive that was *exactly like* ordinary steam locomotives except that it did not produce puffs of smoke.

Still, worries remain. First, although according to epiphenomenalism mental goings-on must be present in order for conscious beings to engage in intelligent pursuits, mental characteristics themselves play no real role in those pursuits. This *inefficacy of the mental* seems, on the face of it, implausible. Second, the status of mental occurrences is puzzling. Thoughts, for instance, are depicted as causal by-products of complex neural events. This requires that we countenance causal relations between events within the physical world and events in some sense *outside* the physical world. Such causal relations are as difficult to understand in their own way as are the mental-physical causal relations envisaged by Descartes. Certainly, the notion that physical occurrences might have effects that fall outside the purview of the physical sciences does not go down well with anyone who supposes that the physical universe is, in respect to its causal relations, self-contained or *closed*. These are matters that would take us far afield. Rather than pursuing them, then, let us turn to nondualist theories of mind. Such theories hold out the promise of a solution to the sorts of difficulties we have noted in connection with dualism.

■ IDEALISM

Dualistic conceptions of mind, while capturing certain intuitions about mental and physical occurrences, give rise to puzzles about the *relation* between the mental and the physical. Interactionism and epiphenomenalism tolerate odd sorts of causal relation, and parallelism requires that we imagine a miraculous correlation between two causally isolated domains. The chronic inability of dualists to provide convincing solutions to such problems suggests that we might improve matters by giving up dualistic conceptions and developing a picture of mind that does not require the postulation of distinct realms. If there is but a single realm, perhaps both mental things and physical things could be understood in terms of it.

Some philosophers, following George Berkeley, have argued for *idealism*, the view that all that exists are minds and their contents. This contention may be understood either as calling for the *elimination* of physical entities or as a claim that physical things are *reducible to* combinations of mental things. Thus, on the one hand, idealists may simply deny that there are any physical things at all. On the other hand, as is more likely, an idealist might argue that physical bodies and events are, at bottom, mental *constructs*. The desk in front of me, for instance, is indisputably a physical object. That is merely to say, however, that it *looks* and *feels* a certain way. Looks and feels, like sounds and tastes, are *sense perceptions*, and sense perceptions are mental states. We naturally suppose that the actual desk lies behind these sense perceptions, that the actual desk is causally responsible for them. As idealists are quick to point out, however, we never encounter any such *actual* desk. We encounter only more and varied sense perceptions. If the physical desk is something that we perceive, we should say that it is nothing more than a pattern of actual or possible sense perceptions. In saying that the desk exists as a physical object, I say only that I am now perceiving it or that anyone *would* perceive it under the right conditions. Physical objects, in John Stuart Mill's phrase, are nothing but *permanent possibilities of sensation*.

An idealism of this sort appears wrong on the face of it. Our awareness of physical objects seems obviously an awareness of bodies at a distance, objects outside us, in space, and independent of our minds. But is this so clear? We sometimes *dream* that we are perceiving familiar objects in the world, yet these experiences are entirely inside us. John Locke, although not an idealist, argued that our awareness of objects as being at a distance from us is merely a learned correlation among sensory experiences. We seem to be visually aware of a sphere resting on a table across the room, for instance; but, according to Locke, what we are actually aware of is a two-dimensional visual disk shaded in a certain way. (Think of a drawing or photograph of a sphere reproduced on a two-dimensional surface, like the page of a book.) We have *learned* that there is a correlation between such visual images and sensations of motion and touch. Before we can feel the sphere, we must move across the room (that is, we must sense our bodies moving in a certain way and simultaneously experience a visual expansion of the sphere and table on which it rests). Once we acquire these correlations (presumably at an early age), the visual image alone can serve as a *sign* of a distant body. Our subjective impression is of objects at a distance, but their *being* at a distance is not a part of our perceptions. This, at any rate, is Locke's conclusion.

It might be thought that none of this establishes that physical things are *only* patterns of sense experiences. Why not allow that physical objects *cause* experiences in us? Thus, although we are only ever aware of the effects of physical objects on us, and never the objects themselves, we can still reasonably suppose that physical objects exist outside our minds.

Idealists, however, have more to say. We have, they insist, no way of knowing whether physical objects persist independently of our sense perceptions in the way just described. Claims that they do, then, are absolutely *unverifiable*. An unverifiable claim, however, is one we could never have reason to accept. There is, then, no reason to suppose that physical objects are anything more than "permanent possibilities of sensation." In fact, as the example of the desk illustrates, our concepts of physical objects are so closely tied to actual and possible sensory experiences that the thought of physical objects existing independently of those sensory experiences, is, at bottom, *unthinkable*.

Idealism sidesteps many of the difficulties associated with dualism. There is only one substance, mind, and no commitment to puzzling causal relations between physical things and mental things. Physical things turn out just to be constructs of mental things. At least one significant puzzle remains, however. What accounts for the orderly pattern of ideas and perceptions that we associate with the material world? The world I perceive differs from worlds I dream up in my imagination. It is natural to suppose that this is because there is an independent physical world that impinges itself on my senses. I perceive this desk every time I enter the room because the desk persists in the room even when I am not about. If the desk is merely "the permanent possibility of sensation," however, what accounts for the orderly character of my experiences of it? One possibility is that my mind contains resources of which I am unaware. As a result, I unconsciously produce for myself the pattern of ideas I associate with the physical world. A view of this sort flirts with *solipsism*, the notion that all that exists is myself and my own thoughts. Another possibility, that advocated by Berkeley, is that God (a *supermind*) sees to it that perceptions are planted in our minds in a regular and orderly way.

Although both of these possible explanations fit our evidence, neither has much else to be said for it. Rejection of the material world carries with it rejection of an important source of explanation for the occurrence of mental states. Surely the simplest, most plausible explanation of our having the perceptions we have of desks, mountains, and other people is that there *are* desks, mountains, and other people, that these things are, on the whole, as we perceive them to be, and that they are in some way causally responsible for our perceptions of them. This may seem to push us back in the direction of interactionism or epiphenomenalism. Perhaps not. Monism—the denial of dualism—need not be idealism.

■ MATERIALISM

Perhaps, then, there is only one sort of substance, *material* substance. Minds are material—that is, physical—entities. To distinguish materialism from epiphenomenalism, we should add that every event and state is a material event or state. The trick now is to account for our mental lives. Consider a simple example. A flashbulb goes off in front of me, and, as a result, I experience a round, greenish afterimage. The afterimage is not an item in my physical environment, but neither would it turn up were you to examine my visual system or brain. Nowhere in my physical constitution is there a greenish item, yet I am indisputably *aware* of such an item. Of course, things are happening in my visual system and in my brain. And these things are no doubt in some sense *responsible* for my experiencing the greenish image. But none of those things *is* the greenish image, indeed nothing inside me need be either round or greenish.

Considerations of this sort may seem to mandate dualism—though perhaps not. Perhaps there are materialistic accounts of mind that can accommodate the phenomena. Before looking over the possibilities, however, it will be useful to distinguish, as we did in discussing idealism, between eliminative and reductive materialism. An *eliminative materialist* holds that there are no minds, no mental states or processes. A *reductive materialist*, in contrast, contends that, although there are mental states and processes, these are in fact nothing more than complex physical states and processes. According to an eliminative materialist, then, I never really experience an afterimage because I never really experience anything at all. Reductive materialists are more cautious. My experiencing an afterimage is just my undergoing a certain brain process, perhaps, or my being disposed to say "I'm aware of a greenish afterimage" when prompted. We shall return to eliminativism later in this chapter. For the moment, however, let us focus on noneliminative, reductive versions of materialism.

■ *The Identity Theory*

One such materialism, the *identity theory*, identifies mental goings-on with physical (typically neural) goings-on. The concept of identity here is one familiar to students of logic. If we discover that Mark Twain *is* Samuel Clemens, we thereby discover that Mark Twain and Samuel Clemens are one and the same person. In the same way, we may discover that water *is* H₂O or that lightning *is* an electrical discharge. The *is* in these cases is the *is* of identity. It is in this sense that the identity theorist holds that mental events or states and physical events or states are identical: Mental things *are* in fact nothing but physical things.

Does this mean that my round, greenish afterimage is really a state of my brain? That seems unlikely. The afterimage, after all, is round and greenish, but no part of my brain is round and greenish. An identity theorist may concede the point but argue that the identity in question holds between mental states (or processes) and physical states (or processes). The distinction is a subtle one. When I experience a round, greenish afterimage, the relevant mental state is my *experience*. That experience is not *itself* round or greenish, hence there is nothing to prevent *its* being identified with—that is, its turning out to *be*—a state of my brain. What of the afterimage? An identity theorist may simply deny that there is any such entity. Rather, when I experience a round, greenish afterimage, something goes on in my nervous system very like what goes on in my nervous system when I visually apprehend a round, green physical object. In neither case is the roundness or greeness *in me*. In the latter case, of course, there is *something* round and green, namely, a particular physical object. The world, then, contains round, green things. It contains as well experiences of round, green physical things. Some of these experiences are *veridical*, that is, some are induced by the presence of round, green things. Some, however, are in one way or another illusory. When that is so, I may experience something round and green even though nothing physical—hence nothing at all—in my immediate vicinity is either round or green.

This dismissal of afterimages and their ilk may seem excessively cavalier. Perhaps it is. In any case, the identity theory provides a straightforward way of understanding how causal interaction between mental and physical events is possible. Because mental events are nothing but physical events, mental-physical interaction is merely a species of physical-physical interaction.

Other problems remain, however. The identity required by the identity theory holds between *types* of mental and physical states or processes. When we say that water *is* (in the sense of *is identical to*) H₂O, we mean that every instance of water is an instance of H₂O. Similarly, when we say that experiencing a round, greenish afterimage is a matter of being in a certain brain state, we mean that every instance of the experience of a round, greenish afterimage is an instance of being in a brain state of *that sort*. But how plausible is it to suppose that this is so? We know, for instance, that other terrestrial creatures have nervous systems importantly different from ours. Such creatures may never be in neural states of the sort we are in when we have visual experiences. If the identity theory is right, however, it seems to follow that such creatures could not have visual experiences like ours: The having of visual experiences like ours is just a matter of being in certain sorts of neural condition; but these creatures, owing to differences in their nervous systems, are never in *those* sorts of neural condition; consequently, these creatures never have visual experiences like ours. Further, it seems possible to imagine alien creatures very different from us biologically, yet similar psychologically. Perhaps the aliens possess a silicon-based nervous system. If these aliens talked about the world as we do, claimed to have experiences of afterimages and the like that they described just as we do, it would seem unreasonable on our part to deny that this was possible solely on the grounds that they differed from us biologically. Yet this, apparently, is what the identity theory requires.

■ Behaviorism

Other materialist routes may be more promising. Thus, *behaviorists* have argued that mental states and processes are really nothing more than behavior or dispositions to do this or that depending on how one is stimulated. Suppose, for instance, I become angry. I turn red, clinch my fists, and, were you to enter the room, I would shout at you. Behaviorists argue that my anger is not some state lying *behind* my behavior, it is that behavior itself (together with its associated dispositions). My anger, then, just is my turning red, clinching my fists, and being disposed to shout should I encounter you. Anger, of course, might be manifested differently by different people or by me at different times. The concept of anger, however, covers familiar patterns of behavior and behavioral dispositions. So it is for all mental concepts. To be in pain is to wince, moan, and to be disposed to seek relief. To believe that it is raining is to carry an umbrella, to be disposed to answer "yes" to the question "Is it raining?" and so on.

It is important to distinguish philosophical behaviorists from psychological behaviorists. Psychological behaviorism is a mish-mash of methodological precepts ("Do not refer to unobservable mental states in explaining behavior") and empirical theory ("The mechanisms responsible for behavior are, at bottom, simple stimulus-response mechanisms"). In fact, psychological behaviorists often disagree about these and other matters, so that it is difficult to characterize the doctrine in any simple way. What is important for our purposes is to distinguish psychological behaviorists of *whatever* stripe from philosophical behaviorists. The latter are notable for defining mental states and processes in terms of behavior. Henceforth, let *behaviorist* mean *philosophical behaviorist*.

Behaviorism, unlike the identity theory, allows creatures with very different biologies to be in the same mental states. Dispositions presumably are realized in a creature's biological structure, but, because dispositions are defined only by their causal inputs and outputs, the very same disposition might be realized in a wide range of physical structures. To see why this is so, consider a simple, nonmental disposition, *fragility*. To say that an object is fragile, is to say (roughly) that it will break if struck by a hard object. A vase's being fragile, then, is a matter of its possessing a certain causal propensity. Perhaps the vase possesses this propensity in virtue of its possession of a particular molecular structure. Now some other object, an egg, might possess the very same propensity, yet do so in virtue of possessing a quite different molecular structure. A range of molecular structures, then, perhaps an open-ended range, might give rise to the same causal propensity. In describing an object as fragile, then, we ascribe to it a causal propensity. This propensity will be realized in some particular, though perhaps unknown, structure. In describing the object as fragile, we abstract from this structure, we describe it at a "higher level."

Behaviorists, in taking mental states to be propensities to respond to stimuli in certain ways, allow that such states might be *biologically realized* in many different ways. Suppose that my perceiving a round, greenish thing, then, is solely a matter of being in a state of a sort typically produced by round, greenish things, a state that disposes me to behave in certain ways—to say, for instance, that I am now perceiving a round, greenish thing, when prompted. There is nothing to prevent a creature with an utterly different biology, even an alien with a silicon-based nervous system, from being in the same dispositional state—that is, a state with the same causal propensities. Every *instance* of a mental state or process would then be identifiable with an *instance* of a physical state or process, but the *kind* of physical state or process might differ from case to case. What makes objects fragile is something about their physical constitution, but that something may differ from one case of fragility to another. Similarly, what gives rise in me to the sorts of behavior and behavioral dispositions we associate with anger may be very different from what gives rise to these in a gorilla or a Martian.

This aspect of behaviorism may seem attractive. It enables us to see how, on the one hand, mental descriptions of intelligent creatures depend on those creatures' physical constitution, while, on the other hand, mental descriptions are not reducible to purely physical descriptions of those creatures. If this sounds strange, think of the parallel case of fragility. That this vase is fragile depends on its physical constitution. In describing the vase as fragile, however, we are not thereby providing a detailed description of its physical constitution. We are rather ascribing a causal propensity to it, one it may share with countless physically dissimilar objects.

The trouble with behaviorism is that it is extremely difficult to come up with plausible behaviorist accounts of particular states of mind. What am I disposed to do given that I have just spotted a round, greenish object? There is no general answer. I may be disposed to say "There's a tennis ball," but not if I do not know what a tennis ball is or I want, for some reason, to keep this information to myself. I might say or do *anything or nothing* depending on *what else* I think and want at the time. There is, it seems, no generally specifiable causal propensity to be identified with my perceiving a round, greenish object. A moment's reflection will reveal that the same could be said about any other state of mind. What do I do or say if I believe that the gun is loaded? That will depend in obvious ways on what else I believe and what I happen to want at the time.

■ *Functionalism*

Perhaps we can take the basic behaviorist insight and modify it so as to avoid such difficulties. Recall that one attraction of behaviorism is that it enables us to associate mental states and processes with physical states and processes identified at a higher level of abstraction. We imagine that mental states resemble fragility in being causal propensities that might be realized in and manifested by many different sorts of physical structure. A spin-off of behaviorism, *functionalism*, endorses this point but extends the notion of a causal propensity to include, in addition to input stimuli and output responses, connections with other mental states and processes. My perceiving a round, greenish object is a matter of my being in a certain state defined by its typical causes (a nearby round, greenish object in clear view), and by its effects on other mental states and processes. My perceiving a round, greenish object, then, typically causes me to *form the belief* that there is a round, greenish object. My subsequent behavior, if any, is determined by my *overall* psychological state at the time.

Functionalists are called functionalists because they take states of mind to be *functional* states of creatures possessing those states of mind. A functional state, like a simple disposition, is a state characterizable in terms of its causal propensities. As in the case of a dispositional state like fragility, we may suppose that every functional state is realized in some physical condition or other, without supposing that a given functional state has always and everywhere the same physical realization. Such a view differs from behaviorism only in regarding causal relations of *other* mental states (all of which are themselves functional states) as being relevant to the character of every mental state. A creature with a mind—a person, for instance—is a creature that possesses a *system* of functional states in virtue of which it responds intelligently to its surroundings.

Functional states, unlike behaviorist dispositions, then, cannot be characterized independently of the system of functional states to which they belong. An object is fragile if it would break when struck, not if it would not. Behaviorists apply this model to states of mind. If I become aware of a round, greenish object, however, there is, functionalists point out, no end to the ways I might react. How I do react will depend on my overall mental condition at the time. According to functionalists, minds comprise organized systems. Particular mental states are what they are in virtue of their place in such an organized system. You and I are in the same mental state providing we are each in a state that figures in a similar system of states. That state is one an alien might be in, as well, despite differences in biology. To return to an earlier example, my being angry is a matter of my being in a state that has certain typical causes and effects. So far this sounds like behaviorism. Functionalists, however, suppose that many, or perhaps all, of those causes and effects are other mental states. Anger, then, is caused by, among other things, my *believing* I have been wronged in some way, and my being angry causes me to form the *intention* to insult you. If we suppose that beliefs and intentions themselves are characterized partly by their relations to other mental states, we can see that the functionalist picture of the mind is a picture of a complex causal network.

Functionalism has won favor with those who find analogies between minds and computing machines illuminating. If the mind is a complex functional system, then it would seem that a suitably programmed computing machine might itself count as a mind. This would be so if we could provide the device with a functional architecture similar to ours. If functionalism is correct, then our accomplishing this feat is at least in the cards. In any case, so far as functionalists are concerned, the fact that a computer is made of plastic, metal, and silicon is no barrier at all to its possessing a mind—unless devices made of plastic, metal, and silicon could not, for some technological reason, come to have a functional structure resembling ours. According to such a view, the possession of a mind amounts to the possession of a highly abstract set of abilities. This accounts for the remarkable idea that minds may be studied by studying computer programs that simulate human cognitive processes (see Chapter 11).

Functionalism is sometimes attacked on the grounds that it is implausible to suppose that *every* sort of mental state is a functional state. Consider, for instance, my experiencing a throbbing pain in my toe. Is this simply a matter of my being in a certain functional state (one that results in my believing that I have a pain in my toe, for instance, and disposes me to rub the toe)? If that were so, it would seem a simple matter to program a computing machine to be in a similar functional state. Yet it is at least odd to imagine that such a device might, solely because of the way we have programmed it, *feel pain*. What seems missing from the functionalist account is the *feeling* of pain. Thus (it might be argued), my being in pain may be *partly* a matter of my being in a certain functional state. It is also, and essentially, a matter of my experiencing a certain *feeling*. And feelings, whatever they are, seem not to be functionally characterizable.

Whether functionalists have a satisfactory answer to this challenge is an open question. They might retreat to the claim that *some*, but not necessarily all, mental states are functional states. So beliefs, for instance, might be functionally specifiable, pains not. Or functionalists might insist, as identity theorists have insisted, that while *pains* are not functional states, one's *experiencing* a pain is a perfectly respectable functional state, one that gives rise to beliefs about being in pain, desires to alleviate the discomfort, and so on. This requires that we can distinguish between, on the one hand, *pains* and their properties, and, on the other hand, *experiences* of pains and the properties of those experiences. It requires, as well, that we dispense with pains as identity theorists dispensed with afterimages, leaving only pain experiences.

Arguments on these points are, so far, inconclusive. It is, even so, worth noting that mental categories encompass two broad classes, and that these may have less in common than is implied by the tradition of lumping them together. One category of mental state, *sensations*, includes such things as feelings of pain, twinges, tickles, feelings of uneasiness, and perhaps sensations obtained by way of the operation of the senses (visual sensations and sensations produced by hearing, touching, smelling, and tasting). As we have just noted, it may be best to suppose that it is the *experiencing* or *having* of sensations, not sensations themselves, that should count as mental states.

A second, very different, category of mental state includes the so-called propositional attitudes. A *propositional attitude* is characterizable by reference to two factors: a particular proposition and a particular attitude toward that proposition. Consider the proposition that it is raining. I may have many different attitudes toward this proposition: I may *believe* that it is raining, *hope* that it is raining, *doubt* that it is raining, *fear* that it is raining, *want* it to be the case that it is raining, and so on. In each case, I am in a distinct state of mind identifiable by reference to my attitude and the proposition toward which I take up that attitude.

Philosophical tradition groups sensations and propositional attitudes together under the rubric *states of mind*. This may be unfortunate. It might easily turn out that accounts of sensation are, of necessity, very different from accounts of propositional attitudes. Sensations, for instance, seem to possess—essentially—particular introspectable qualities. Pains *hurt*, tastes are *sweet* or *salty*, sounds are *loud* or *soft*. Such qualities raise difficulties for the identity theory and for functionalism. Propositional attitudes, in contrast, seem not to possess—at least not essentially—introspectable qualities. My belief that it is raining exhibits no special feel (though, of course, my coming to have the belief may give rise to a variety of feelings: anxiety, disappointment, happiness).

It may be too much to ask of a particular theory of mind that it provide a single, unified account of sensations and propositional attitudes. In fact, in recent years philosophers have concentrated on providing theories of mind that can cope with propositional attitudes. The strategy seems to be one of divide and conquer. For surely if we could come up with a really satisfactory explanation of one class of mental state, such an explanation need have nothing much in common with proposed explications of another class. Let us consider, then, some recent attempts to provide materialistic accounts of the propositional attitudes.

■ Instrumentalism

Instrumentalist approaches to the propositional attitudes focus on the role these have in the explanation of behavior. The term *instrumentalism* comes from the philosophy of science, where it designates the view that scientific theories neither provide nor purport to provide true or false descriptions of the world. Instrumentalists are distinguished from *realists*, who take scientific claims to provide descriptions, true or false, of reality. Instrumentalists believe that theories enable us to come to terms with our experiences of the world, but that they may do so without being true. Physicists talk about photons and quarks. Realists imagine that such talk refers to entities that may (if the theory is true) or may not (if it is false) exist. The existence of such unobservable, *postulated* entities explains why observable objects behave as they do. Instrumentalists imagine that we need only suppose that the world is *as if* there were photons and quarks. The theory may work nicely; it may fit all of our observations (now and forever) without there being any photons and quarks.

An instrumentalist approach to the propositional attitudes supposes that all of our talk about beliefs, desires, intentions, hopes, and fears is wonderfully useful, even indispensable, but doubts that the talk should be taken literally as referring to actual states and processes inside intelligent creatures. According to this view, to say that I have a mind is just to say that my behavior can be described and explained using the familiar mental vocabulary: I behave *as if* I had inside me beliefs, desires, and intentions, and these were responsible for the production of my behavior. In fact my behavior results from complex neurobiological goings-on. Because our understanding of these is slender, however, we are obliged to resort to talk about beliefs, desires, and the like. This way of talking enables us to make sense of, predict, and, within limits, control, the behavior of others. The instrumentalist's point is that mental concepts may serve this function even if there are, strictly, no mental states or processes, even if our behavior is completely determined by nonmental, neurobiological processes.

Even were we neurobiologically sophisticated, however, we might find this vocabulary indispensable. The concepts of agency, responsibility, warrant, belief, and the like are *constitutive* of human societies and institutions in the way the concepts of queens, knights, capturing, and checkmating are constitutive of chess. It is possible to describe a chess match by referring only to the masses of particular pieces, their relative motions, and the like. Such a description, however, leaves out most of what interests us about the game. Similarly, so long as our aim is to make sense of one another as social beings, we seem bound to resort to mentalistic terminology.

■ Eliminativism

Realists contend that beliefs, desires, intentions, hopes, and fears are genuine, causally significant states of persons. Instrumentalists, in contrast, suppose that talk about states of mind serves an important explanatory function, one with practical significance, but one that stops short of the assumption that there really are beliefs, desires, and intentions. A view of this sort leads quite naturally to more radical *eliminativist* thoughts about the mind. Eliminative materialism—*eliminativism*—begins with the reflection that our talk about mental states and processes constitutes a somewhat primitive *folk theory* of human behavior, a theory we learn at our mother's knee. According to this folk theory—*folk psychology*—human beings are animated by beliefs, desires, and intentions. If you know what I want and what I believe, then you can, in many cases, anticipate what I shall do. If you grasp my intentions, you can, as often as not, infer what I believe and want. Folk psychology, as instrumentalists have emphasized, is remarkably successful. Novelists and playwrights make use of its subtlety and power. Experimental psychology represents an on-going attempt to refine and systematize its categories.

Despite this admirable track record, folk psychology is, eliminativists argue, radically false. That is not to say that it is not of tremendous practical value. Consider a parallel, *folk medicine*. Folk medicine may have endless useful applications. That is not, however, because the theoretical vocabulary of folk medicine— talk of *humors*, for instance, or of *yin* and *yang*—refer to actual features of the body. To the extent that folk medicine works, it does so not because it correctly comprehends the underlying mechanisms of disease and infection. Its aptness lies exclusively in its instrumental capacity for prediction and control. It can be successful on this dimension without incorporating a correct account of the relevant mechanisms. Folk medicine may tell me that I can cure a rash by applying a certain herb. The treatment may work despite the fact that folk medicine's *explanation* for its working—the herb restores my yin-yang balance—is wildly off base. The *real* explanation of the herb's efficacy is a pharmacological one utterly foreign to the categories of folk medicine.

The phenomenon of elimination on which eliminativists focus is quite general. As science evolves, theories replace theories. When this happens, entities postulated by the replaced theory are eliminated in favor of entities postulated by the new theory. At one time chemists explained combustion by reference to *phlogiston*, a fluid that was said to be driven out of objects when they were heated. When it was noticed that heated bodies in fact *gained* weight, this was accommodated by the supposition that phlogiston had *negative* weight: Its addition to a body resulted in that body's becoming lighter. The oxygen theory of combustion eventually replaced the phlogiston theory. As a result, talk of phlogiston was eliminated from chemistry, and chemists no longer regarded beliefs that phlogiston existed as reasonable.

Eliminativists envisage a similar fate for the propositional attitudes. Beliefs, desires, and intentions, like phlogiston, are *theoretical entities* postulated to explain the observable properties of certain objects. It is reasonable to suppose that such things exist only so long as it is reasonable to accept the theory in which they have a place. Advances in the neurosciences, however, suggest to eliminativists that folk theories of behavior are on the verge of being replaced by neurobiological theories that purport to explain intelligent behavior without reference to beliefs, desires, intentions, or anything comparable. There is, they insist, good reason to doubt that beliefs and the rest exist.

We may, of course, continue to *use* folk psychology—and folk medicine—while at the same time doubting that the theoretical vocabularies of either refer to anything at all in the world. For folk medicine, pharmacology plays an eliminative role analogous to the role played by neurobiology in the case of folk psychology. As strange as it sounds, if eliminativists are right, there are no beliefs, desires, or intentions. There are only neurobiological states and processes.

Some philosophers have expressed concern that eliminativism is ultimately *self-defeating*. Thus, eliminativists presumably *believe* in their theory, and present it in such a way as to encourage belief on our part. But, were eliminativism true, no one would believe anything: Beliefs are among the states of mind eliminated by the theory. Worse, perhaps, the theory, if true, is not one for which *evidence* could be offered, and certainly not one anyone could ever *reasonably accept*. The concepts of evidence and reasonable acceptance are closely associated with the concept of belief. If the latter goes, so do the former.

Considerations of this sort show that eliminativists are bound to find it difficult to *formulate* their thesis. Our current ways of talking essentially incorporate propositional attitude concepts. It does not follow that the thesis is false. It might be true of me that everything I say is false. Were that true, of course, it would not be something I could truly *formulate*. Indeed, if I announce, "Everything I say is false," my utterance seems paradoxical: If it is true, then it is false! Eliminativists appear to be in the same boat. If their theories are correct, then attempts to express them in everyday language are bound to have a paradoxical air. Perhaps this will change if advances in the neurosciences provide us with a new vocabulary. Even if this were not to happen, it would be hasty to conclude that eliminativism must be false because its formulation seems in certain respects paradoxical.

It does not follow, of course, that it is reasonable for us to *accept* eliminativism. If we imagine that folk psychology provides us with a reasonably satisfactory picture of ourselves and our fellows, we may doubt that it could be threatened by an advancing neuroscience. We understand everyday physical objects in our environment in terms of their solidity, color, and weight. These notions have no counterparts in basic physics. Objects we designate solid, for instance, in fact consist mostly of empty regions populated by tiny particles spaced far apart. We are not, however, inclined to deny that objects are solid on this account. Our "folk" depiction of objects coexists with our best physical theories. In fact, it is tempting to suppose that those theories *explain* what it is for objects to be solid, or colored, or weighty. Perhaps this is how we should regard the neuroscience envisaged by eliminativists. That science will tell us what it is for intelligent creatures to have beliefs, desires, and intentions.

■ INTENTIONALITY, INTERNALISM, AND EXTERNALISM

We have thus far focused almost exclusively on the *mind-body problem*, the problem of understanding the relation of minds and their contents to bodies. This scarcely exhausts the concerns of the philosophy of mind, however. In the space remaining, we shall focus on another central problem in the philosophy of mind, the problem of meaning, or *intentionality*. States of mind are said to have intentionality insofar as they are *of* or *about* something. My belief that snow is white has intentionality, it is *about* snow. Your desire for a Whopper concerns—is *for*—a Whopper. The intentionality of states of mind identified already as propositional attitudes is expressed in the propositional component of attitude descriptions. Nonpropositional states of mind may also possess intentionality. Your image of your grandmother is an image, not a proposition, yet it is *of* your grandmother.

States of mind are not alone in exhibiting intentionality. The English sentence, "That's a Whopper," is *about* a Whopper (as is the French sentence, "C'est un Whopper"). A squiggly road sign indicates that the road ahead twists and turns. The intentionality of sentences, signs, and the like is sometimes said to be *derivative* intentionality. Such things apparently owe their aboutness to relations they bear to people and, ultimately, to states of mind. The words printed on this page have a meaning—they are about various things—because they are used by human beings to express meanings. Were the page the random product of a zillion monkeys pounding on a zillion typewriters, it would be empty of meaning. Of course, owing to its coincidental resemblance to a nonaccidentally produced page of text, someone might *mistake* it for a collection of meaningful sentences. It might even come to be *used* in a book like this one. Were that to happen, however, appropriate connections to the practices of English speakers would have been established, and from that point on, the marks on the page would have meaning. The point is a general one. The inscription *snow* means what it does, not because of its shape or sound, but because it is used by English speakers with the aim of referring to snow. Let us suppose, then, that the intentionality exhibited by utterances, inscriptions, and other meaningful artifacts is derived from relations these bear to intentional states of mind. On what, it may be asked, does the intentionality of states of mind depend?

On one familiar picture of the mind, thoughts come by their meaning *intrinsically*. Descartes, for instance, supposes that minds contain thoughts that remain unaffected by alterations in the circumstances of those minds. He imagines an evil demon who tricks us into having false beliefs about almost everything by doing away with the physical world while feeding us illusions that nothing has changed. We can concoct a variation on this theme by imagining that a mad scientist has anesthetized you and removed your brain from your body. Your brain is placed in a vat of nutrients. Its input and output (afferent and efferent) nerves are connected to a computing machine programmed to provide appropriate stimulation. When you decide to raise your arm, the machine stimulates your nerves appropriately. You *feel* your arm go up and, at the same time, *see* it. The device is so programmed that you fail to recognize your plight. You continue to believe that you are about in the world, seeing trees, eating Whoppers, and cavorting with fellow philosophy students.

Thought experiments of this sort reinforce the view that the intentionality of thoughts is due entirely to their intrinsic properties. What are these? An *intrinsic property* is a property a thing possesses *on its own*, without, that is, requiring the existence of any other thing. An *extrinsic property*, in contrast, is one that is not intrinsic. A billiard ball's being *round* is an intrinsic property of the billiard ball. Its being *next to* another ball is an extrinsic property. We can add or subtract that property without disturbing the billiard ball—simply by adding or removing the second billiard ball. Two billiard balls in different environments might be identical with respect to their intrinsic properties, but different extrinsically. If the contents of thoughts, their intentionality, is an intrinsic property of thoughts or thinkers, then thoughts will remain unaffected by changes in thinkers' circumstances. A brain in a vat hooked to a computing machine and a normal brain situated in your body might be exactly alike intrinsically. If, despite conspicuous differences in their circumstances, their thoughts, too, have the same *content*— are *about* the same things—then it would follow that intentionality is an intrinsic feature of thoughts. Let us call the view that thoughts possess the intentional content they possess independently of their circumstances, *internalism*.

The brain-in-a-vat thought experiment suggests that internalism is correct, that thoughts are what they are whatever the circumstances of thinkers. It is possible to doubt that this is so, however. To see why, let us ask what makes your thought about your grandmother, a thought *about your grandmother*. One possibility is that this thought is about your grandmother because it in some way *resembles* your grandmother. Your thinking about your grandmother might, for instance, be a matter of your having an *image* of your grandmother before your mind's eye, where an image is taken to be something picturelike. Suppose, however, that someone far away, someone who has never met or heard of your grandmother, has an aunt who happens to look very much like your grandmother. Suppose that this person has a thought-image of his aunt. His aunt-image might well be indistinguishable from your grandmother-image. If the images could somehow be switched, neither of you would notice any difference. Even so, although your images are intrinsically alike, his is *of his aunt*, yours *of your grandmother*.

The imaginability of cases of this sort suggests two things. First, something more than bare similarity is required for intentionality. Your thought is as similar to the aunt as it is to your grandmother, yet it is of your grandmother, not the aunt. Indeed, it is possible for your grandmother-image to resemble the aunt more closely than it does your grandmother. This seems not to affect the fact that it is of your grandmother and not the aunt. Second, whatever *else* is required for intentionality, it must be something in addition to the intrinsic properties of intentional items. As the example illustrates, two thoughts, despite being indistinguishable intrinsically, might nevertheless be thoughts *of* different people.

Perhaps the missing element is a *causal* one. Your thought is of your grandmother, rather than the aunt, in part because it was *caused by* your grandmother, and not by the aunt. If this is right, if intentionality includes a causal component, then we shall need to rethink our earlier thought experiment. A brain in a vat, after all, is causally connected to the world very differently than a normal brain. In our original case, we imagined a brain removed from a body, smuggled into a vat, and connected to a computing machine. Were that to happen, the brain's thoughts would have, up to that point at least, more or less normal causal histories. Thus, the brain's images of its grandmother *would* stand in more or less appropriate relations to its grandmother. For that reason, it might be right to describe the brain's thoughts just as we should describe the thoughts of an embodied counterpart.

Now, imagine a different case. Imagine a brain just like yours that has spent its *entire life* in a vat. Suppose that this brain is connected to a computing machine that, purely by chance, provides it with a pattern of stimulations indistinguishable from the pattern you have received in the course of your life. In this case, the envatted brain is intrinsically indistinguishable from your brain. What is no longer obvious, however, is whether its thoughts have the same significance as yours. The grandmother-aunt example suggests that they may not. If intentionality incorporates a causal component, and the brain's causal history is vastly different from yours, there is no more reason to suppose that *its* thoughts are of or about what *your* thoughts are of or about than there is to suppose that your grandmother-induced image is of the same person as someone else's aunt-induced image.

If these musings are on the right track, they yield an *externalist* conception of mind very different from the traditional internalist conception. Minds are not self-contained organs directing thoughts outward onto the world in the way a flashlight directs a beam of light outward from an internal source of illumination. Instead, minds are taken to be items whose character depends partly on their intrinsic features and partly on their circumstances. A conception of this sort is a revolutionary one. Its implications are now being hotly debated by philosophers. As yet there are no settled answers.

It would be a mistake to conclude from the fact that there is today disagreement among philosophers on such matters either that, in philosophy—as distinct from science—*nothing is ever settled*, or that, in philosophy—again, in contrast to science—*there is no progress*. At the cutting edge of science, there are always more questions than answers. Moreover, the perception that science continually progresses is guaranteed by the fact that we count as a scientific conclusion only what has in fact been settled. Philosophy, in contrast, suffers the opposite fate. Once an issue that excites philosophers is settled, it ceases to be counted a philosophical issue. What is clear is that our perspective on the mind has expanded manyfold since the time of Descartes. Puzzles remain, but our grasp of their parts—and of what makes them *puzzles*—has steadily matured.

Plato remarked that philosophy begins in wonder. Philosophers are those possessing the capacity to find puzzling what others take for granted. If one day no questions about the mind remain, the philosophy of mind will have run its course. From where we now stand, however, that day is well beyond the horizon.

■ QUESTIONS

1. Descartes believed that nonhuman creatures—dogs, cats, gorillas—lacked minds. When such creatures behaved in ways that seemed intelligent, this was due, he argued, to their being ingenious *machines*. The test for whether a creature possessed a mind was whether it could use language intelligently. What are the advantages and disadvantages of such a test? How would *you* distinguish creatures with minds from those who merely behave *as though* they had minds?

2. Materialism is sometimes accused of disregarding the subjective, qualitative aspect of mental states. An afterimage may seem to me greenish and blurry around the edges; a headache feels dull and throbbing. Nothing in my nervous system, however, appears to have these characteristics. Materialists argue that, in one sense, *nothing at all* has such characteristics. My *experience* of the afterimage or pain is identified with some state of my nervous system, but afterimages and pains, themselves, vanish from the picture. Explain the argument here, indicate how a materialist might answer the charge that materialism ignores the qualitative aspects of mental states, and say how the maneuver is or is not plausible.

3. Could a machine think? feel pain? fall in love? How might a dualist answer this question? a functionalist? How do *you* think the question should be answered?

4. Many philosophers have seen the impossibility of mental-physical causation as a fundamental stumbling block to interactionism. Why is causation of this sort thought to present a problem? *Does* it? Explain.

5. Suppose that externalists are right; suppose that the intentional character (the meaning or significance) of mental states depends on things and events outside the body. Could we still say that mental states have a causal role in the production of behavior? Why, or why not?

6. Imagine that you are an astronaut and land on a distant planet—planet Ork. You discover that the only inhabitants of Ork are brains, anatomically similar to ours, floating in vats and connected to computing machines. How would you decide whether the brains had thoughts and, what, if anything, those thoughts were about?

7. What are the chances that your mind will survive the death of your body? If your mind survived, would *you* survive? Explain your answer.

8. Do you have any reason at all to think that you are not a brain in a vat on planet Ork? If you do not, then is it rational for you to continue to believe that you are a normal human being on planet Earth? Why, or why not?

9. Eliminativists and epiphenomenalists agree that mental states play no causal role in the production of behavior. In what respects do they *disagree*? Which doctrine seems more correct?

10. Functionalism may be seen as a natural successor to philosophical behaviorism. Identify some alleged difficulties with behaviorism and explain how functionalism purports to overcome them. Is functionalism successful in this regard? Why, or why not? ■

■ FOR FURTHER READING

Berkeley, George. A *Treatise concerning the Principles of Human Knowledge*. Originally published in 1710, available in various editions.

Chappell, V. C., ed. *The Philosophy of Mind*. Englewood Cliffs, NJ: Prentice-Hall, 1962.

Churchland, Paul. *Matter and Consciousness*. rev. ed. Cambridge, MA: Bradford/MIT Press, 1988.

Dennett, D. C. *The Intentional Stance*. Cambridge, MA: Bradford/MIT Press, 1987.

Descartes, René. *Meditations on First Philosophy*. Originally published in 1641, available in various editions and translations.

Fodor, J. A. *Psychological Explanation: An Introduction to the Philosophy of Psychology*. New York: Random House, 1968.

Leibniz, G. W. V. *Discourse on Metaphysics*. Written in 1686, available in various editions and translations.

Putnam, Hilary. *Reason, Truth, and History*. Cambridge: Cambridge Univ. Press, 1981.

Ryle, Gilbert. *The Concept of Mind*. London: Hutchinson, 1949.

Smith, Peter, and O. R. Jones. *The Philosophy of Mind: An Introduction*. Cambridge: Cambridge Univ. Press, 1986.

■ CHAPTER ELEVEN

Cognitive Science

KENNETH AIZAWA

■ INTRODUCTION

A common misconception about philosophy is that it is an unscientific discipline. Although there are unscientific, and even antiscientific, strains of philosophy in the twentieth century, a concern with science has assumed a prominent role in philosophical thinking. Perhaps nowhere is philosophy's interest in scientific developments more evident than in the fledgling field of *cognitive science*. Over the last twenty years, the disciplines of computer science, psychology, artificial intelligence, neuroscience, and philosophy of mind have contributed to the formation of a field specifically dedicated to the investigation of processes such as thinking, perceiving, remembering, inferring, learning, believing, and knowing.

At the heart of this new discipline is the theoretical and technological research that has given rise to the now ubiquitous electronic digital computer. Cognitive scientists believe that the use of computers to guide rockets through space, route telephone calls, store information about personal credit histories, and keep track of airplane reservations is among the more intellectually superficial of innovations promised by the theoretical and technological development of computation. Cognitive scientists see in this twentieth-century marvel a means of unlocking the secrets of human cognition and, indeed, of the very idea of cognition itself. The cognitivist's view of human cognition is that the brain is a type of computer, and that thinking, perceiving, and so on are matters of running a program on that computer. The project of psychology, or at least of "cognitive psychology," is to discover what sort of computing device the human brain is and what programs humans run when they think, perceive, remember, and so forth. A second principal interest of cognitive scientists is in the development of intelligent machines or machines that think. This branch of cognitive science is generally called *artificial intelligence* (AI). Where AI differs from cognitive psychology is in the relevance of what humans do. Cognitive psychologists want to find out how humans think, but AI investigators want to develop a thinking machine, regardless of whether it thinks like a human or not.

While cognitive science shares some interests with more traditional philosophy of mind, it differs from philosophy of mind in two primary respects. First, cognitive science works in the context of rather widely shared background assumptions. It assumes that some form of materialism is true, most notably either the identity theory, functionalism, or eliminativism (see Chapter 10). Second, whereas philosophy of mind is concerned with virtually all the fundamental questions of what takes place in minds, cognitive science focuses on but a single more or less vaguely defined portion of the mental—namely, the cognitive, the things associated with thinking, perceiving, remembering, and learning. Cognitive science thus generally ignores questions concerning the nature of the emotions and their role in mental life; it also is somewhat indifferent to questions concerning the nature of pain.

In this chapter, we shall survey a few of the leading philosophical questions and problems facing cognitive science. In order to fully understand many of these questions, however, we must have some knowledge of what a computer is. Our first section, therefore, will be a partial introduction to an extremely simple type of computing device, the Turing machine. In the second section, we will review what philosophers and computer scientists have had to say about intelligence—what it is for a machine to think, or to have a mental life. Although these may seem to be questions of mere academic interest, in fact, when the possible theories of the mental are presented, most everyone has a rather strong view on the matter. In our third section, we shall examine what is emerging as the leading methodological question in cognitive psychology, namely, should we, or should we not, try to use our knowledge of the biology of the brain as an aid to our understanding of psychological processes? At present, opposing answers to this question sharply divide the two leading theories of cognition. Those who might be called *classical cognitivists* maintain that the needs of cognitive psychology are best served by avoiding the use of neuroscientific concepts, while *connectionists* try to use what is known about neurons as a guide to psychological theorizing. By the end of this chapter, we will have an extended example of how and why it is that contemporary philosophy comes to be knee-deep in science.

■ WHAT IS A COMPUTING DEVICE?

Philosophers have always been interested in questions of the form "What is X?"; questions such as "What is truth?" "What is beauty?" and "What is virtue?" As much as philosophers would now like a *definition* of what a computing device is, at present all we have are a large number of *examples* of computers. This situation may be explained by an analogy. Everyone knows that a prime number is defined as a number that is an integer multiple of only one and itself; everyone also knows that 3, 5, 7, and 11 are examples of prime numbers. That is, we both know the definition of *prime number*, and we have examples of prime numbers. When it comes to *computer*, we only have examples, but no definition. This point made, let us consider a particularly simple example of a type of computer, the Turing machine. Although we will not provide definitions of all the ideas that the cognitivist scientist uses, we will give a sufficient number to illustrate what is involved and to convince the reader that all the relevant concepts can be defined.

The Turing machine is not really a physical object, or machine, like a pocket calculator you can buy at the bookstore. It is instead a mathematically specified formalism in much the way a blueprint is a mathematical specification of a building. The Turing machine was conceived by Alan Turing, a brilliant English mathematician and logician, during his work on the foundations of logic and mathematics beginning in the 1930s. A Turing machine (TM) may be thought of as having two parts: a so-called finite state control (FSC) and an indefinitely long tape divided into squares. Each square on the tape contains one of two *tape symbols*, either a 0 or a 1. The FSC can assume any one of a finite number of states denoted by *state symbols* in the set $Q = \{q_0, q_1, \ldots, q_n\}$ and has a read-write head that is able to "scan" a single square on the tape at a time. Depending on what the head scans on the tape and what state it is in, the FSC can do one of four things: (1) It can move one square to the right, so that it scans the square to the right; (2) it can move one square to the left, so that it scans the square to the left; (3) it can write a 1 over whatever it scans in the square; and (4) it can write a 0 over whatever it scans in the square. A dependency between what appears on the tape and the state of the FSC is specified by an instruction the TM has in its FSC. Each *instruction* is a quadruple of symbols: a state symbol, a tape symbol, a tape symbol or a direction symbol, another state symbol. So, one instruction might be "q_0 1 0 q_1," and another "q_{12} 1 R q_3," and another "q_{31} 1 L q_{23}." The first instruction may be read in English to mean, "If the FSC is in state q_0, scanning a 1, then it should write a 0 and change to state q_1." The second may be read "If the FSC is in state q_{12}, scanning a 1, then it should move one square to the right and change to state q_3." Thus, if the first two symbols in an instruction describe the state of the FSC and the square being scanned, then that instruction is executed. A TM *program* is a set of instructions.

Turing machines differ among themselves in having different sets of instructions, or programs. So, one TM will be specified by the program

q_0 1 L q_1
q_1 0 1 q_2

another will be specified by the program

q_0 1 L q_0
q_0 0 L q_0

and yet another will be specified by the program

q_0 1 R q_0
q_0 0 1 q_1
q_1 1 R q_1
q_1 0 L q_2
q_2 1 0 q_2

A Turing machine is said to be *deterministic* if each instruction differs from all the others in either its first state symbol or its first tape symbol. In other words, a deterministic TM is one that does not have two instructions that both begin with the same two symbols, say, "q_0 1." This condition renders a Turing machine deterministic, because for any given state-tape symbol pair, there is at most one thing the Turing machine will do. In other words, the initial symbols of an instruction determines what the Turing machine will do. Another sort of TM is the *probabilistic* Turing machine. A Turing machine is said to be probabilistic if (1) it is allowed to have more than one instruction that begins with the same first two symbols, and (2) each of the instructions sharing the same first two symbols is executed with a fixed probability. One may, therefore, think of probabilistic TM instructions as quintuples:

q_0 1 R q_0 0.5
q_0 1 R q_1 0.5

meaning something like, "If in state q_0 scanning a 1, then go right and change into state q_0 with probability 0.5," and "If in state q_0 scanning a 1, then go right and change into state q_1 with probability 0.5."

A computation begins with an *initial state* in which the FSC is in state q_0 scanning the 1, if any, appearing farthest to the left on the tape. If there is an instruction beginning with "q_0 1," that instruction is executed, making changes specified by the remainder of the instruction. Instructions continue to be applied as long as there is one whose conditions are satisfied, that is, as long as there is one whose first two symbols describe the state of the FSC and the square being scanned. If no instruction begins with the current state of the FSC and the symbol on the tape being scanned, the Turing machine *halts*; otherwise it continues to apply instructions indefinitely. If there is always an instruction that applies, the Turing machine may be said to go into an "infinite loop." If the Turing machine eventually halts, the position of the FSC and what appears on the tape when the program halts constitute the *final state*.

In order to gather some idea of how Turing machines operate, we shall consider some of the computations performed by the first program listed above. Suppose we have an initial state in which the FSC is in state q_0 and is scanning the leftmost of three consecutive 1's with the remainder of the tape containing 0's. We might represent this initial state by "0 q_0 1 1 1 0," where by convention we assume that all the symbols to the right of the rightmost 0 are 0's and all the symbols to the left of the leftmost 0 are 0's. The position of the state symbol q_0 indicates what tape symbol the read-write head of the FSC is scanning; it is scanning the tape symbol to the right of the state symbol. This sort of representation is an *instantaneous description*. The TM program

$$q_0 \; 1 \; L \; q_1$$
$$q_1 \; 0 \; 1 \; q_2$$

will apply the first instruction because it is in state q_0 scanning a 1. The FSC will move one square to the left and will go into state q_1. In other words, the instantaneous description will change from "$0 \; q_0 \; 1 \; 1 \; 1 \; 0$" to "$0 \; q_1 \; 0 \; 1 \; 1 \; 1 \; 0$." In new terms, the Turing machines will make a *state transition* from "$0 \; q_0 \; 1 \; 1 \; 1 \; 0$" to "$0 \; q_1 \; 0 \; 1 \; 1 \; 1 \; 0$." Next, the TM will execute its second instruction, because it is in state q_1 scanning a 0. The FSC will write a 1 in place of the 0 it is scanning and go into state q_2. Thus, the instantaneous description will change from "$0 \; q_1 \; 0 \; 1 \; 1 \; 1 \; 0$" to "$0 \; q_2 \; 1 \; 1 \; 1 \; 1 \; 0$." At this point, there are no instructions beginning with q_2 and 1, so the TM halts. A little thought reveals that, as long as there is at least one 1 on the tape in the initial state, this first TM program will always simply look at the first 1 in an initial string of 1's, move one square to the left, then change the 0 to a 1 and halt. If, however, no 1's appear on the input tape, the TM does nothing. That is, it halts in the initial state.

Turing machine computations may be used for a multitude of purposes. For example, they may be used to compute a variety of familiar mathematical functions, such as addition, multiplication, and exponentiation. More interesting, however, is the possibility of producing a Turing machine program that can carry on a conversation in English, prove theorems in geometry, or enable a robot car to drive safely around town. The way to get a Turing machine to do these various tasks is to allow strings of 0's and 1's to encode names for things. We might, for example, code the number one as a string of one 1, two as a string of two 1's, three as a string of three 1's, and so on. As another example, it is possible to let strings of 0's and 1's stand for letters of the English alphabet. For example, we can let 00000 stand for a, 00001 stand for b, 00010 stand for c, 00011 stand for d, and so on. Using this code for letters of English, we can have what is written on the tape of the Turing machine stand for words and sentences of English. With this encoding, and with a considerable amount of effort and cleverness, we could write a Turing machine that will check the spelling of the words written in the code on the tape. With even greater effort, it may be possible to write a Turing machine program that uses this code to take English sentences as input and produce English sentences as output. It also seems to be possible to use strings of 0's and 1's to code problems in geometry and logic.

These sorts of possibilities bring us to the exciting possibilities that lie in the suggestion that cognition is a type of computation. Namely, it allows us to provide a sort of mathematical theory of cognition. Let us consider some examples of the ways in which various simple aspects of human cognition can be described mathematically in terms of computation. Human cognitive processing involves receiving environmental stimuli, such as recognizing a person's face, and producing various sorts of motor responses, such as waving or saying hello. According to cognitivists, stimuli are inputs on which a program runs, and responses are the outputs of computations run on those inputs.

Another obvious fact of cognition is that different people know different things. One person may know that the Japanese Meiji Restoration took place in 1868, while other people know nothing about Japan. Another person may know when the Spanish-American War was fought, even though others have only the vaguest idea. According to cognitivists, each piece of information a person learns constitutes part of that person's cognitive input. One person knows things another does not in virtue of having received different input. Cognitivism also neatly accounts for another obvious fact: Different people have different responses to the same stimuli. For example, a person will respond differently to his or her mother's face than will other people. This is because the person has different information stored in his or her memory.

Yet another analogy between computing and cognition is the fact that both seem to involve a sequential, or step-by-step, process. When a person adds large numbers together, say, 34,572 and 22,336, he may first add the 2 and the 6, then the 7 and 3 carrying the one, then the 5 and 3 and the carried one, and so on. When playing chess, a person will consider a move, then some of the possible responses of his or her opponent, then his or her own possible responses to the opponent's possible moves. Computers perform steps in a similar way; they can add 34,572 and 22,336 by first adding the 2 and the 6, then the 7 and the 3 carrying the one, and so on, and they can examine one possible chess move, an opponent's possible moves, and their own possible responses.

One might imagine alternative cognitivist explanations of the preceding sorts of phenomena, and one might also imagine further analogies between cognition and computation. This is part of the tremendous attraction of cognitivism. In fact, such intuitions convince many that cognitivism must be true. Yet, there remain in the minds of many others metaphysical questions about what properties a being must have in order to have a mind, and epistemological questions about how one might ascertain exactly what mental properties humans have. We turn to these two types of questions in the next two sections.

■ ARTIFICIAL INTELLIGENCE

The thesis that cognition is computation suggests that, in principle, it is possible to build an intelligent machine, a machine that thinks. More dramatically, it suggests that one day people may be able to hire a computer as a lawyer or doctor. It suggests that it is possible that one day one will be able to have a philosophical argument with a computer. It suggests that one day, a computer may go to the Supreme Court in order to secure equal rights for computers under the United States Constitution. Although such possibilities are presently little more than science fiction, cognitivism suggests that such eerie possibilities in fact exist. All that need be done is build the right sort of machine with the right sort of program.

Many people bristle at the suggestion of machines that think and have minds just like humans. To these anticognitivists, humans, and perhaps other biological life-forms, are somehow different from machines in such a way as to allow them to have minds where machines do not. The philosophical question these people must answer is what it is that separates machines from humans. One sort of answer is that there is a God who gave humans, and perhaps other biological species, minds, and that God did not give machines minds. This is why machines will never think as people do. This sort of *theistic anticognitivism* makes sense, but it also goes against the leading scientific inclinations of the day that seek to account for what takes place in the world around us without appeal to God and many of the traditional religious ideas. *Scientific anticognitivism* seeks an alternative theory of the differences between humans and machines.

Both cognitivists and anticognitivists must explain the difference between cognitive beings and noncognitive beings. Both must draw a dividing line between thinking things and nonthinking things. Anticognitivists believe the dividing line falls between humans and machines: Humans have minds, and machines, including computers, do not. The cognitivist, however, must presumably draw the line between humans and certain machines, on the one hand, and other sorts of machines on the other. Presumably, not every machine or computer is intelligent. Presumably, a Turing machine that always goes into an infinite loop, for example, the Turing machine

$$q_0 \; 1 \; L \; q_0$$
$$q_0 \; 0 \; L \; q_0$$

is not intelligent. Yet, a Turing machine that could use the sort of special coding mentioned above to carry on a normal conversation with a human being, if there exists such a machine, might be considered intelligent. Or as another example, a machine that opens the door for people at the supermarket might not seem to be intelligent, but machines as sophisticated as *Star Wars'* C3PO or R2D2 are likely candidates for intelligent beings. Insofar as cognitivists are willing to make a distinction between the intellectual capacities of computers with different programs, we need some theory of what that difference is. We need some rationale for saying that some machines are intelligent, whereas others are not.

Although it will not be possible to review all that has been said on these matters, a famous proposal put forth by Alan Turing can provide a nice introduction. Turing's benchmark is now known as the *Turing test*. Not long after Turing had completed his work on problems in the foundations of mathematics leading up to the description of the Turing machine, World War II broke out. During the war, Turing applied his mathematical skills to problems in cryptology, aiding the British intelligence operations in breaking the secret code used in German military transmissions. After the war and soon after the technological emergence of vacuum-tube computers, Turing turned his attention to more philosophical matters. In "Computing Machinery and Intelligence," Turing proposed a standard for the possession of intelligence.

The idea was based on a parlor game in which two individuals, a man and a woman, are placed in one room, and an interviewer is placed in another. The object of the game is for the interviewer to determine which of the two subjects in the distant room, initially known to the interviewer only as "Subject A" and "Subject B," is the man, while both pretend to be the man. The basis of the interviewer's determination are questions put to the two subjects, passed back and forth by a third party. A subject may answer the interviewer's questions in any way he or she may see fit, honestly or dishonestly, in an attempt to convince the interviewer that he or she is the man.

In Turing's variation of this parlor game, the man and the woman are replaced by a computer and a person (either a man or a woman), and both are to be interviewed by a person via teletypewriter. Both the person and the computer then try to convince the interviewer that he/she or it is the person. The interviewer may ask anything he or she believes may be of some help in determining which subject is the computer and which is the person. Presumably, the interviewer will ask questions that probe for things a person would know, or think, or believe, that a computer would not. For example, the interviewer might ask, "Subject A, can you give me a word that rhymes with *Hello?*" or "Subject B, is red a hot color or a cold color?" or "Subject B, if you were standing naked in front of a crowd of people, what would you feel?" or "Subject A, is red an even number or an odd number?" Turing's suggestion is that if no interviewer could reliably determine which subject is the human and which is the computer, that is, no interviewer could make the correct determination more than about half the time, then we must say that the computer is intelligent.

An obvious variation on the game is a type of solitaire in which an interviewer asks questions of an individual on the other end of a teletype connection. If the individual can fool the interviewer into thinking the individual is a person, or has a mind, then the individual has a mind. Something like this idea appeared in a science-fiction movie *Bladerunner.* In the movie, there are androids that appear completely human and can only be distinguished from humans by measuring their responses to a series of questions. For example, an android might be asked, "Suppose you found a tortoise lying upside down in the hot sun and that it could not right itself. It will die if you do not help it. What do you do?" The police officer, or bladerunner, assigned to hunt down the androids felt great remorse at killing them because they seemed so human; they could only be detected by this very sophisticated form of Turing test.

Although Turing's idea is presented in the form of a question-and-answer game, with obvious variations, the idea underlying the Turing test is simple and can be stated quite generally: If no one can tell the difference between the computer's apparent thought and genuine thinking, then there is no difference between the computer's apparent thought and genuine thinking. The computer really thinks. Turing's idea is that if a computer can prescribe medicine as well as a normal human doctor, then it is intelligent; if a computer is as good a trial lawyer as a human, then it is intelligent; and if a computer can carry on a normal conversation, then it is intelligent. By the standard Turing suggests, we would have to say that we already have intelligent computers among us, because there are computers that play very good games of chess.

Although there is some plausibility to the Turing criterion, the most common complaint about it is that it is too easy; it counts as intelligent things that are not intelligent. It is felt that in order to be truly intelligent, to really have a mind, something more is needed. An extremely popular suggestion is that in order to have a mind, to be intelligent, to be more than a mere machine, a being must have emotions. This intuition accords with the anticognitivist sense that humans, who have emotions, also have minds, while machines, which lack emotions, also lack minds. It also accords with the cognitivist distinction between the mindless machines that open doors and the emotional and minded science-fiction androids R2D2 and C3P0. The reason we think R2D2 and C3PO have minds and think is that they are at times afraid and at other times happy.

Although there is some inclination to believe that true cognition requires emotion, it seems quite possible to find cognitive processing in completely unemotional beings. Perhaps there could be child prodigies who learn skills in math, science, and engineering at an early age, but who are emotionally defective. They might not feel anything. If we were to find such children, would they not be cognitive beings? We might make the same point using another example from science fiction. In the television show *Star Trek*, Mr. Spock, or at least all the pure Vulcans, completely lack emotions. In fact, it is sometimes suggested that if a Vulcan were to experience an emotion he or she would die. Nevertheless, people never say that Mr. Spock and the Vulcans are not intelligent, or that they have no mental lives, or that they do not really think. Indeed, the Vulcans are assumed to be a very intelligent species. We might even return to our example of the androids in the movie *Bladerunner*. Perhaps we should say only that these androids are intelligent and have minds, but that they lack our humans emotions. These new observations cast some doubt on the necessity of emotions to cognitive life.

A second theory of the difference between humans and computers is that computers always do the same thing in response to the same input, whereas humans will respond differently to the same input on different occasions. Every time one starts a computer program for adding and asks it to add 1223 and 345, it will always produce the same output. The Turing machine program

q_0 1 R q_0
q_0 0 1 q_1
q_1 1 R q_1
q_1 0 L q_2
q_2 1 0 q_2

always replaces two inputs on its tape with the sum of the two inputs. In contrast, when people see the same movie twice, or see the same person twice, they may respond in different ways on the different occasions. The first time, they may not enjoy the movie; the second time, they may. Perhaps they will see things the second time that they did not see the first. Perhaps seeing a person for the first time will produce no reaction, but after getting to know the person, seeing him or her for the second time may be a pleasant experience. This, it is sometimes thought, represents one reason why thinking cannot be the same thing as computing. In order to be able to think, a being must be capable of responding differently to the same stimulus.

This objection, however, involves a misunderstanding of computation; this should be clear given our earlier introduction to Turing machines. It is perfectly possible to have a computer provide different responses to the same input on different occasions. In fact, there are two ways in which this might be accomplished. One would be to suppose that the computer is a probabilistic computer, such as the probabilistic Turing machine defined above. If this were the hypothesis, the fact that people sometimes have different responses to the same stimulus would be due to their intrinsically probabilistic nature. The second possible explanation would appeal to differences in input. For example, seeing a movie the first time counts as a part of the input to a computer, and seeing it the second time counts as more input. From this perspective, different reactions to the same movie on different occasions would simply be a natural consequence of the additional inputs.

A variation on the preceding objection to the Turing test is that humans sometimes make mistakes, whereas computers never do. Computers are very "logical," whereas humans are often not. This objection presupposes that in order to have a mind, a being must not be entirely logical and must sometimes make mistakes. This criterion does not serve the anticognitivist as a means to separate humans from machines. The reason is simply that it is possible to write computer programs that make mistakes. A probabilistic Turing machine might be written that usually computes addition when it is supposed to, but which occasionally makes mistakes. Setting aside the fact that machines can be made to make mistakes, it would also seem that the making of errors would be a miserable criterion by which to separate intelligent machines from unintelligent machines. Why should making mistakes be a mark of intelligence?

A fourth condition that is sometimes thought to be relevant to being intelligent is speed. To be intelligent, a being must not only go through the appropriate cognitive processing, it must also do it at an appropriate rate. For example, a person who can solve multiplication problems quickly is often thought to be more intelligent than a person that multiplies more slowly. A person who can read more quickly and memorize more quickly is also thought to be more intelligent than his or her slower counterparts.

Although these observations strongly support the idea that the demarcation of intelligent from unintelligent behavior must involve some condition on speed of processing, the idea is not entirely uncontroversial. Person A might be a slower multiplier, or slower reader, than person B, for two possible reasons. The first is that A goes through the same mental steps as does person B, but that it takes A's brain longer to make the transition from one state (specified by an instantaneous description) to another than it does for B's brain. In other words, A and B run the same "mental program," but each step takes A longer to execute. A second possibility is that A and B run different mental programs, go through different sequences of instantaneous descriptions when doing multiplication or reading, and that A takes longer to do multiplication or to read simply because she goes through more mental steps in multiplying or reading. She might, for example, double-check each step in her calculations, whereas B does not, or she may read every word in a text, whereas B does not. B may skim over many of the words, without losing the content of the text.

Once we realize that there are two possible explanations for why A multiplies faster than B, our assessment of their relative intelligence becomes more complicated. We might want to say that having a faster-running brain does not make the difference between being intelligent and not being intelligent, so that if it turns out that A has a slower brain than B, then we should not say that A is less intelligent than B. Speed of processing is not to be measured in real time, in seconds and minutes; it is to be measured only in terms of the number of useful state transitions that are involved and how many, if any, are pointless. By this standard, we should say that A is less intelligent than B if A goes through a lot of idle steps in her mental processing. Because double-checking one's results will count as an intelligent thing to do, even though A may take longer to carry out some multiplication, A counts as intelligent. She is doing something sensible with her state transitions. According to this theory of the significance of the speed of mental processing, speed does not matter. All that matters for having a mind is doing something sensible at each step of mental processing.

Other more involved objections have been leveled against the Turing test, but the ones presented here constitute some of the more popular objections and misconceptions about the Turing test and cognitivism. It should be noted that we have not proved, or even argued very convincingly, either that the Turing test is a good criterion of intelligence or that it is a bad criterion. We have tried to present considerations that support and considerations that oppose the use of Turing's test as a benchmark for intelligence. At present, we do not have the evidence or the insight to say with great certainty whether the criterion is a true mark of intelligence or of having a mind, or not. This concession, however, should not be misinterpreted as saying that nobody is right and nobody is wrong. The concession means only that we cannot tell who is right and who is wrong. Time, we hope, will tell who is right.

■ COGNITIVE PSYCHOLOGY

Within the cognitive-science framework, the goals of *cognitive psychology* are to determine what sort of computing device humans are, what sorts of programs they run, and what sorts of mental processes take place in the brain. The brain is quite unlikely to turn out to be a Turing machine; that would be a virtually impossible coincidence. The ideas Turing developed as a simple example of computation are not likely to be the same as the type of computer designed by evolution by natural selection. The actual computer of the brain will likely involve different types of instructions than those in the Turing machine. The memory of the brain is almost certainly not laid out in something equivalent to a tape of squares.

Given the scientific goals of determining what sort of computing device humans are and what programs they run, we need to ask how ought we go about reaching them. This is the most divisive methodological question in cognitive psychology today. The question is "Should cognitive psychologists try to use data about the human brain in understanding cognition, or should cognitive psychologists ignore neuroscience as, at present, too primitive to contribute much of interest to our understanding of thinking?" Philosophers say that this sort of question is a methodological, or *epistemic*, question, because it concerns the methods by which we might figure something out, the methods by which we might come to know something. At present, this epistemological question is closely associated with, one might even say confused with, metaphysical questions about the nature of mental states. This metaphysics will serve as our point of departure for the examination of our epistemological question.

Consider a person, call him "Jones," who as a child learns how to do long division of 14,595 by 21. Doing long division is simply one kind of mental processing; others include thinking about moves for playing chess, painting a portrait, writing a paper, playing the piano, and balancing a chemical equation. Our example could involve any of these other mental processes. Jones could do long division as a boy, as a young man, as a mature man, and as an old man. Over all these years, Jones has been able to go through the same mental operation, even though his body has changed considerably over the years and the vast majority of the molecules making up his body as a boy have been replaced by others several times over by the time he becomes an old man. In other words, Jones can for many years go through the *same* mental process, even though his body is in various respects *different* over the years.

Obviously enough, Jones is not the only person ever to have been able to solve this long-division problem. Many other people can do the same thing he does, even though they differ from him in all manner of characteristics, such as age, height, weight, the foods they like, their allergies, the languages they speak, the music they like, how much they know about science, and on and on. All manner of people seem capable of going through the same mental process. Moreover, it is not too fantastic a piece of science fiction to suppose that there could be alien beings who also do long division, even though their bodies are made out of chemical compounds wholly undreamt of by humans. Perhaps they have silicon-based chemistry, whereas humans have carbon-based, and perhaps they run their metabolic engines on hydrogen sulfide, rather than water. Perhaps spirits made of "ghostly ectoplasm" could also do long division.

These intuitions about the sameness of mental process through biological change form the basis of functionalism, a metaphysical thesis about mental processes. According to functionalism, mental processes are not defined in terms of simpler physical, chemical, or biological processes such as electrical discharge, current flux, oxidation, hydrolysis, catalysis, hydrogen bonding, covalent bonding, approaching chemical equilibrium, DNA replication, protein synthesis, or phosphorylation. Instead, mental processes are a species of *functional* process; they are defined in terms of the *functional* interactions between psychological, and ultimately, biological, chemical, and physical objects, such as a language faculty, neurons, potassium ions, and electrical charges. So, for example, any physical process that plays the "appropriate" role in answering the question "What is 14,595 divided by 21" counts as performing long division. The physical process can be an electrical current in neurons, or an electrical current in insulated gold wires, or a marble rolling down an inclined plane, so long as it serves to enable a being to perform the right sort of behavior. The fact that mental processes are functional processes explains why beings that radically differ in their familiar physical processes can be identical in their mental processes.

The metaphysical thesis of functionalism encourages a methodological, or epistemic, attitude that denigrates the significance of biological facts. The attitude is that if the biological processes that underlie mental processes in humans are not definitive of mental processes, then it is misleading to look at them. If we were to look at the biological processes in the brain, we might be misled into thinking they define cognitive processing, that they are essential to cognitive processing. We know from our previous functionalist observations, however, that the usual physical, chemical, and biological processes with which we are familiar are not definitive of psychological processes. To put the functionalist argument bluntly, we should not look at biological data, because these will be misleading.

This argument is not a very good one. There is no reason to think that we *must* be misled by the use of biological data. We need not mistake biological contingencies of our brains for necessities in cognitive processing. Biological data does seem to be able to illuminate the nature of human cognitive processing. Perhaps an example, controversial though it is, will illustrate the point. Human speech processing generally involves the left half of the brain in right-handed people. One area of the brain, Wernicke's area, takes care of speech recognition, while Broca's area takes care of speech production. Some of the evidence in support of this hypothesis are the many observations of speech disorders in persons with brain damage from, say, tumors or gunshot wounds. Those with damage to Broca's area cannot speak, while those with damage to Wernicke's area can speak to some extent, but they often do not know what they are saying. These findings would presumably count as biological. Moreover, they suggest that perhaps there are distinct computer programs for speech production and speech perception, and that the program for recognizing speech is stored in Wernicke's area, and that the computer program for producing speech is stored in Broca's area. This is an extremely speculative view, and the brain is certainly not as simple as this example suggests, but the important point is that it is possible to use biological data, such as lesion data, in support of psychological hypotheses. For this reason, it seems to make sense to use biological data.

Even more commonsense reasons suggest that psychologists ought to use biological data in their psychological theorizing. Without using biological data to explore the brain, one is limited to behavioral tests. Although it is not possible to do justice to the full range of behavioral tests in cognitive psychology, we may venture two simple examples. A typical memory test might involve having a person listen to a list of numbers, then after having heard the last one, write the list from memory. By lengthening the list of numbers, one may test for limitations on how much information can be stored in so-called short-term memory. Other tests might examine reaction times in facial recognition and word recollection, while one might also observe the mistakes people make in learning, such as the sorts of mistakes children make when learning a natural language such as English. In the computational terms discussed in the first section of this chapter, the idea of these tests is to try to figure out the program the brain runs and what type of computer the brain is by running the program of the brain on various inputs. One knows the input of the computation, and perhaps some of the intermediate stages of processing during the computation, as well as the output of the computation. Here we have an example of how we might describe behavioral testing in cognitivist terms.

Although there is a tremendous amount that can be learned from these techniques, and a vast literature based on these techniques, it seems to be impossible to verify many of the details of cognitive processing using only these tests. It is known that for any computing device like the Turing machine, for any function on the natural numbers, if there is one program for computing the function, then there are infinitely many programs for computing the function. The question naturally arises, then, whether it is possible to discover exactly what program the brain runs, using only the behavioral-test methodology. Perhaps it is, but perhaps it is not. No one knows at present. Those sceptical of the adequacy of behavioral tests liken the difficulty of determining how the brain works based on its operation to the difficulty of trying to figure out how a radio works by fiddling with the knobs and switches.

Given the difficulty of ascertaining the program of the mind from only behavioral evidence, it would appear that we should try to find any further source of evidence that we can. In particular, what might be extremely helpful is a knowledge of how the neurons in the brain contribute to cognitive processing. Scientists have, in fact, had this very sensible idea of explaining psychological facts in terms of the operations of neurons for over a century. For example, one of earliest theoretical endeavors by Sigmund Freud, around 1895, was the articulation of a version of a neural network theory of cognition. *Connectionism*, as this theory has come to be known, has two principal tenets. First, the predominant form of cognitive processing in the brain is the passage of electrical activity between nerve cells in the brain. Such electrical activity is thought to account for spinal reflexes, motor skills, face recognition, short-term memory, speech recognition, and speech production.

All manner of biological evidence supports the importance of electrical activity in cognitive processing. For example, we have electroencephalograms that measure the waves of electrical activity over the surface of the brain. In a spinal reflex, such as the well-known knee-jerk response, external environmental stimuli induce electrical activity in the patellar tendon in the knee. This propagates to the spinal cord, which in turn sends electrical activity up the spinal cord to the brain and back to the appropriate muscles that extend the knee. In facial recognition, light striking the retina in the posterior portion of the eyeball disinhibits retinal cells, causing electrical activity in the neurons leading into the brain. Once the electrical activity reaches the brain, it is supposed to be coordinated with information stored in the brain that may be used to determine whether or not a presently visible face is familiar.

The second tenet of connectionism is that learning or remembering something is fundamentally different from other sorts of cognitive processes. Learning a person's phone number, or how to play the violin, or that Immanuel Kant was a philosopher involves modifications in the synapses that connect individual nerve cells together, hence the name *connectionism*. The reason for postulating a second biological mechanism for cognitive processing is based on the observation that people are frequently able to remember facts for decades. Because the pattern of electrical activity in a set of neurons does not appear to last for decades, some more durable substrate must be involved, and the modification of neural synapses may be that more durable substrate.

In the 1980s, connectionism has enjoyed a tremendous resurgence in popularity under the name of *parallel distributed processing*. The theory now involves a tremendous amount of mathematics used to specify the operations of the individual neurons, their interactions at synapses, and various ways in which synapses might be modified, but in essence the theory is a "jazzed-up" version of late-nineteenth-century ideas.

Although the theory is rather simple in outline, and the methodology seems eminently reasonable in theory, in actual practice, neuroscience and connectionism at present form a rather meager basis for the elaboration of a genuinely explanatory and predictive theory of cognition. The reason is that much of the neuroscientific information that would most usefully guide connectionism is not available; that is, even though we know a tremendous amount about the brain and neurons, we simply do not have some of the facts most crucial to a connectionist theory of cognition. Neuroscience in this century has succeeded in determining the chemical and biochemical mechanisms underlying the electrical activity of individual neurons and their pairwise interactions at synapses. Beyond this firm basis in neuroscientific fact, connectionism becomes extremely speculative. Some of the leading open questions in this area include "What features of the electrical activity of individual neurons really matter for cognitive processes?" "What information is transmitted through the brain via the electrical signals?" and "How is it transmitted?" This difficulty may be clarified by an analogy. Suppose one listens to repeated sequences of long tones and short tones. One will readily discern that the sequences are made up of a series of short and long tones, but it will be extremely difficult to figure out what the sequence means. One does not know how the individual tones are combined into larger units, whether two, three, four, or more tones are to be combined into a single unit, or even what the units are supposed to be. The units might be words in English or some foreign language, or letters in English or some other foreign language, or perhaps some units with meanings, though not words in themselves. With the brain, we know that neurons signal each other using some code made up of so-called action potentials, but as yet we do not know what the code is nor what sorts of messages are written in the code.

Another extremely important question concerns the very idea of the existence of synaptic modifications in the cortex of the brain and its possible correlation with learning and memory. The cortex of the brain is the most evolutionarily developed portion of the human brain. Its size relative to our body weight in part explains why humans are smarter than other animal species. Yet, neuroscience has not been able to provide convincing evidence that synaptic modification takes place in the cortex, or that it is correlated with learning and the formation of memories.

Finally, there do not yet exist neuroscientific techniques that will allow scientists to ascertain the organization of neurons into circuits in the relevant regions of the brain. Many things are known about the pathways sets of neurons take in the brain, but little is known about the exact patterns of wiring that exist between individual neurons. This point may also be brought out by an analogy. Our knowledge of neural circuitry is similar to knowing how bundles of wires work their way through a television set, without knowing how the individuals wires are connected to their terminal points. At present, connectionists deal with our present ignorance by investigating those circuitry patterns that most readily admit of conceptual and mathematical analysis.

In this section, we have considered two methodological options for cognitive science. One is to try to use biological facts to build a psychological theory, the other is to ignore biological facts as either misleading or of little use. In support of the use of biological facts are the observations that there must eventually be some account of the role of neurons in cognition, and the fact that purely behavioral evidence gleaned from running the human mental computer seems to be insufficient to pin down the details of cognitive processing. In support of setting aside the use of biological facts is the apparent unfeasibility of the project as witnessed by the difficulties facing connectionism. Although we might like to use biological facts to guide our psychological theorizing, the facts that would be of greatest value are presently unavailable. It thus appears that both methodologies are unpromising. This is rather unsatisfying; we want to know how we ought to go about doing psychological research. We want some answers. Unfortunately, at present, we do not have the evidence that would allow us to say with justification which method is in fact superior.

■ CONCLUSION

Many scientific disciplines have their origins in philosophy. Aristotle, one of the greatest of all philosophers, was also a biologist, chemist, meteorologist, physicist, logician, and astronomer. René Descartes was a philosopher, but he invented analytical geometry and made contributions to optics and physics. Isaac Newton referred to himself as a natural philosopher, though we always think of him as a physicist. In the late nineteenth century, psychology announced its independence from philosophy. The emergence of a new scientific discipline from a philosophical beginning is a rare event in intellectual history. The emergence of cognitive science is one of those rare events, stemming from arcane questions in the foundations of mathematics and logic during the 1930s, from programming efforts in early computer science, and from a psychological tradition looking for a new perspective on the mind. In this chapter, we have touched briefly on some of the theoretical work in computer science. We have also considered one of the philosophical questions that arises when one attempts to use the mathematics of computation as the mathematics of cognition. Finally, we have considered the leading methodological question of contemporary cognitive science, to use or not to use biological evidence in psychological theorizing. What we have seen, therefore, is that new scientific developments can raise rather difficult philosophical questions, questions that we do not yet know how to answer, but which we must nevertheless face if we are to make progress in our scientific endeavors to understand the world around us.

■ QUESTIONS

1. Suppose you have a machine that plays chess and that the time it takes to make a move depends on how fast you turn a crank on the side of it—that is, the faster you turn the crank, the faster it makes a move. Does the machine get smarter or more intelligent when you turn the crank faster?

2. It seems reasonable to suppose that there are computations that existing computers can perform that no human could ever perform before his or her death. For example, no human could ever perform all the computations necessary to guide a rocket to the moon. The person would not live long enough to do the math. Does this mean that existing computers, such as the ones used to navigate in space, are smarter than people? Why, or why not?

3. Connectionists try to use both biological and psychological evidence in the development of their theories. Is this an important method to be followed? Why, or why not?

4. Connectionists say that cognition involves two fundamentally different processes, weight change and activation propagation. These correspond to learning and memory storage, on the one hand, and all other cognitive processes on the other. Does a cognitivist posit one mechanism for learning and another for other cognitive processes, or is learning just another cognitive process?

5. What is an appropriate response to the following argument? "Computers do not lie; they always tell the truth. In contrast, humans sometimes lie, so, no computer can think like a person does."

6. What is an appropriate response to the following argument? "Computers only do what humans tell them to do, but humans can do whatever they want to do. So, computers cannot think."

7. How might an advocate of cognitivism account for the scientific observation that humans have certain natural instincts, say, fear of fire, fear of large animals? How might a connectionist account for instincts?

8. How might a cognitivist say that humans differ from other primates and other higher mammals? How might a connectionist say that humans differ from other primates and other higher mammals?   ■

■ **FOR FURTHER READING**

Cutland, N. J. *Computability: An Introduction to Recursive Function Theory*. Cambridge: Cambridge Univ. Press, 1980.

Graubard, Stephen. *The Artificial Intelligence Debate*. Cambridge, MA: MIT Press, 1980.

Haugeland, John. *Mind Design*. Cambridge, MA: MIT Press, 1981.

———. *Artificial Intelligence: The Very Idea*. Cambridge, MA: MIT Press, 1985.

McCorduck, Pamela. *Machines Who Think*. New York: Freeman, 1979.

Turing, Alan. "Computing Machinery and Intelligence." *Mind* 59 (1950).

Writing Philosophical Papers

LEEMON McHENRY

The art of philosophy is perhaps like the art of fencing at least in one respect: You can not learn it just from watching or reading books. Just as the novice fencer must take up the foil, learn basic techniques of offense and defense, and then engage in battle with an opponent, the student of philosophy must eventually take up the issues and problems, learn basic logical skills, and argue a thesis. In neither endeavor is there only one recipe for success. The progress is slow, but the more you practice, the more likely you are to get the swing of it.

One of the best ways to learn philosophy (though certainly not the only way—as Socrates clearly demonstrated) is to commit your ideas to writing. Here your imagined audience is your instructor, your classmates, and ultimately yourself because you are writing about what you believe to be the truth. Your task is to devise a convincing argument that shows you have done your work and know the material.

Philosophy papers are probably not very much like other papers you have written for English or history classes, even though basic writing skills such as spelling, grammar, and overall structure are just as important. What distinguishes a philosophy paper is the emphasis on critical analysis and argument of a thesis. In this respect, it is not a mere summary or paraphrase of an author's point of view. Nor is it a *collection* of quotations from several philosophers or commentators. Rather, a philosophy paper is the result of your taking up some problem, issue, or interpretation; subjecting it to careful analysis; and developing your own point of view. Thus, your *thesis* is the main *conclusion* of your paper that you support with *premises*. This gives your paper its essential logical structure such that the development of your essay is a process of articulating reasons for your main conclusion.

One point cannot be emphasized too much: *Your thesis is a proposition or statement that demands demonstration.* Therefore, the thesis should be less obvious than the reasons used to support it. An argument is a set of statements that support a conclusion, but if you begin to defend some point that is already well established or uncontroversial, the paper is doomed from the start because there is no argument or any point that needs demonstration. A genuine thesis, on the other hand, should elicit this response from the reader: "Interesting, but let's see you prove it!"

There are two fundamental types of philosophy papers. The first is the topic or problem paper, in which your aim is to take up some philosophical issue or problem (for example, "What is knowledge?" "Must morality be based on religion?" "Is capital punishment just?" or "What is a possible world?") and attempt to argue for an answer. You develop your thesis by taking a stand on the issue and giving reasons to support what you believe. You may also want to criticize the views of those who hold the thesis that directly contradicts your view. In this way, you strengthen your thesis by refuting your opposition, and, in the process, clarify for yourself the merits of the position you are defending.

The second type of philosophy paper is expository or interpretative. This type of paper will require the use of primary sources (original works) and secondary sources (commentaries on these works). In expository or interpretative papers, you concentrate on an original work or works written by some important philosopher(s) and attempt to uncover and explain the real point(s). For example, such a paper might discuss the definition of justice in Plato's *Republic*, Descartes's examination of the piece of wax in *The Meditations*, or the concept of duty in Kant and Ross. Here you defend some interpretation of these difficult-to-understand passages or works, answering such questions as "What do they mean?" and "What is the author really trying to say?" Your task is to illuminate and expose so that you make clear the key ideas, assumptions, implications, or meanings of terms. You may want to accomplish your exposition by referring your reader to other works or commentators to clarify the passages under analysis. This leads you to secondary sources that you may use either to support your interpretation or reject as inadequate to the proper understanding of the ideas, texts, and so on. Note especially that the expository paper still argues a thesis; it is your idea about how we should most properly understand and appreciate an idea, a text, and so on.

In either kind of paper, you will typically have a beginning, middle, and end, or:

1. a statement of your thesis or position—the view or conclusion for which you are going to argue
2. an exposition and/or argument, with proper documentation of your sources
3. a conclusion—a final statement of the thesis, together with a brief summary of how you have reached it

Because the thesis and defense are crucial parts of any philosophy paper, it is essential that you include a brief statement of your thesis in the first paragraph. Doing so clarifies for your reader what you intend to accomplish in the paragraphs that follow. For the most part, the paper will be evaluated in terms of how successful you are in doing what you said you were going to do. You might clearly identify your thesis by saying: "In this paper, I will argue that. . ." or "This essay will defend the view that. . ." Now you can proceed to discuss the thesis and provide background information that explains its importance. Make certain that the reader is left with no doubt as to what you intend to accomplish. This sets up the body of your paper, which contains the support for your particular thesis. To bring your paper to a close, you will need to summarize briefly what you have done and how you have done it.

Getting started is often the most difficult obstacle to overcome. In many cases, a thesis will not be the first thing you think of, although it is often helpful to have some rough idea (and outline) before you plunge into the body of the paper. You should regard your initial ideas as tentative and subject to revision as you explore the thicket of arguments for and against the view you hope to defend. Mozart once said that his musical compositions were committed to paper quickly because everything was already finished in his head before he picked up the quill. Most writers, however, rarely write papers in the fashion that Mozart wrote music. Leaving aside cases of extraordinary genius, for the most part philosophy papers grow out of successive revisions in which ideas clarify themselves as you engage in the process of writing.

The following suggestions should help you get started.

First, find some topic with which you feel comfortable. If the problems of metaphysics and epistemology are too obscure and remote from your own personal concerns, then find a problem in ethics, aesthetics, or the philosophy of religion that excites your imagination or addresses some issue in your own life. In addition, do not try to cover too much territory. Narrow your topic, and do not try to defend a thesis that would require a book-length discussion. Find a topic suitable for the length requirement of the paper, and pursue it in sufficient depth, showing that you have mastered some aspect of the problem or text. In many respects, your achievement will grow in proportion to what you decide to leave out.

Second, study the readings carefully, think about the material, and make notes.

Third, formulate a thesis about a problem and begin to explore what you think about the problem. In the most basic sense, your main task in writing a philosophy paper is to come up with some fairly original thesis or novel interpretation of the text. As we have noted already, this will probably be rather tentative at first.

Fourth, consider preparing an outline to help you formulate the logical structure of the paper.

Let us pretend that you are a Christian and want to defend the soul theory. You bring to this project certain assumptions that you have acquired from your background—home life, church teachings, and personal experience. These may include a belief in an immortal soul that is distinct from the body and survives death in an otherworldly paradise or in an otherworldly hell, depending on one's moral behavior and pious devotion in this earthly existence. You therefore begin to think about your beliefs within the context of the philosophical issue of personal identity, and construct your tentative thesis: "This essay will demonstrate the truth of the Christian view of the soul."

This is an ambitious project because you begin with the strong claim that you will demonstrate the "truth" of the Christian view of the soul, but it is a good starting place. Having read the various chapters in this book relevant to your thesis however,—"Personal Identity" (Chapter 9), "Metaphysics" (Chapter 3), "Philosophy of Mind" (Chapter 10) and "Philosophy of Religion" (Chapter 8)—you are confronted with some serious objections to the very notion of a soul and some inconsistencies in the Christian interpretation.

You might be troubled by these problems, but you remain confident that your original thesis can be defended against these objections if you modify it and proceed with careful analysis. Furthermore, you are advised by your instructor to read the relevant parts of Aristotle and St. Thomas Aquinas that defend the soul theory, and now you revise your thesis to be slightly more modest: "This essay will attempt to demonstrate that there are souls distinct from our bodies that survive the death of our bodies." Notice that the revised thesis is narrower in scope because it does not commit you to all of the claims connected to the Christian view. For example, your thesis involves defending the independence of the soul from the body, but it does not commit you to arguing for the existence of heaven or hell.

This now gives you something on which to build an outline and begin writing the essay. At this point, your argument will involve addressing the objections to the notion of the soul and attempting to overcome them with the help of Aristotle and St. Thomas Aquinas. You will also need to show that your view holds up better than the opposition, for example, a purely materialistic interpretation that holds persons do not survive the death of their bodies.

To sum up then, you have found a topic, constructed a tentative thesis, and modified the thesis in light of further reading and reflection. You can now get down to the business of writing and thinking through the problems.

This, of course, is the hard part. You must always guard against dogmatism. If in the process of defending your thesis, you discover that your view really doesn't hold up against the opposition, or that you have been assuming the truth of your position without critical examination, you must follow the argument where it leads you. Ultimately, your first and foremost obligation is to truth and honesty.

As you write and revise your paper, be aware of some logical errors or fallacies that are commonly found in philosophical arguments: the straw man, irrelevant appeal to authority, and begging the question. Some of these fallacies and a number of others are discussed in Chapter 2. Check yourself to see if you have committed any of these fallacies. For example, when you are guilty of the straw man fallacy, you misrepresent the view of the opposition in the attempt to refute that view. Be careful, then, to ensure that you understand and fairly represent the view you set out to attack; otherwise, you are simply attacking your own misunderstanding.

In light of what you discover in thinking and writing about your topic, you might have to abandon your original beliefs and begin to think afresh about your paper. If, in fact, this happens, in no way does it mean failure, for the whole point of writing is to confront yourself with this process of critical examination. What survives this process is worthy of defense; what does not survive and forces you to reconstruct your beliefs is an intellectual step forward.

Once your paper is finished, read it over, looking for spelling and typographical errors, faulty grammar, logical errors, or incoherence in the flow of your argument. It is always a good idea to write your paper well in advance of the deadline so that you can lay it aside for a while and come back to it again with a fresh eye before you deliver it to your instructor. It is also helpful to have someone else look over the paper for you, but make sure that you choose someone whose judgment you can trust. After you have made corrections and incorporated suggestions, you are ready to prepare the final copy.

■ FOR FURTHER READING

Hole, George T. "How to Write a Philosophy Paper." APA *Newsletter on Teaching Philosophy* 4 (4): Winter 1984.

Kahane, Howard. *Logic and Contemporary Rhetoric.* Belmont, CA: Wadsworth, 1988.

Martinich, A. P. *Philosophical Writing.* Englewood Cliffs, NJ: Prentice-Hall, 1989.

Strunk, William, Jr., and E. B. White. *The Elements of Style.* New York: Macmillan, 1979.

GLOSSARY

Act utilitarianism   In ethics, the form of **utilitarianism** that holds that it is the consequences of the action under consideration that need to be taken into account. See also **rule utilitarianism**.

Aesthetic experience   In aesthetics, pleasurable experience typically resulting from contact with works of art or natural beauty. See also **sublime**.

Aesthetics   The theory of art. Philosophical investigation of the beautiful and **sublime**.

Analytic   In epistemology, a proposition in which the predicate merely spells out what the subject implies. See also **synthetic**.

Antecedent   The component of a **conditional** proposition that immediately follows the word *if*. See also **consequent**.

Anthropomorphism   The attribution of human characteristics to a nonhuman being or thing.

Anti-intentionalist   In aesthetics, the view that interpretations of works of art should ignore the artist's intentions. See also **four-factor theory, object for interpretation**.

A *posteriori*   Latin for "from what comes after." In epistemology, a claim that involves knowledge dependent on experience (see **empirical**). See also *a priori*.

A *priori*   Latin for "from what is before." In epistemology, a claim that involves knowledge independent of experience. Anything known in this way cannot be refuted by experiment or observation. See also *a posteriori*.

Argument   A group of statements arranged such that one (the conclusion) is intended to follow from the others (the premises).

Artificial intelligence   The branch of cognitive science concerned with the development of intelligent machines.

Atomism   In metaphysics, the theory that reality is composed of tiny, indivisible material **particulars** or atoms and the **void**.

Aural experience   In aesthetics, a sensory experience due to the sense of hearing.

Axiology   Value theory including ethics, aesthetics, and political philosophy.

Behaviorism, philosophical   The view that mental states and processes are identifiable with or reducible to behavior or dispositions to do this or that depending on how one is stimulated (see **identity, reduction**). See also **functionalism** and **behaviorism, psychological**.

Behaviorism, psychological   A collection of methodological precepts and empirical theory. Behaviorists avoid references to unobservable mental states and focus on simple stimulus-response mechanisms in explaining behavior. See also **behaviorism, philosophical**.

Body theory   In the theory of personal identity, the view that person X = person Y if and only if X's body = Y's body. See also **brain theory, psychological continuity, soul theory**.

Brain bisection   The operation of separating the two hemispheres of the brain by severing the connecting band of fibers known as the **corpus callosum**. Brain-bisected subjects raise the philosophical question of whether there can be two persons existing in one body.

Brain theory In the theory of personal identity, the view that person X = person Y if and only if X's brain = Y's brain. See also **body theory, psychological continuity, soul theory**.

Categorical imperative In ethics, an "ought judgment" with no *ifs* about it; an unconditional command. See also **hypothetical imperative**.

Circular definition A definition is circular if it makes use of the expression to be defined (or any expression whose definition contains the expression to be defined).

Cognitive A mental **event, state**, or process relating or pertaining to knowledge.

Cognitive science The study of mental processes such as thinking, perceiving, remembering, inferring, learning, believing, and knowing, constituted by contributions from computer science, psychology, **artificial intelligence**, neuroscience, and **philosophy of mind**.

Cognitivism In philosophy of mind and cognitive science, the view that cognition is computation.

Coherence In epistemology, a relation between a belief (proposition) and other beliefs (propositions). Beliefs (propositions) cohere to the degree that they mutually support one another's truth or likelihood of being true.

Coherentism In epistemology, the view that the justification of a belief is a product of its **coherence** with other beliefs. See also **correspondence theory of truth**.

Concept A mental construct that contains all of the objects or events classified together according to their common **properties**. An abstraction or general idea to which particular objects or events belong.

Conditional A type of proposition, the standard form of which is "if such-and-such is the case, then so-and-so is the case" (If p, then q). Other forms of the conditional include "p if q," and "p only if q." See also **antecedent, consequent**.

Connectionism In cognitive science, the theory that neurobiological processes in neurons and their synapses, or mathematically specified processes in nodes and connections, have an explanatory role to play in human **cognitive** processing.

Consequent The component of a **conditional** proposition that immediately follows the word *then*. See also **antecedent**.

Consequentialism In ethics, the general theory that holds that the rightness or wrongness of an action is determined by the consequences the action would have if it were performed. See also **non-consequentialism**.

Content See **intentionality**.

Contingent proposition An ordinary descriptive proposition of the sort usually expressed in a declarative sentence. Neither necessarily true (see **tautology**) nor necessarily false (see **contradiction**). See also **logical form, necessary proposition**.

Contradiction Two propositions that cannot both be true; neither can they both be false. One is the denial of the other. One proposition is self-contradictory if it denies itself. Such a proposition must be necessarily false. See also **logical form, tautology**.

Correspondence theory of truth In epistemology, the view that a belief is true if it correctly describes reality. When reality corresponds or agrees with its depiction, the depiction of reality is said to be "true." See also **coherentism**.

Cosmological argument In the philosophy of religion, an *a posteriori* argument for the existence of God that attempts to deduce God's existence from the alleged necessity for a first cause of the universe or an ultimate explanation of the universe. See also **ontological argument, teleological argument**.

Counterfactual A **conditional** proposition that has an unrealized **antecedent**; for example, "If the moon were made of green cheese, mice would worship it."

Cultural relativism In ethics, the claim that different societies have different beliefs about what is morally right or wrong. See also **ethical relativism**.

Deduction In logic, a method of reasoning in which the premises of an **argument** are claimed to provide necessary support for the conclusion. See also **induction**.

Deontic logic The logic of obligation; the branch of logic that formulates and systematizes principles that are specific to concepts such as "obligation," "rightness," "wrongness," "permissibility," and the like.

Descriptive claim In ethics and aesthetics, a claim that says what is the case without commenting on whether it is good or bad. See also **normative claim**.

Desert theory of distributive justice In political philosophy, the theory that a distributive system is just if and only if it distributes rewards in accordance with what everyone deserves. See also **distributive justice**.

Deterministic Turing machine In cognitive science, a **Turing machine** that always does the same thing when in the same state scanning the same type of symbol. More technically, a Turing machine whose program contains instructions each of which differs from the others in either its first state symbol or its first tape symbol (see **Turing machine state symbol, Turing machine tape symbol**).

Diminishing marginal utility of material goods In political philosophy, the phenomenon of a given amount of a material good being less beneficial to someone the more of that material good he or she already has.

Distributive justice In political philosophy, justice in the distribution of benefits and burdens.

Divine command theory In ethics and the philosophy of religion, the theory that ethical statements are made true or false by God's decreeing how we should act.

Dualism In metaphysics and the philosophy of mind, the view that minds and bodies belong to distinct, nonoverlapping metaphysical domains. Minds are nonphysical entities; bodies are nonmental. See also **ontology, monism, pluralism**.

Eliminativism In the philosophy of mind, the view that, as science progresses, we will have reason to doubt the existence of the entities, states, and processes referred to in **folk psychology**. Eliminativism is distinguished from reductionism (see **reduction**).

Empirical Knowledge derived from sense experience—sight, sound, touch, smell, or taste (see *a posteriori*).

Empiricism The theory that all knowledge of facts is derived from sense experience. No knowledge is innate or constructed by reasoning independent of experience (see **rationalism**).

Enthymeme In logic, an argument with an unstated, taken-for-granted, premise or premises.

Epiphenomenalism In the philosophy of mind, the view that physical events can have mental effects, but mental events are causally impotent. What appear to be the effects of mental occurrences are in reality caused by the physical events responsible for those mental occurrences.

Epistemology   The theory of knowledge. The philosophical investigation of the nature and conditions of knowledge.

Ethical relativism   In ethics, the thesis that whatever beliefs a society has adopted about what is morally right or wrong is morally right or wrong. See also **cultural relativism**.

Ethics   The philosophical study of morality; the study of the nature and defense of moral judgments.

Event   A particular, nonrepeatable, dated occurrence, typically involving a change.

Evidence   In epistemology, a natural relation between things or events such that one carries information about the other.

Expression as articulation   In aesthetics, the attempt to specify the thoughts, perception, likes, and dislikes that underlie an emotional state.

Externalism   (1) In epistemology, the view that knowledge may depend on factors beyond one's grasp, awareness, or control. (2) In the philosophy of mind, the view that the intentionality of states of mind is determined in part by the **extrinsic properties** of agents (see **intrinsic property**). See also **internalism**.

Extrinsic property   A property possessed by an object that depends on the existence of some distinct object or state of affairs. See also **intrinsic property**.

Fallacy   In logic, an error in reasoning. A fallacy need not be obvious; it is not to be confused with the purely factual error of reasoning on the basis of false information. See also ***non sequitur*, invalid argument**.

Family resemblance   A relation among objects such that each object is similar in a specific way to another, but no other object need be similar in the same way.

Finite state control unit   In cognitive science, the portion of a **Turing machine** that contains the **Turing machine program** and that scans the squares of the **Turing machine tape**.

Folk psychology   The psychological theory we learn as we learn our language. Folk psychology explains behavior by reference to postulated beliefs, desires, and intentions (see **propositional attitude, theoretical entity**), which are taken to be the hidden causes of that behavior.

Form   (1) In Plato's metaphysics, a "Form" is an immaterial and independently existing entity that determines the nature of **particular** things in the material world. (2) In Aristotle's metaphysics, a form is the essential characteristic of an individual **substance**, but does not exist independently of the substance.

Foundationalism   In epistemology, the view that for some belief to be known or justified there must be basic beliefs that do not depend on other beliefs to be known or justified. These basic beliefs are said to be known or justified foundationally.

Four-factor theory   In aesthetics, the view that whether an object is a work of art depends on four distinct factors: its function, the intention with which it is made, the medium in which it is made, and when it is made. See also **institutional theory of art, open-concept theory of art**.

Functionalism   In the philosophy of mind, the view that **states** of mind are functional states of creatures possessing them. A functional state is a state characterizable in terms of its causal propensities. See also **behaviorism, philosophical**.

Hedonism   In ethics, the conception of the good life that takes pleasure as the ultimate good.

Higher-order psychological states   Psychological states that are *about* psychological states—for example, a belief about a belief.

Hypothetical imperative   In ethics, a judgment that involves a condition; a command of the form "If you desire D or goal G, then do action A." See also **categorical imperative**.

Idealism   In metaphysics and the philosophy of mind, the theory that ultimate reality is composed of mind or spirit. There are no material (or physical) **substances, states, or events**. See also **materialism**.

Identity   A relation of selfsameness holding between some item and itself. If A is identical with B (A = B), then A and B are one and the same.

Identity theory   In the philosophy of mind, the view that mental phenomena are identical with physical phenomena (see **identity**). **Type-identity** theories hold that mental properties are identical with certain physical properties (perhaps complex neural properties) of conscious agents. **Token-identity** theories hold that every mental particular is identical with some physical particular.

Induction   In logic, a method of reasoning in which the premises of an **argument** are claimed to provide probable support for the conclusion. See also **deduction**.

Inference   In logic, the process of reasoning expressed by an **argument**. See also **deduction, induction**.

Institutional theory of art   In aesthetics, the view that an object is a work of art if and only if it acquires a special status in a social institution known as the artworld. See also **four-factor theory, open-concept theory of art**.

Instrumentalism   In the philosophy of science, the view that scientific theories neither provide nor purport to provide true or false descriptions of the world. See also **pragmatism, realism**.

Intentionality   The property of being *of, for,* or *about* something; associated with states of mind and meaningful utterances and inscriptions. Items possessing intentionality—thoughts, sentences, gestures—are said to have propositional or intentional content. See also **propositional attitude**.

Interactionism   The view that, despite fundamental differences, minds and bodies causally interact. Mental events produce changes in bodies, and physical occurrences have mental effects. See also **dualism**.

Internalism   In the philosophy of mind, the view that the intentionality of states of mind is to be explained exclusively by reference to the **intrinsic properties** of agents. A pair of intrinsically indiscernible agents in very different contexts must, according to internalism, have the same thoughts. See also **externalism**.

Intrinsic property   A property possessed by an object independently of any other object or state of affairs. See also **extrinsic property**.

Intuitionism   In ethics, the theory that certain basic moral statements are self-evident and therefore can be known to be true by all reasonable and thoughtful people.

Invalid argument   An **argument** in which the conclusion does not follow from the premises. An argument that commits a **fallacy** of *non sequitur*. See also **valid argument**.

Logic   (1) In the narrower, more usual, sense, *logic* refers to the systematic investigation of the general principles of valid inference (see **inference, valid argument**). (2) In the broader, less usual, sense, it refers to any conceptual investigation.

Logical form   (1) The logical form of a deductive argument is the aspect of its structure that determines its validity or invalidity (see **deduction, valid argument, invalid argument**). The various techniques of symbolizing and diagraming are tools for clarifying logical form. (2) The logical form of a **proposition** is the structure that determines whether the proposition is contingent or necessary (see **contingent proposition, necessary proposition**).

Logical positivism   Philosophical movement of the Vienna Circle in the twentieth century. A variety of **empiricism** that stresses the tautological nature of logical and mathematical propositions, together with the criterion of verifiability for factual propositions (see **tautology, verification principle**).

Matter   In Aristotle's metaphysics, the indeterminate stuff that receives determination by being imbued with a **form**. In modern thought, matter is the basis of physical reality subject to quantitative analysis and is usually contrasted with mind. See also **materialism, substance**.

Materialism   The theory that reality is fundamentally composed of **matter**. Mind or spirit has no independent reality. Only physical matter and its properties exist. See also **idealism**.

Metaphysics   Systematic investigation into the most general principles of reality.

Monism   In metaphysics, the theory that there is only one **substance**, or that all of the constituents of the universe are of one kind, usually either mental or spiritual (see **idealism**), or material (see **materialism**). See also **dualism, pluralism**.

Moral philosophy   See **ethics**.

Natural religion   In the philosophy of religion, a religious belief or religious practice grounded in the normal operations of human reason and not based on revelation (see **revealed religion**).

Naturalism   The belief that all the phenomena of the universe can be accounted for by the same methods of explanation—considerations of the nature of human beings, human society, and the like, without reference to the supernatural.

Necessary condition   A is a necessary condition of B if and only if B could not occur without A. See also **sufficient condition**.

Necessary proposition   A proposition that is necessarily true or necessarily false in virtue of its **logical form** alone. A necessarily true proposition is one that cannot be denied without a **contradiction** or inconsistency (see **tautology**). A necessarily false proposition is one that (1) either *is* or *implies* a contradiction or (2) is a contradiction in terms. See also **contingent proposition**.

Necessary and sufficient conditions   A condition that is both a **necessary condition** and a **sufficient condition** is normally expressed in terms of the language *if and only if*.

Non-consequentialism. In ethics, the general theory that holds that the rightness or wrongness of an action is determined by factors other than the consequences the action would have if it were performed. See also **consequentialism**.

Non sequitur. Latin for "it does not follow." The largest class of **fallacies**. To say that an **argument** commits a fallacy of *non sequitur* is the same as saying that it is **invalid**.

Normative claim   In ethics and aesthetics, a claim that says whether something should be the case, or whether it is good or bad. See also **descriptive claim**.

Object for interpretation   In aesthetics, the view that an object should be interpreted according to the aims we bring to it rather than the intention with which it was made. See also **anti-intentionalist**.

Ontological argument   In the philosophy of religion, an *a priori* argument for the existence of God that attempts to deduce God's existence from the concept of God. See also **cosmological argument, teleological argument**.

Ontology   The branch of metaphysics that attempts to determine what exists. The study of being or existence.

Open-concept theory of art   In aesthetics, the view that there are no **necessary and sufficient conditions** for an object to qualify as a work of art. See also **four-factor theory, institutional theory of art**.

Paradox   (1) An apparently contradictory **proposition** (see **contradiction**). (2) An **argument** whose conclusion *must* (it seems) be true (because it follows necessarily from clearly true premises) and yet cannot possibly be true (because it is patently absurd).

Parallel distributed processing   In cognitive science, a strain of contemporary **connectionism**.

Parallelism   In the philosophy of mind, the view that minds and bodies do not interact causally, but function in parallel. Mental occurrences may be correlated with changes in bodies, and physical events may coincide with mental happenings, but the relations are not causal.

Particular   In metaphysics, a concrete individual entity.

Personal identity   Persons X and Y are identical just in case X and Y are the selfsame person (see **identity**).

Philosophy of mind   Distinguishable from psychology, though not sharply. Psychology concentrates on empirical aspects of mind. The philosophy of mind, in contrast, focuses on conceptual matters.

Physicalism   See **materialism**.

Pluralism   In metaphysics, the view that the world is composed of many distinct **substances** or many different kinds of substance. See also **monism, dualism**.

Political philosophy   The study of whether the state is justified, of what the purpose of a justified state would be, of what obligations citizens have to their state, and of what the state should do for its citizens.

Possible world   In metaphysics, any real or imagined, but logically consistent, state of affairs.

Pragmatism   American philosophical movement that rejects absolute metaphysical foundations or principles in favor of theories or beliefs that are useful and result in effective modes of adaptation. See also **instrumentalism**.

Prima facie   Latin for "at first appearance." In ethics, a *prima facie* duty is a conditional duty, one we should do if there is not an overriding, more important, duty that applies in the particular case.

Probabilistic Turing machine   In cognitive science, a **Turing machine** that does different things with different probabilities when in the same state scanning the same type of symbol. More technically, a Turing machine that may have a program with more than one instruction that begins with the same first two symbols and for which each instruction sharing the same first two symbols there is a fixed probability.

Property   In metaphysics, the repeatable characteristics of individual **substances** or **events**.

Proposition   The content or meaning expressed by a complete declarative sentence; an assertion that is either true or false.

Propositional attitude   A state of mind characterizable by reference to two factors; a particular proposition, and a particular attitude toward that proposition. See also **proposition, folk psychology**.

Psychological continuity   The idea common in theories of **personal identity** that a person consists of a continuous series of psychological **states** or **events**. See also **body theory, brain theory, soul theory**.

Quality   See **property**.

Rationalism   The theory that knowledge is gained chiefly through intuition and reason independent of experience. This theory contrasts with **empiricism**, the view that knowledge is gained only by experience.

Realism   In the philosophy of science, the view that scientific claims provide descriptions, true or false, of reality. See also **instrumentalism, pragmatism**.

Reduction   Applies to concepts or entities, and sometimes distinguished from elimination (see **eliminativism**). A concept or entity, A, is reduced to another, B, when it is shown that A's are nothing but B's.

Reliabilism   In epistemology, the theory that identifies knowing that something is true with having a true belief that is based on **evidence** that would not exist unless what it is evidence for were the case.

Representational art   In aesthetics, art that depicts, describes, or in any other way is *about* something, real or imaginary.

Revealed religion   In the philosophy of religion, a religious belief or religious practice based on purported communications or disclosures by a divine being. See also **natural religion**.

Rule utilitarianism   In ethics, the form of **utilitarianism** that holds that it is the consequences of a type of action that are relevant to deciding whether to perform a particular action of that type. See also **act utilitarianism**.

Scepticism   In epistemology, the view that knowledge or rationally justified belief, as we usually conceive of it, is unobtainable.

Solipsism   In the philosophy of mind, the view that all that exists is myself and my own thoughts.

Soul   (*psyche*, Greek; *anima*, Latin) (1) principle of life; (2) a person's inner-life, self, or personality; (3) subject of conscious experience.

Soul theory   In the theory of personal identity, the view that person X = person Y if and only if X's soul = Y's soul. The soul theory is held by a number of religions and is thought by many people to be the only theory of personal identity that allows for an afterlife. See also **body theory, brain theory, psychological continuity**.

Sound argument   A **valid argument** with all true premises.

State   A particular, nonrepeatable, datable condition. Distinguished from an **event** by the absence of change.

Statement   See **proposition**.

Sublime   In aesthetics, an awe-inspiring experience. See also **aesthetic experience**.

Substance   In metaphysics, a **particular**; the essential reality of a thing that is fundamental and exists independently; that which has or underlies **properties**.

Sufficient condition   A is a sufficient condition of B if and only if the truth or presence of A is all that is required for the truth or presence of B. See also **necessary condition**.

Syllogism   A species of deductive argument consisting of two premises and one conclusion. See also **deduction**.

Synthetic   In epistemology, a proposition in which the predicate expands on the meaning of the subject. See also **analytic**.

Tautology   A proposition that is necessarily true in virtue of its **logical form**. See also **contradiction**.

Teleological argument   In the philosophy of religion, an *a posteriori* argument for the existence of God that attempts to establish God's existence on the basis of the alleged need to account for the elements of purpose and harmony in the universe. See also **cosmological argument, ontological argument**.

Theoretical entity   An entity postulated to explain some observable condition or **event**.

Turing machine   In cognitive science, a simple type of mathematically specified computing device consisting of a **finite state control unit** that scans single squares on an infinite tape divided into squares. The machine's behavior is governed by what the finite state control unit scans on the tape and the program contained within the finite state control unit.

Turing machine initial state   In cognitive science, the condition of a **Turing machine** when a computation begins, namely, when the **finite state control unit** is in state q_0 scanning the *1*, if any, appearing farthest to the left on the tape.

Turing machine instantaneous description   In cognitive science, a description of what appears on the **Turing machine** tape, the state of the **finite state control unit**, and the location of the finite state control unit's read-write head. More technically, a string of symbols beginning and ending with a zero and with a **Turing machine state symbol** in between. The Turing machine read-write head is taken to be scanning the tape symbol to the right of the state symbol.

Turing machine instruction   In cognitive science, an ordered four-tuple consisting of a **Turing machine state symbol**, a **Turing machine tape symbol**, a Turing machine tape symbol or direction symbol, and another Turing machine tape symbol.

Turing machine program   In cognitive science, a set of **Turing machine instructions**.

Turing machine state symbol   In cognitive science, a symbol standing for one of the finite states of the **Turing machine finite state control unit**.

Turing machine state transition   In cognitive science, the change from one **Turing machine instantaneous description** to another in accordance with an instruction of a **Turing machine program**.

Turing machine tape symbol   In cognitive science, a symbol that appears on the infinite tape of a **Turing machine**.

Turing test   In cognitive science, a standard by which to determine whether a machine is intelligent. If under specified conditions the machine can pass for a human, then the machine has intelligence.

Utilitarianism   In ethics and political philosophy, the view that the morally best dispositions, actions, and social institutions are a matter in some direct or indirect way of what would reasonably be expected to produce the greatest overall well-being. See also **consequentialism**.

Utility   In ethics and political philosophy, the good, or well-being, of individuals.

Utterance meaning   The message a speaker gets across by using a sentence on a specific occasion in a specific context.

Valid argument   An *argument* whose conclusion follows from its premises. In a valid deductive argument, the conclusion follows necessarily from its premises (see *deduction*). To claim that its conclusion "follows necessarily" from its premises is to claim that it cannot possibly be false *unless* one or more of its premises is also false. See also *invalid argument*.

Verification principle   The fundamental principle of **logical positivism** that attempts to determine the meaningfulness of factual propositions by **empirical** content. If no sense experience can count in favor of the truth of a proposition, it is meaningless.

Void   Empty space; vacuum; the receptacle for atoms.

Wisdom   A knowledge that involves theoretical as well as practical understanding. Thought by some philosophers to be the goal of philosophical reflection.

Worldview   A general and coherent way of understanding the world; from the German *Weltanschauung*, one's view of the big picture.

NOTES ON THE CONTRIBUTORS

Frederick Adams, coeditor, is chairman and professor of philosophy at Central Michigan University. He has previously taught at Lawrence University, University of Wisconsin, and Augustana College. He has published in the philosophy of mind, epistemology, and cognitive psychology.

Kenneth Aizawa is assistant professor of philosophy at Central Michigan University. He has also taught at the University of Pittsburgh and Carnegie-Mellon University. He has published in cognitive science and the philosophy of mind.

William H. Brenner is associate professor of philosophy at Old Dominion University. He has published in the history of philosophy and the philosophy of Wittgenstein.

Gary Fuller is associate professor of philosophy at Central Michigan University. He has previously taught at the University of Oxford and the University of Florida. He has published in the philosophy of mind, philosophy of the human sciences, and personal identity.

John Heil is professor of philosophy at Davidson College. He has published in the philosophy of mind and epistemology.

Joyce Henricks is associate professor of philosophy at Central Michigan University. She has published in ethics, social and political philosophy, philosophy of social science, and women's studies.

Brad Hooker is assistant professor of philosophy at Virginia Commonwealth University. He has previously taught at the University of Oxford. He has published in social and political philosophy and ethics.

Leemon McHenry, coeditor, is assistant professor of philosophy at Wittenberg University. He has previously taught at the University of Edinburgh, Old Dominion University, Davidson College, and Central Michigan University. He has published in American philosophy, metaphysics, and the philosophy of science.

Galen K. Pletcher is associate provost and professor of philosophy at Southern Illinois University at Edwardsville. He has previously taught at the University of Michigan. He has published in the philosophy of religion, ethics, and twentieth-century analytic philosophy.

Robert Stecker is associate professor of philosophy at Central Michigan University. He has previously taught at the Massachusetts Institute of Technology, University of Houston, and the National University of Singapore. He has published in aesthetics, ethics, and the history of modern philosophy.

INDEX